It Didn't Happen On My Watch

George E. Murphy

Triangle Books

Triangle Books
are published by
Research Triangle Publishing, Inc.
PO Box 1223
Fuquay-Varina, NC 27526

ISBN 1-884570-31-3

Library of Congress Catalog Card Number: 95-68646

Cover Design by
Kathy Holbrook

Edited by
Bonnie Tilson

Printed in the United States of America
10 9 8 7 6 5 4 3 2

DEDICATION

This book is dedicated to those who answered their country's call to serve in the Merchant Marine during World War II and whose legacy of a strong U.S. maritime policy is all but forgotten through government bureaucracy.

ACKNOWLEDGMENTS

Looking back on my life I realize I have enjoyed the best of many of life's experiences—experiences which could probably be categorized by three distinct "families" who inspired this writing.

My wife and sons who encouraged me to put down on paper the many sea stories I bored them with for so many years would be the first of these families.

The second, though short lived, would have to be without a doubt my class at Massachusetts Maritime Academy. We grew to become a cohesive group of young men just out of high school, a tightly knit group allied to stick it out through those early tormenting days of being an underclass cadet, meeting secretly nearly every night to convince one or another to hang in there, and we did survive, all of us!

And the third family must be all those fine people with whom I worked in United States Lines. Those who worked on the piers, in the offices, and on board ship under the broad, worldwide wingspread of the Blue Eagle.

All of the above are a part of this writing.

My thanks also to Richard F. O'Boyle for his assistance in writing the manuscript, a difficult task because I submitted it to him piecemeal and in no semblance of order. To Mike Moriarty, for his review and comments, and finally to my son, Tim, for his review, critique and humorous comments in the margins of the original manuscript; I treasure them.

My sincere thanks also to Captain Arthur R. Moore, author of *A Careless Word.. A Needless Sinking,* a voluminous writing of the American Merchant Marine in World War II, and to Captain Charles Dana Gibson, author of *Merchantman? or Ship of War*, a detailed history of the war at sea, 1939-45. I found their writings invaluable for references in putting this work together. These two individuals also figured prominently in World War II merchant seamen gaining veterans' status from the federal government in early 1988.

My sincerest thanks to all.

PREFACE

I have often heard it said, "There are hundreds of seagoing stories out there, it's too bad some of them aren't being written before they become lost."

Many have been written, but for some unknown reason most have been written by ships' captains, few by marine engineers. I decided to write some of these sea stories from an engineer's point of view, as seen from the engine room floorplates rather than from the bridge of a ship.

It has been said, "The difference between a sea story and a fairy tale is: A fairy tale starts out—'Once upon a time.' A sea story starts out—'Now this is no shit!'"

I have attempted to be fair in the accounts related here, to tell them as I heard or witnessed them. Some readers may sense a twinge of envy or jealousy when writing about some of our captains, but I assure you it is not so.

While a cadet at Massachusetts Maritime Academy in 1942, our wartime course was accelerated. We had to select either the deck or engineering course at the time of our appointment, so I had the opportunity to go either way. I selected the engineering route and have never regretted it. I joined United States Lines, a prominent steamship company, during World War II and remained there for forty-three years. During this period I had the pleasure and privilege to sail and work with many fine shipmasters, chief engineers, and company officials from my days as a third assistant engineer through chief engineer and on to port engineer.

I was also fortunate early in my career to sail with young third mates and third assistant engineers who went on to become masters and chiefs. Thus later when husbanding a ship as a port engineer in a shipyard or for voyage repairs, knowing these men for so many years made my job that much easier.

In April 1941, my high school class was returning from its Washington/New York trip to our small Massachusetts town of Leicester. This trip was an annual affair taken by each senior class and looked forward to after twelve arduous years in school.

We were leaving New York via overnight boat due to dock in Providence, Rhode Island, the next morning. As we proceeded through New York's upper bay, I was sitting in the ship's lounge when a classmate called to me to step out on deck to view the New York skyline. He said, "This is probably the last time you will ever have a chance to see it from the deck of a boat." Boy, was he ever wrong!

Although I didn't realize it at the time, I was looking at a squat twelve-story building nestled among the lower Manhattan skyscrapers. The address was Number One Broadway, world headquarters of United States Lines, Inc., where in a couple of years I would be employed for the next forty-three years.

This is a review of those years, eighteen spent at sea, the remainder in the company office as a port engineer. Many of these anecdotes are personal experiences while others were told to me by shipmates and friends. I strongly suspect some of those told to me might be stretching the truth a bit; my own, however, are nothing but the truth! It has been necessary to change some names for reasons that will be obvious to you as you read along. Occasionally, I may use a person's real name when it suits the situation.

CHAPTER ONE

MASSACHUSETTS MARITIME ACADEMY

Upon graduation from high school, I applied for admission to Massachusetts Maritime Academy located at the time in Hyannis, Massachusetts. I was informed I would be required to pass a U.S. Naval Reserve physical exam prior to taking the written entrance examination. The academy also notified all prospective entrants that a twelve-week refresher course was available at Massachusetts Institute of Technology. I enrolled in the course with twelve other prospects from various sections of Massachusetts.

Upon completion of the course, we were summoned to the Naval Reserve Center in Boston for physicals. All of the MIT fellows passed except one, me! I was rejected for a reason that defied all logic—my teeth did not bite correctly in front; the dental term is malocclusion.

I asked the Navy doctor why this was so important and he said it was a carryover from the Revolutionary War days. It seems any-one shooting a musket would have to extract the plug from his pow-der horn with his teeth and hold it there while pouring powder into his gun. Afterward, he would jam the plug back into the horn with his teeth. I told the doctor that to the best of my knowledge the U.S. Navy stopped firing muskets over a hundred years ago, but it fell on deaf ears.

After several months of orthodontia treatment, my teeth were biting correctly so I took the physical again. This time I passed and was then pleasantly informed that due to wartime conditions and the need for Navy and Merchant Marine officers, the written test had been waived and admission was to be based on one's high school records. I was finally in!

I discovered upon entering the academy that my friends from MIT were now upperclassmen so I thought "how lucky to be among friends." On my first day I was called into one of their rooms and found all of them gathered there to greet me. I was told in no uncertain terms that any friendships developed prior to my entry at MMA were no longer in effect. I was to treat all upperclassmen with the utmost respect, and I was nothing more than a lowly "young man," a term used to designate fourth classmen, the lowest type of animal in the academy.

We were assigned to various duties, such as orderlies (a runner for the officers) and mess punks (waiting on tables, cleaning the galley, operating the dishwasher, etc.). I was selected to be a mess punk.

Our food was prepared by "professional cooks" and it was, in a true sense, a two-pot ship—officers enjoyed one menu, the cadets tolerated another. Officers were served daily soup, we had none. During dinner one day while serving a first-class table, I was told to bring a bowl of soup to an upperclassman whom I'll call O'Hara. I told him there was no way in the world the cook, a Philippine man named Morro, was going to give me a bowl of soup for a cadet, but he said if he didn't have soup in front of him within two minutes, I would suffer the consequences.

I went to the galley and determined the officers' soup was clam chowder; the cadets were having beef stew. I drained the liquid from some of the stew into a bowl and served it to O'Hara. He slopped it up as though he was eating from a trough, and just as he finished, his classmate noticed the resemblance between the stew and O'Hara's "soup." O'Hara rushed into the galley and confirmed the officers' soup to be clam chowder. I was doomed! He ordered me to bring a large pot of the stew into the mess room after the meal and forced me to eat it with a ladle. He stood over me and upended the ladle periodically, so in the end, I was covered with it. I realized then that this was the beginning of a strained relationship between O'Hara and me, and he still had six months to go before graduation!

Maintenance at the academy, such as cleaning, painting, and policing the grounds, was performed by cadets under the supervision of first classmen. Each upperclassman was assigned a "Top," an area for which he was held responsible for its upkeep and cleanliness. Under his supervision were five or six "young men" who were to do the work. I was assigned to O'Hara's top. The top assignments were randomly selected, however I strongly suspect O'Hara requested that I be assigned to him.

Working under him after the soup incident, I realized, could make for a miserable existence for me so I began to ponder ways to escape from this tyrant. My dream came true in a matter of days when a notice was posted on the bulletin board, "Bugler Wanted, $5.00 a month, two-hour Wednesday afternoon liberty." Having played the trumpet in high school and served in a drum and bugle corps, I quickly applied for the job. I got the job after an interview by the executive officer and a short demonstration of my expertise on the bugle. I felt quite proud until I learned I was the only applicant.

The job consisted of playing eighteen bugle calls a day from reveille at 0615 until taps at 2200 hours. I was to play the calls every other day, alternating with the other bugler, a first classman named Mayo. It meant waking up fifteen minutes before everyone else and turning in after everyone had gone to bed, but it also meant I would have the head (bathroom) to myself early in the morning and could wash up at ease instead of fighting for a place at a wash basin. Best of all, however, it relieved me of all "mess punk" duties and orderly watches, as well as a limited time in O'Hara's top.

I reported to Mayo for instructions and was informed that the method of payment was by a single check for $10.00 made out to Mayo monthly. He was to cash it and hand over $5.00 to me. That may have been the rule, but Mayo quickly informed me that because I was a "young man" I did not rate earning any money, therefore he would keep the entire $10.00. To further aggravate me, he informed me that I would be playing all the calls! In spite of these drawbacks, it still beat working for O'Hara every day.

Playing the bugle sometimes had its problems. One morning when I approached the duty station to remove the bugle from its rack, I was informed by the cadet officer of the deck, who was on watch, that I was to sound reveille that morning in the room of one of his classmates, instead of on the stairway landing where it was usually played. The cadet officer had the bugle in his hand and said he would accompany me to the fellow's room and would hand the bugle to me at the appropriate time. He looked at his watch and at 0615 handed it to me and told me to hold it next to the head of his classmate and let go! I didn't object to this because the sleeping cadet wasn't exactly one of my favorites. I inhaled to fill my lungs with air and let loose with what should have been the first notes of reveille but, unknown to me, the cadet officer had filled the tubing of the bugle with water. When the sleeping cadet felt the water striking his head, he awoke with his arms flailing, striking the bell of the bugle which split open the inside of my upper lip, and sent the bugle, end over end, sailing across the room where it collided with a steel bunk, putting a deep dent in the bugle. The entire cadet corps had to be awakened that morning by the fire alarm. On another occasion, someone had pounded an apple core into the bell of the bugle and the first note that morning blocked my ears for hours.

Realizing I had at least sixteen months of bugle playing ahead of me, I decided to bring my trumpet from home on my next week-end pass. I now had an excuse to keep the trumpet in my room instead of at the duty station because the academy didn't want to be responsible for it. One evening when the upper class learned I was using a trumpet for calls, I was instructed to play *Brahms' Lullaby* instead of taps.

Having been warned by the executive officer about jazzing any bugle calls, I had second thoughts about Brahms. Then I remembered the senior officer on duty that night was a Navy lieutenant and a pretty good guy, so I complied with the request. At its completion, chuckles could be heard throughout the building and even some applause. The lieutenant came out of his quarters and said, "Well done, Murphy, now go to bed."

One of the perquisites of being a first classman was the privilege of sleeping in a few extra minutes each morning. The underclassmen had to rise at the sound of reveille, wash up, quickly dress, and report to formation from which they were dispatched to various areas to clean and sweep and generally police the grounds.

Thirty minutes later when the first call to assembly for breakfast was sounded, these upperclassmen would bound from their bunks, rush to the heads, dress, and make it to formation in ten minutes, and don't get in their way! Shortly after some of my classmates became aware of this privilege, they devised a payback plan to upset it.

Late one evening after taps had been sounded, my roommates quietly removed the hinge pins from the doors leading to five first-class rooms on the second deck. The next morning when the bugler sounded call to breakfast, they awakened, dashed from their rooms in a flurry, and the doors fell. They stood there bewildered, some of them standing on the doors they had just opened, others leaping around trying to dodge the falling doors!

As the doors fell one by one, they made a tremendous noise which could be heard by the officers on the deck below. When they came dashing up one flight to see what caused it, there stood twelve cadets in their Skivvies looking at each other with puzzled looks.

Of course no one knew anything about it, but I was one cadet who could appreciate it because I had sounded the bugle call to breakfast at one end of the hall where it happened. We had saved the hinge pins and later they were "found" in a bag in one of the heads on the upper-class deck and replaced that day by the carpenter.

O'Hara's graduation day finally arrived. I saw him on the mess deck while he was saying good-by to some friends and approached him to ask if he would consider swapping boots in the rear end with me. Kicking an underclassman's rear was called "assuming the ancient and honorable position" and was used as a means of discipline for young men when they got out of line. The officers at the academy turned the other way when hazing such as this was carried out. Although the regulations contained procedures one could use against anyone involved in hazing, I never saw anyone attempt to use these procedures because it would mean a miserable existence for him down the line. Also, there was an unwritten rule that anyone who thought he was being hazed beyond reasonable limits could challenge the upperclassman to put on the gloves in the gym during our free period. If the upperclassman failed to appear for the bout, he lost face not only with the underclasses, but also with his own classmates who would no longer consider him one of their own.

In assuming the "ancient and honorable position" the man being booted would bend over, lift his private parts out of the way, and get kicked. If at all possible, he would not flinch or let on that it hurt so as not to give the upperclassman the satisfaction of knowing he did a good job.

O'Hara said, "Murphy, you don't know how to kick ass, you're a young man." I replied, "At least let me have one shot at you before you leave. We may never see each other again." He agreed, telling me I could kick him first, and then he could have his last shot at me.

He bent over and I stepped back about fifteen feet to get a running start. I ran toward him and connected with his rear end so hard I fell down and he went sprawling flat out on the deck. I recovered before he did and took off up the stairway, out of the building, across the great lawn, and hid in an adjacent building that housed the machine shop. Moments later I heard him enter the shop and just as he started his search, the assembly bell rang calling all hands to parade formation to begin the march to the graduation ceremonies. Of course they had to use the assembly bell because the bugler was nowhere to be found! O'Hara turned and left the shop while I remained behind. I missed the formation, and I later received ten demerits at the captain's mast for missing the bugle call, but they were demerits well and justly earned.

One favorite expression used by young men to show their disdain toward certain upperclassmen was to stand in their midst when some of their own classmates were present and shout loudly:

"Three cheers for Johnson!" (The upperclassman's name.)

"Hip, Hip - SHIT!"

"Hip, Hip - SHIT!"

"Hip, Hip - SHIT!"

Of course, none of us would stay around after this to hear any comments!

With the graduation of O'Hara's class, the pressure eased up on mine; a new class entered to become young men while we became third classmen no longer subject to hazing, but still without upper-class privileges. A few of the new first class tried hazing us but were soon put in their places. We were in a state of limbo. Mayo, the bugler, had graduated and there were no buglers in the new class. I became the sole bugler, but more importantly, I could keep the entire ten dollars.

In 1942 the war of the Atlantic was raging between the German submarines and American shipping. Allied ships were being sunk at an alarming rate so the War Shipping Administration (WSA) ordered all the academies to accelerate their curriculums to get cadets out to sea as early as possible. This meant that subjects normally required by the State Board of Education for a degree, but not required to pass the United States Coast Guard examination for a license, be eliminated and deck and engineering subjects be more concentrated. With this speed up of the teaching process, the first class soon graduated and we were suddenly second classmen. The short period of time those graduates served as first classmen was still long enough to haze the new fourth class to the point where the fourth class vowed to get even.

During the previous month, the academy officials had decided to hold future graduations in Faneuil Hall, Boston, in order to accommodate parents, officials, and invited guests. A group of seven young men was bused to Boston, carrying steamship company house flags and alphabetical and numerical signal flags to decorate the hall. They were told the graduating class would be seated on the stage and the first two rows in the audience reserved for dignitaries: the governor, speakers, invited guests, etc. The cadets hung eight alphabetical signal flags on the stage wall behind the graduates.

The following day at graduation with a full auditorium, the governor entered and was seated in the front row next to the academy superintendent. Just after the ceremonies began, a Coast Guard officer in the front row interpreted the eight flags. They spelled out B A S T A R D S!

He quickly relayed this information to those surrounding him, but it was now too late because the governor was about to begin his speech. The fourth class had the last laugh after all, and could say, "Revenge is Sweet."

Massachusetts Maritime Academy, since its inception in 1891 as Massachusetts Nautical School, had always been an "onboard" type of school. Cadets lived aboard ship, ate aboard, held classes aboard and worked aboard ship. The most recent training ship on which they performed all these functions was called *Nantucket*, a former Navy gunboat obtained by the school in 1909.

It was barkentine rigged with a horizontal, reciprocating steam engine. Its length was 177 feet with a beam of 32 feet and had a draft of 32 feet. It remained as the school ship until 1941, being berthed at various times at the Charlestown Navy Yard and North End Park in Boston.

Wherever the "Nancy," as it was affectionately called by the cadets, was berthed, that was the location of the Massachusetts Nautical School. The school has stayed in continuous operation since its beginning, thus the claim on the school stationery letterhead, "The Oldest Continuously Operating Maritime Academy in the United States" as compared with the claim by "The State University of New York Maritime College" at Fort Schuyler, New York, of "The Oldest Maritime Training School in the United States."

The school at Fort Schuyler was founded in 1874 as "The New York Nautical School," but ceased operations for a brief period early in its history, and then resumed operations when budgetary problems were solved.

These claims have made for interesting discussions over the years between the alumni of both schools, but their mutual admiration and cooperation have enabled both to survive in times of economic need or when the U.S. Government goes on periodic thrift binges.

In 1942 the *Nantucket* was declared unseaworthy, so the school moved for the first time in its history to a shore facility in Hyannis, Massachusetts. The *Nantucket* was towed from Boston to the newly formed United States Merchant Marine Academy at Kings Point, New York, where it was berthed to be used as a receiving ship for arriving cadets and renamed *Emery Rice*.

At Massachusetts Maritime Academy the course of study was originally two years, but this was soon accelerated to sixteen months due to the need for Merchant Marine and Navy officers during the war. The new shore facility for the school was a group of buildings formerly used as a state teachers college. In order to familiarize all new cadets with shipboard language, the building became known as the "Ship," various floors became "Decks," corridors were "Passageways," and so forth.

On the main deck, the gunners mate had built a rifle rack to hold about 200 old World War I Springfield rifles which we used for drilling. The guns were rendered inoperable by plugging the barrels. Whenever we were scheduled for a drill, each cadet would pass by the rack, grab the next rifle in line, and carry it to formation along with his bayonet. Drilling was held at the athletic field twice a week.

Word was received one day that Governor Leverett Saltonstall was in the area and had requested to review the cadet corps. Our two gunners mates, one a retired Navy chief petty officer and the other a third class on active duty, went frantic cleaning and polishing the dummy 3-inch and 5-inch guns in preparation for his visit, but nothing was done to the Springfields.

When the governor arrived at the academy, the regiment was assembled outside the administration building and marched to the athletic field. There we went through various maneuvers and eventually assembled in regimental formation ready for his inspection. He walked up and down the ranks, accompanied by Captain Bassett, our superintendent, and Executive Officer Jack Thompson.

My company, Company Five, was standing at "attention" as the governor approached. He asked Captain Bassett if he could examine one of the Springfields saying he hadn't held one since the last war. The captain was standing in front of me at the time, so in a loud authoritative voice commanded, "Murphy, INSPECTION ARMS!"

I brought the rifle from attention to the inspection-arms position, which meant releasing the bolt mechanism to the open position, quickly looking into the chamber, and then looking straight ahead. He took the rifle from me and handed it to the governor. The governor looked into the chamber and then held the butt of the rifle high over his head while he attempted to sight through the barrel from the muzzle end.

He turned the butt end around in circles, but when he couldn't see through it, asked me to remove the bolt mechanism. I released the latch, removed the bolt, and handed it back to him. Again, he attempted to sight through the barrel, when I blurted out, "You can't see through the barrel, Governor, because it's plugged, sir!"

He turned to the captain and said, "Why didn't you tell me that, Captain?"

I realized I had just lost many points with the captain and resigned myself to a royal chewing out after the formation, but he never said anything to me.

The governor never inspected anything the gunners had cleaned and polished and they were embarrassed because the only thing he did look at was the plugged guns!

Smoking by cadets was permitted only during specified hours and in specific areas outside the buildings. Anyone found smoking in the buildings at any time was subject to heavy penalties, any cadet, that is! Officers were free to smoke in their rooms or in the officers' lounge at any time.

Whenever work periods, classes, or study halls were finished, an orderly would pipe "smoking lamp is lit" and all the smokers, with their cigarettes and matches at the ready, would light up. Sometimes, it seemed that there was competition among them to find who could smoke the most during the brief period when smoking was permitted. Only cigarettes were allowed because the butts were easily disposed of when "smoking lamp is out" was piped some time later.

Young men were required to carry a book of matches at all times, ready to light the cigarette of an upperclassman if he should request it. If we failed to produce a match, our penalty was to wear several matchbooks secured to a lanyard around our neck for a week.

When the words "smoking lamp is out" were piped, the smokers were to snuff out their cigarettes, split the paper in the butt, and sprinkle the tobacco over the ground, then roll the paper into a tiny ball between their fingers and put it in a trash barrel. Adhering to these rules was almost enough to make some men quit the habit, but at least the grounds remained free of butts.

Cadets had to take many courses, regardless of whether they were studying engineering or deck subjects, such as first aid, rowing, lifeboat drills, and a certain amount of seamanship. These courses were all calculated to be of some practical use in the future, particularly since we would be going to sea in the middle of a war.

One of the seamanship drills was the technique needed to pull ourselves aloft in a boatswain's chair, tie off, and stay suspended in the air. This course was conducted in a building with high ceilings which was equipped with pulleys suspended overhead. A rope reaved through the sheave of the pulley was secured to the boatswain's chair and the other end coiled on the deck.

For training purposes, we had to sit in the chair, which was simply a short board with a loop of rope at each end, pull ourselves up from the deck a few inches, and following the directions of the boatswain, single-handedly tie ourselves off. We were suspended only a few inches from the floor because we were not very successful the first few times we tried this.

Our "final exam" for this drill was to be seated in the chair, blindfolded, and hoisted by the boatswain to the ceiling where we were told to reach up and touch it with one hand. This was to let us be aware of how high we were. The boatswain then lowered us a short distance and then raised us and kept this up until we had no idea about the distance between us and the floor!

And then we heard the orders we weren't looking forward to—"Tie Off!"

When securing yourself in a boatswain's chair, the moment of truth arrives when you slack off your grip on the "married" lines you have held squeezed together in your hand as a "friction brake" and the chair settles downward an inch or two and you stay up there!

After being suspended for a few minutes, which seemed like an eternity, the boatswain told us to remove the blindfolds. We found ourselves hanging only a few inches from the floor of the room, much to our embarrassment!

While I personally thought this was useless training for an engineering cadet at the time, several months later I was to discover just how valuable it would be.

Another method of torture was called "bayonet sitting." If an upperclassman thought a young man needed more discipline, as they referred to it, he would be required to assume a sitting position with his back against a wall (but without benefit of a chair beneath him) and with a bayonet standing on end, point up under his rear. The bayonet would be placed beneath him while he was sliding downward against the wall until the point of the bayonet, standing on its hilt, would just touch his body enough to be supported without falling over.

This position could only be held for a few minutes before the person's body began to slide downward. So in order to escape after enduring as much as he could tolerate, the young man would throw himself sideways to prevent injury. This form of hazing backfired one time, as I recall, when a young man reached for the bayonet just as he was falling sideways and grasped it by the hilt, while at the same time, an upperclassman reached for it and grabbed it by the blade!

Each man attempted to pull it loose from the other when the blade sliced through the palm of the upperclassman's hand. He was rushed to sick bay where several stitches were required to close the wound.

The medic in sick bay was told that the upperclassman cut it on a piece of broken glass and everyone present was sworn to secrecy to prevent any repercussions from the officers and possible dismissals.

With the heavy merchant ship losses in the North Atlantic in 1942 from German U-boats, it was inevitable that the academy would soon be learning about some of its graduates making the ultimate sacrifice. After receiving several of these notices in a few weeks, the academy officers selected a large wall on the main deck to be a wall of honor for them. It was painted a dark blue, bordered in gold leaf, with the names and graduation year of these men stenciled in gold.

Word was received one day late in 1942 about the sinking of a U.S. Lines freighter named the SS *American Leader* by a German raider vessel. Several men lost their lives, while others were taken prisoners aboard the German ship. One of those reported dead was the third mate, George W. Duffy, a Massachusetts Nautical School graduate, Class of 1941. A stencil was made and his name added to the growing list on the honor roll, but a few months later it was learned he had not perished. He was among those taken prisoner.

His name was painted over with blue paint and another name put in his place. A few months later, we again heard he had died as a prisoner of war, so another stencil was made and his name added further down on the list from its previous location.

Two months later word was received that he was not dead, but had been transferred to a Japanese ship as a prisoner and now was in a Japanese POW camp in Java. Once again his name was painted over. Then someone suggested not breaking down the stencil this time in case it wasn't true, but everyone agreed the stencil should be dismantled to give him every chance or at least benefit of the doubt.

Happily, Duffy survived the POW experience so his name was never added to the honor roll again!

As a young man we were always required to carry a watch and be prepared to answer an upperclassman's request for the time at any moment. Our answer couldn't be a mere "It's 10:15" or other simple answers. Upon being asked, we would be required to reply, "Not knowing to any certain degree of the accuracy of my chronometer, I dare not designate exactly, lest I might err; however, my chronometer does indicate the present time as being 10:15."

This is a lot of words just to tell a fellow the time, but it was a requirement as a young man. It was not unusual to have an upperclassman request the time, go through the above, and a couple of minutes later be asked again by another in the same group.

Another expression commonly used was the number "86." This was used by an underclassman when an upperclassman or officer approached a group and some in the group didn't want to be overheard. It was also used after taps in the evening when everyone was forbidden to talk.

The number "86" was used because it is one of the few numbers which can be uttered without moving your lips, therefore the tip-off man could not be observed. Often a cadet officer would wander through the sleeping compartment after taps hoping to catch some young men talking. But when he appeared in the doorway, the lookout would come out with "86" and the compartment would be suddenly silent. The cadet officer would give the third degree to the group, but, of course, no one would admit saying it and finally he'd leave.

When we graduated from MMA in 1943, we were presented with a diploma, ensign's commission, a license, and a Bible, courtesy of the Massachusetts Bible Society. The one document lacking was a degree. Our course of study had been accelerated to speed up our time in the academy so that we might get out to sea to aid the war effort. Thus the subjects and semester hours required for a degree were not in the curriculum.

At the end of World War II, I contacted the academy to inquire what subjects and hours would be required for a degree. They furnished this information, but it would have required returning to the academy for the courses and hours. By now I was a full-time seagoing employee of U.S. Lines, so returning to school in Massachusetts was out of the question.

Forty years later in 1983, I again inquired about a degree and was asked to submit a brief resume of my career, background information, licenses obtained, Naval Reserve rank, etc. Upon receipt of this data, they informed me that I had fulfilled the requirements for a degree and if I could be present at the graduation exercises that June, it would be presented to me along with those of the cadets.

I was unable to attend, however, because I was on a boiler repair job on a ship stationed in Diego Garcia, half way around the world. My degree was accepted for me by Don Kadlac, port engineer for U.S. Lines, who was at the graduation to present the U.S. Lines award to an engineering cadet.

Several years later, my youngest son, Tim, graduated from college and I felt relieved—the last of my kids would finally be on their own. At least that's what I expected. But he informed me that he wished to continue in college for another few years. I asked him if he was going to be one of those young people who take several years to get their degrees and he replied, "What's wrong with that, Dad, you did!"

He had me and he knew it. He continued studying at another college and while there met a young lady who is now our daughter-in-law. Talk about things happening for the best.

CHAPTER TWO

TRAINING SHIP *AMERICAN PILOT*

The USCG required a total of six months sea time for cadets in 1942 and 1943 to sit for a license. Thus after a few months in the academy at Hyannis, it became time for our first cruise. It was to last three months, one half of the sea time needed.

The entire student body of Massachusetts Maritime Academy was then bused to Fort Schuyler to board the New York State Maritime Academy training ship, *Empire State,* renamed *American Pilot*, a World War I Hog Island Class of cargo vessel. Upon boarding we found we were to share the ship, not only with New York cadets, but with cadets from Maine Maritime Academy as well.

A routine was quickly developed whereby New York cadets would hold classroom work, Massachusetts cadets would do the ship's maintenance, such as cleaning and painting, and Maine cadets would operate the ship for one-week intervals and then rotate. This gave each school the opportunity to conduct classes, operate the ship, and maintain it.

One of the failures of this routine was that fire and boat drills would only be a function of the operation of the vessel, thus only the school conning the ship could conduct them. Cadets from one school would be on deck painting when suddenly the fire alarm would sound and the loudspeaker would announce the fire drill for one of the other schools. Water would be pumped to the fire stations, cadets would man the hoses and wet down much of the newly painted areas, including the cadets who were doing the painting. Often times, tempers flared when some wet cadets accused those of another school of the washdown being deliberate.

Never once during the two three-month cruises was a fire and boat drill held concurrently with the three schools. I can only imagine the pandemonium that would take place if ever there was a real fire or need to abandon ship.

My duty station during fire drills was to dog down the water-tight door which led from the machine shop to a compartment which happened to be where New York cadets and officers were berthed. During one of these drills I heard the alarm, went to my station, and began dogging the door closed. Just as I pulled one dog down it sprang up almost immediately. The door had six dogs and it became apparent that someone on the other side of the door was attempting to open it to gain access to the machine shop.

I asked another cadet to pass a sledgehammer to me, which I then used to beat the dogs onto their wedges. I held my hands on two of the dogs and could feel the person on the other side pushing and pounding on them. A moment later a voice came through the door, "Open up this door, New York Officer!" I shouted, "Massa-chusetts fire and boat drill, sir!" He replied, "I don't care, open up!" I refused until the all clear signal was sounded which came a mo-ment later.

I had to use the sledgehammer to release the dogs, but just as the last dog was released, the door nearly tore from its hinges as it was pulled open from the other side. There facing me, his face a beet-red color, stood Lt. Doyle known to New York cadets as "Ducky." His first words were, "What's your name, Cadet?" I replied, "Murphy, sir." He screamed, "First of all, square that hat!" I pulled my sailor hat down over my eyes and then listened to a tirade of threats of insubordination, failure to follow orders, etc. My only reply was, "I was only doing what I considered to be my duty, sir." After venting his wrath some more, he left the shop.

On another occasion while still a young man, I was assigned to clean the paint on the outside of the exhaust trunk between the high-pressure and low-pressure turbines. This is a large diameter pipe which carries steam from the outlet side of the HP turbine to the inlet side of the LP turbine. It rose vertically from the HP for ten feet, then made a right angle turn and ran for ten feet, then another downward turn to the LP. With its thick asbestos insulation, the diameter was about twenty inches. This insulation had been painted white several years previously and my job was to attempt to clean it.

The only way to approach the job was to be lowered down from a point above it by rope, straddle the pipe, and hang on. My classmate lowered me down, then heaved up the rope with the intent of getting a bucket of soapy water and lowering that to me. While straddling the pipe and holding on for dear life, but with no bucket yet, Ducky Doyle entered the engine room via a ladder which ran adjacent to the pipe about eight feet away. He saw me and shouted, asking what I was supposed to be doing there. I told him about the bucket and my assigned cleaning detail. Ten minutes later I hadn't received the bucket when Ducky returned. When he saw I hadn't started the job, he said, "Murphy, you're a goof-off. If you ever decide to go to sea in peacetime and you walk aboard a merchant ship and see me, make a U-turn at the gangway. I wouldn't carry you for ballast." Fortunately for both of us, I never saw him again after our sea time aboard the *American Pilot*.

The head (toilet) in the Massachusetts compartment aboard the ship was made up of four open stalls with no doors and half-high bulkheads separating the seats. The entire unit was constructed of pipe supports and bracing. While I was sitting on one of the bowls one afternoon, two first classmen entered the head. They were discussing the fact that General Eisenhower could chin himself three times using only one hand, an extremely difficult feat.

Deciding to try it, they reached up and gripped the horizontal pipe between the compartments and attempted to do the same, but found it impossible. At that point in walked my nemesis, O'Hara, and observed their actions. When they told him what they were attempting, he said, "I'll show you how," but he found he wasn't tall enough to reach the overhead pipe.

When I saw this I reached next to me, tore off a piece of toilet paper, and placed it on the deck next to him. I said, "Here, O'Hara, jump up on this!" He glared at me and said, "Murphy, you'll pay for this," and I did, many times over.

There was another head in our compartment, but it was only used when repairs were being made to the main head. This consisted of a long, flat board set at an angle, mounted over a sloping trough through which seawater flowed from the high end to the low end and then overboard. Cadets would sit on the board with their rear end hanging over the edge to allow the droppings to land in the water and be flushed overboard. A favorite trick was for a cadet to wait until the board was filled with other cadets, crunch up some toilet paper, and lay it on the water at the high end and set it on fire. Every man on the board would let out a cry or yelp as the paper traveled beneath him!

In addition to the officers and cadets from the three academies, the *American Pilot* also had a permanent crew of maritime service sailors who served in such capacities as ABs, firemen, watertenders, oilers, storekeepers, boatswains, and pharmacist mates.

One morning the storekeeper reported that someone had broken into his storeroom and stolen several dozen sets of underwear. We were in the middle of Long Island Sound at the time and preparing to heave up the anchor to practice maneuvering. It was decided to remain at anchor and search the ship for the missing underwear, so all cadets were to standby their locker for inspection by an officer. When this failed to turn up the missing goods, a general ship search was conducted but this also failed.

The ship remained at anchor all day and into the night. The officers suspected that the culprits would throw the goods overboard that evening under the cover of darkness, so they stood watches on the bridge wings, playing a searchlight fore and aft, port and starboard into the night. We became annoyed at the bright light shining in our portholes every few minutes (one cadet said it reminded him of time he had spent in jail), so we devised a plan. Each cadet contributed a pillow case or sheet which we tore into sixteen-inch squares and distributed to the cadets in all compartments. When the ship's bell struck four bells for 2:00 A.M., cadets stationed at the portholes threw out the torn pieces of cloth. The officers on the bridge thought they had found the culprits until they fished some of the pieces out of the water with a boat hook and realized they had been had. The searchlights were turned off and we settled down to sleep for the rest of the night. We never found out who stole the underwear or where or how they disposed of it.

Just off the coast of the United States reports of German submarine activity were in the news daily, so the *American Pilot* was limited to cruising in the confines of Long Island Sound. The ship would be navigated and maneuvered by daylight and anchored each night. Its schedule suited us, however, because we would leave on Monday morning from Fort Schuyler and return on Friday just in time to have a liberty on either Saturday or Sunday.

While cruising Long Island Sound we would receive news reports from local radio stations reporting the daily loss of ships to German submarine activity. One Massachusetts cadet seemed overly nervous after hearing these reports and was quite frightened, especially at night. He was on watch one evening on the generator flat and had the duty to manually adjust the field rheostat on the main switchboard to maintain the ship's voltage at a constant 120 volts. The generator flat had a low overhead and was directly below the machine shop. Another cadet who was aware of his nervousness pulled a stupid trick to frighten him. He entered the machine shop, picked up a heavy sledgehammer, raised it over his head, and slammed it on the steel deck directly over the cadet on watch. The noise on the generator flat was like an explosion and the cadet's first thought was, "We're torpedoed!" At the same time the force of the hammer blow tripped the circuit breaker off the switchboard and the ship blacked out. This further frightened the cadet on watch who ended up in a cold sweat and near panic. An engineering officer soon arrived at the switchboard and reset the breaker to restore power. The cadet in the machine shop was long gone, but the hammer was still on the deck. At least they knew what caused the power failure although they never knew who caused it.

One weekend while at Fort Schuyler, I was walking through a section of the fort when I met Lt.(j.g.) Ed Tierney, my math teacher and baseball coach in Leicester High School. He had requested a leave of absence from his teaching position to enter the Navy's officer training school at the fort. He was wearing his uniform for the first day, so I asked him if I had to salute him and he replied, "You bet your ass, you do, or I'll have you court-martialled. Can't you see I'm an officer of the United States Navy?" We saw each other from time to time, and shortly after completing the course, he was shipped out.

After the war he returned to Leicester to resume his teaching career and, shortly thereafter, was promoted to school superintendent. He retired several years later.

CHAPTER THREE

SS *CLARA BARTON*

At graduation all the members of my class were presented with their diplomas, their license as either third mate or third assistant engineer, and their commission as ensign USNR. The required oaths were taken at the same ceremony and finally we were dismissed for the last time.

Some of my classmates immediately left for active duty with the Navy, while others opted to enter the Merchant Marine. The Recruitment and Manning Organization of the War Shipping Administration requested, but did not order, us to apply for duty with the Merchant Marine rather than the Navy because of the acute shortage of engineers and mates. Also, by taking this option, we could always request active duty with the Navy if we didn't care for the Merchant Marine after one trip. Those who entered the Navy directly did not have a second choice.

In addition, the "Ninety Day Wonder Schools," which the Navy operated at several colleges, were turning out ensigns at a rapid rate and the Navy was becoming saturated with them. Thus the Navy was just as pleased with our choice to join the Merchant Marine.

One of my classmates, Jason (Jake) Providakes, and I decided to ship out together, so we reported to the Boston Office of the WSA where we presented our new licenses and seamen's documents. Jason, who held a third mate's license, was sent to one address, while I was sent to another, each of us with an assignment letter from the WSA.

My address was a rather sleazy looking building where I found the office from which I would receive my final orders and the location of my first ship. This runaround I thought at the time, was all part of wartime security and I swelled up with pride to think I was now a part of it. When I presented myself to the portly gentleman seated behind a massive desk, he looked at my papers from the WSA and shouted to another man in the adjoining room, "Charlie, take that third assistant's job off the blackboard for the *Clara Barton*, we got one here."

I asked who Clara Barton was. I thought it was some sort of wartime code because I knew the birthplace of Clara Barton, the founder of the American Red Cross, was only a few miles from my home in Massachusetts.

"That's the name of the Liberty ship you've been assigned to here in Boston. Its code name is BO484, expected to sail next Thursday or Friday, soon as they can get enough ships to make up a convoy," he said.

I became irritated at this and told him he shouldn't be divulging this information for all to hear. I had spotted a large poster over his desk which read: "LOOSE LIPS SINK SHIPS!"

He laughed and asked, "First ship?" I told him it was and he handed me an assignment card to be presented to the chief engineer and purser. He also gave me directions to Castle Island where the *Clara Barton* was berthed.

"There is just one more thing to take care of, young man. Can you give me a down payment toward your initiation fee?"

"I have to pay an initiation fee to join the Merchant Marine?" I asked.

"No, to join the MEBA. You're gonna join, aren't you?"

"What's that, that War Risk Insurance I heard about from the WSA people?"

"No, it's a labor union, the Marine Engineers' Beneficial Association. You'll never get a job in the Merchant Marine after the war if you don't join."

No one in the maritime academy had ever clued us in to something like this, so I was completely naive about these matters. I was somewhat astounded to think I had to join a labor union to help my country during wartime.

I gave him $5.00 toward the fee with the balance to be paid at the end of my first trip. Little did I realize the benefits I would subsequently receive because of his efforts to recruit me.

I left the union hall with my seabag slung over my shoulder, looking somewhat like another wartime poster showing an old salt saying, "SURE, I'M GOING BACK TO SEA!"

I hailed a cab, told the driver, "Castle Island," and I was on my way.

We arrived at the pier and as I climbed out of the cab, I stared at what appeared to be the biggest ship I had ever seen. My first ship I kept thinking. It was about 6:30 P.M. so I went directly to the chief engineer's office and presented my papers to him.

He was a very large, elderly man, and my first thoughts were, "What in the world is he doing here at his age; he should be retired and taking things easy!" I learned he was one of many who answered our country's call for retired Merchant Marine officers and crewmen to return to sea to aid the war effort. Immediately, I felt a great deal of respect for him.

He directed me to my room, gave me a big handshake, and said, "Welcome aboard, young man!" He made me feel at home at once, except for that last remark, "Young man!" "First at the union hall, and now here," I thought; "will I ever get over the horrors connected with that expression!"

The first thing that caught my eye as I entered the room was a rack near the sink on which was hung clean bath and face towels, soap in the soap dish, and clean sheets on the already-made-up bunk. This surprised me because as a cadet we had to furnish our own linens, towels, and soap and, once again, we were never told at the academy what to expect in the industry we were trained to enter.

I immediately opened my seabag, removed the towels, sheets, and soap my mother had packed for me and stowed them in a drawer beneath the bunk. I didn't want someone to come into my room and see that I brought my own aboard and have a good laugh at my expense.

I walked around the passageway and found that Jason also had just reported aboard. He, too, had gone the same route I had earlier in the day, union hall, shipping list, etc. I told him to quickly unload his sheets, towels, and soap to save the two of us any embarrassment.

When I opened the drawer to put the towels away, I found a letter addressed, "To the new Third Assistant." I opened it and was startled at its contents. It read, "If you are a Jew, get off this ship right now; don't even sign on. This first assistant is a terror, a nervous wreck, and despises Jews. His favorite expressions are 'Jew Bastard' and 'no good Jew.' Please destroy this letter after you read it."

The letter ended with a PS " I am not Jewish, I'm of Irish extraction. The first assistant is Irish, but I can't take him any longer, and these are the reasons I quit."

I folded the letter, replaced it in the envelope, and hid it in my clothes locker. Then I changed into my work clothes and headed for my first visit to the engine room. When I reached the floorplates, I met the watch oiler who directed me to the first assistant.

The first assistant was dirty, greasy, and smelled of a week's perspiration and didn't even attempt to shake my hand when I offered it to him, introducing myself as the new third. He growled, "Be on the floorplates tomorrow morning at 0800, no later. Is that clear?"

I assured him I'd be there and as I walked by the log desk, I saw a battery operated emergency lantern. I reached over and flipped the switch on and off to see if it was working. He saw me do this and came rushing across the engine room and said, "Murphy, don't you ever let me catch you doing that again except in an emergency. Is that clear? We may need that if we get torpedoed next trip!"

I said, "In school they told us the third assistant engineer is in charge of all electrical equipment on a Liberty, so I thought I'd test it."

"Well, on here, you ain't in charge of nothing unless I tell you," he growled.

I returned to my room, removed the letter, closed my door, and reread it. I could already understand why the previous third had quit. He was right when he said the first was a nervous wreck.

The following morning I was on the floorplates at 0755 for good measure. The first assistant appeared at 0800 and told me to repack the fresh water pump, "I want to see how good you are," he said. Moments later a young man appeared and asked if I was Mr. Murphy, the new third. I replied that I was and he introduced himself as the cadet, and said that he had been told by the first to assist me on the pump. He was a Kings Point cadet and Jewish.

The pump was located in a rather secluded area, so he and I had a chance to talk about the ship, but more importantly, about the first. The cadet had made one trip on the ship, which had been his first trip to sea, and was thoroughly discouraged by the treatment he had received from the first.

This was to be my first exposure to anti-Semitism. I assumed he was telling me about the difficult time he had aboard because I was the only one in the engine room gang close to his age. After telling his horror stories, he felt better just getting them out in the open. I was furious about the abuse he had taken, so I told him he didn't have to tolerate anything like that from anyone and that he should tell his district training supervisor and request a transfer.

He said the training supervisor was due aboard that day to collect his cadet's sea project and to interview the officers with whom he had worked. He would be interested in the cadet's attitude, behavior, interest, and ability; all subjects he feared if the supervisor were to talk to the first.

I told the cadet about the letter and that I would be happy to show it to the supervisor if it became necessary to convince him of the cadet's concern. Later that day the cadet came to me in his dress uniform to tell me he was being transferred. I said, "You wouldn't be dressed like this in the middle of a work day with that terror around if you weren't being transferred!" He laughed, and then in a serious note, thanked me for letting him talk it out and encouraging him to speak out about his treatment.

I said, "The training supervisor never approached me for the letter, so you must have sounded sincere and genuine to him, congratulations!" I wished him the best of luck on his next assignment and he left. For some reason even I felt good the rest of the day. I returned to the engine room and something inside me kept saying, "First, just try giving me some of your crap, now!"

I went home that evening by train out of South Station, Boston, mainly to see my parents again before sailing, but also to bring the sheets, towels, and soap back to my mother. My folks had a big laugh over this! I took an early train from Worcester to Boston the next morning to be sure I'd be on board and on the floorplates by 0800 to face the terror.

I arrived on board in time for breakfast and saw the first eating his meal in his dress clothes. I assumed he was taking a day off and didn't give it another thought. I went below at 0800 anyway and did some odd jobs until nearly noon when a large man came up to me and asked if I was the third assistant engineer. I replied, "Yes, may I help you?"

He gave me the biggest, friendliest smile I had seen on that ship up to this time and said, "I'm the new first assistant engineer!" It was music to my ears; I beamed a broad smile and said, "Am I glad to see you!" and then my thoughts went back to the day before when the cadet left. If we had only known.

Apparently, the training supervisor reported the conduct of the first to the chief. The chief advised the first to quit because of the "strain" he was under due to the war and to take a much needed rest! Later that day it dawned on me that the cadet was responsible for the first leaving, but the cadet never realized it!

A few days after the new first came aboard, he asked me if I was a member of the class that had just graduated from Massachusetts Maritime Academy and I proudly said I was. He asked me if I knew a young fellow whom I'll call "Harold Burns" and I replied,

"Know him? He was my roommate!" And then it struck me—the new first's last name was the same as Burns' girl friend!

After completing our course of studies at the Maritime Academy, we assembled in Boston at the U.S. Coast Guard Marine Inspection Office to sit for our license exams. On our last night in Hyannis, Burns jumped ship after taps to have a final date with a girl he had been seeing for several months.

He had returned that night about one o'clock while the rest of us in the room were busy packing our gear to leave for Boston the following day. He began to worry because he had given his girl a line about "soon going into the subinfested waters of the North Atlantic and maybe never returning." She had finally succumbed to his wile, and now he was worried that she might become pregnant.

We tried to reassure him not to worry, that the chances of that happening were extremely remote, but in reality none of us knew what we were talking about. We were only trying to put his mind at ease because of the pending license exams.

The first continued, "Do you know where I can find that son of a bitch?"

"Gosh no, I have no idea where he might be now, or even who he shipped with. I don't even have his home address!" I said. I was trying to distance myself as far as possible from further questioning.

"Well, if you ever see him again, tell him I'm looking for him."

I assured him I would, and then I worked up enough courage to ask why he was looking for Burns. He replied, "He took my daughter out on a date that last night you fellows were in Hyannis. Just before he left my house to go back to the school, I told him it was too dark to try to grope his way there and attempt to sneak into the building from the rear of the academy grounds. So I loaned him my flashlight and the bastard never returned it!"

"Is that the only reason you're looking for him?" I asked, relieved.

"Yes," he said laughing, "He was a nice fellow and I'm really not worried about the flashlight, but if you ever do see him again, remind him of it just to give him a hard time."

I told him I would be more than happy to do that, more than he knew. I never saw Burns again, nor heard what ever happened to him, but if he's out there hiding, I'd like to put his mind as ease after fifty years.

In a few days the *Clara Barton* left Castle Island. It was deeply laden with Army vehicles in the cargo holds, fighter planes on deck, a crew of forty-four Merchant Marine personnel, and the armed guard made up of twelve Navy sailors and one ensign, whose designation was "gunnery officer," and one U.S. Army security officer.

We rendezvoused outside Massachusetts Bay with other ships from the New York area and together sailed to Halifax where we were joined by more ships to be formed into a massive convoy which seemed to stretch to the horizon. It's easy to simply say in words, "formed a convoy," but the maneuvering and several near collisions that occurred while backing and filling for position to locate proper stations in the convoy, the signal flag messages from the commodore, the whistle signals from the many ships, plus the destroyers and destroyer escorts scrambling in and out of the formation made for one day of total mass confusion!

Our armed guard sailors had made the previous trip to Europe while most of the merchant crew was embarking on their first trip aboard, me included. This mix of personnel meant a lot of adjusting had to be made. The Navy men claimed certain squatters' rights by virtue of being "old timers," but after a few days we became aware they were only trying on the merchant guys for size.

The captain, a Norwegian with a heavy accent, the chief engineer, and gunnery officer, a former school teacher and product of a ninety-day wonder school, held a meeting to lay the ground rules for all hands. These rules were relayed to all departments and soon we had a cohesive crew, getting along nicely.

Gunnery drills were run through daily, using not only the Navy boys, but the merchant crew as well. The gunners' mates instructed our guys in various duties, such as passing ammunition, loading guns, as well as firing them because the merchant men were the backups for the Navy men in the event some were knocked out of action.

The Navy had installed a dummy 5-inch 50-mm gun on board for training purposes. It was useful in teaching, except it was manually operated almost to the point of slow motion—a completely unrealistic situation compared to the real thing.

The North Atlantic, that most treacherous of the world's oceans especially in December, soon forced the convoy to spread out. We had to increase the distance between ships while attempting to maintain position lest we face imminent collision situations. Our position was in the middle of the convoy which made station keeping a constant vigil, increasing or decreasing speed by one or two revolutions of the propeller every few minutes. This required the watch engineer to stand by the throttle continuously.

As confining as our position in our station seemed to be, we still felt a little more secure than those ships in the outside rows. Veteran seamen always said the outside and the corner ships were most vulnerable to torpedoing. To add to the confusion caused by heavy weather, we were constantly zigzagging our course which further complicated station keeping.

A few days before leaving Castle Island, the new second assistant engineer had reported aboard. He introduced himself to the chief and first assistant engineers who were in the chief's office at the time. I didn't meet him until an hour later when he appeared in the engine room. As we shook hands, I noticed he was wearing two silver bars on the collar of his work shirt. Before I could ask about them he said, "I see you're looking at my collar emblems. I'm a lieutenant in the United States Maritime Service, which is the rank for a second assistant engineer."

He continued, "I usually wear them for the first few days I'm aboard a new ship, until the crew learns I'm an officer and not a crew member." I let this pass without comment, wondering what we had here.

I asked him if he had ever served on a Liberty before this and he said he hadn't.

"I'm a high-pressure man, just got off a C-2."

I felt a twinge of envy at that remark. As cadets, it had always been our ambition to sail on one of the "C" Class ships, or a Victory ship, rather than a slow Liberty. The Liberty was considered a low-pressure job with its boiler pressure about 200 pounds, while the "C" ships steamed at 450 pounds and were state of the art for those days.

Also, the Liberty machinery was nearly all steam reciprocating; main engine, pumps, steering gear and all deck machinery, while the "C" Class ships had turbines for main propulsion, generators, and feed pumps. Deck machinery was electric motor driven and the steering machinery electro-hydraulic The only electric motors aboard the Liberty drove the refrigeration compressor and gyro-compass motor-generator set, plus a few room fans. The second also said because of his high-pressure experience, he would be capable of learning this plant very quickly. Again, I wondered.

Two days out of Boston, in convoy, the exhaust steam back pressure began to drop slightly on his watch. The correction for this was to close in slightly on the system valve to the main condenser. This valve was located on the top of the main condenser midst a cluster of other valves. I had offered to point out its location to him, but he said that was not necessary, he would find it when he traced out the exhaust system. The purpose of this arrangement was to maintain ten-to twelve-pounds pressure of steam which is routed to a feed heater to warm up the water before it enters the boiler, an economy measure to conserve fuel.

The back pressure continued to drop in spite of his closing in on the valve, but he was too proud to call for help. Suddenly, the bridge called the engine room and the chief engineer to tell us the steering gear was no longer functioning. The bridge went into panic—we were out of control!

The mate on watch ran up the "out of command" flags on the halyards and all the ships in the convoy scrambled to stay clear of us. The chief and first found everything normal in the steering gear room, but they couldn't get the steering machinery to move, even from its local steering station located in the room. They then rushed to the engine room where a quick check revealed that the exhaust valve from the steering gear was closed.

The second had slowly closed it in his effort to regulate the back pressure. This valve was located next to the valve he should have been closing, the one I had offered to point out to him the previous day. The steering gear operated normally as soon as its exhaust valve was opened, but it took hours for the convoy commodore to get all the ships back into their proper stations.

To prevent a recurrence of this, the chief wired the valve in the open position. The captain was fuming at the steering gear failure and began spouting off in Norwegian at the engineers! The chief wanted to protect the second, so he lied, saying the exhaust valve probably vibrated closed. He assured him it couldn't happen again because it was now wired open.

This experience brought the second assistant down from high pressure to our level, and he became quite humble after that.

We maintained a log sheet in the engine room to log the speed changes and times. Sometimes the weather would subside for a few hours and no speed changes would be required for a couple of hours. This gave us a little relief.

One morning the weather was quiet and I had received no speed changes on my watch which had started at 8:00 A.M. About 9:00 A.M. the captain called on the engine room phone and asked how many revolutions I was making. I referred to the last entry on the log sheet which had been entered by the man I relieved an hour earlier and replied, "Sixty-eight, Captain."

He replied, angrily, "No you aren't, you're turning seventy; now reduce to sixty-eight!"

I slowed the engine to turn sixty-eight and from then on it was up two, down one, for the balance of the watch. I thought, "What difference did it make as long as we were on station?" Incidentally, Liberty ships were not equipped with revolution counters. The engineer had to hold his hand on the linkage to the counter mechanism, similar to an odometer on an automobile, count the strokes for fifteen seconds, and multiply by four for the revolutions per minute.

When I went off watch, I talked to Jason, who had been on watch on the bridge, and asked why the captain had called me about the revolutions. He told me the captain had asked him about the revolutions when he arrived on the bridge and he also told him sixty-eight. The captain then counted the revolutions by listening to the exhaust of the engine through the engine room ventilator and had counted seventy. The captain climbed all over Jason, too. Later when I entered the saloon to eat lunch, the captain said to me, "Murphy, if you ever lie to me again, I'll put you in the logbook!" I asked what lie he was referring to and he said, "The lie about the revolutions this morning!"

This was my first brush with the captain. The chief engineer told me to forget about it, he was a nervous wreck from the trip before, just like the first assistant engineer who quit in Boston.

On our second day in convoy, the bridge called the engine room on my watch to inform me our stack was belching heavy, black smoke and to cease at once. I told the fireman to check on it and to speed up the forced draft blower to clear it up. He did so, and the bridge called to tell me it was now clear and to keep a close watch on any smoking. The convoy commodore had sent a message to us stating if we had repeated smoking violations, we could leave the safety of the convoy and go it alone.

Such harsh rules soon impressed upon us the importance of not giving away our position to any submarines lurking on the horizon. The following morning we got another warning about smoking. Again, I told the fireman to pay closer attention to the combustion in the fireboxes.

He was a new fireman, making his first trip after finishing a short course at Sheepshead Bay Training Center, and of course, he had to be on my watch. Eventually he got the knack for firing the boilers cleanly, but only after a few more warnings from the commodore.

The oiler on my watch was his classmate at Sheepshead Bay, so he too was just as inexperienced. His duties were to squirt a stream of lubricating oil into the exposed moving parts of the main engine as it turned between sixty-five to seventy-five revolutions per minute. These areas consisted of up and down moving crossheads, horizontally moving eccentrics, and a rotating crankshaft.

Each area presented a different moving target so it took considerable time for him to perfect the technique. Experienced oilers took great pride in using only one quart of oil per watch, hitting their targets on every squirt. My oiler was using an average of four quarts.

Some experienced oilers even sanded the brass bottom of their oil can to thin it down to gain better control over the stream. My oiler was issued a new oil can at the start of his first watch and promptly spilled oil over his hands while simply filling it from a large barrel. He attempted to squirt a stream on his first round of the engine. But, because his hands were slippery, the can squeezed out of his hand and dropped into the crank pit. It made a loud clatter as it was struck by the rotating crankshaft.

I was standing at the throttle with my back to him when I heard the noise. I turned around and he said, "I just dropped my oil can into the crank pit!" I issued another to him and before the watch was finished, he had dropped that one too.

Between the fireman smoking and the oiler dropping oil cans periodically, I was slowly losing patience. To be honest, however, I wasn't much better than they.

During heavy weather with the ship heading into the seas and pitching badly, it became necessary for me to stand by the "butterfly valve" to prevent the engine from racing. The butterfly valve acted as a quick closing valve, much like a stovepipe damper, to quickly shut off the steam to the engine whenever the propeller came out of the water and to reopen it when the propeller was submerged.

This procedure required a certain technique and coordination not easily learned when one is feeling somewhat seasick. In a short while the chief engineer came below to demonstrate how to achieve this. With the valve lever in his hand, he positioned his feet firmly on the floorplates so as to feel the ship's motion and proceeded to open and close the valve smoothly without any problems.

After a few minutes of demonstration, he turned it over to me and told me to try it. I assumed the same stance he had and tried to synch myself with the feel of the ship's motion. On my first attempt, I opened the valve exactly opposite to what would be the correct time just as the propeller came completely free of the water. The engine raced so rapidly, the eccentrics picked up a large glob (about the size of a softball) of emulsified lubricating oil from the eccentric pit and flung it directly at the chief engineer.

It struck him squarely in the middle of the chest, saturating him with warm, slippery oil. Luckily, he was a good-natured and patient man and assured me I would catch on to it soon. He then left the engine room to take a shower and change clothes.

A few days later we received a submarine warning from the commodore. Apparently our destroyer escorts had picked up sounds on their detecting devices, so they began to lay down a smoke screen around us and ordered all ships to commence making smoke from their stacks.

When the bridge called to tell me this, I shouted to the fireman. I told him to make as much smoke as he could and that this was his chance to look good after having been chastised so much prior to this. I couldn't assist him in the fire room because we were getting speed changes constantly and I couldn't leave the throttle.

The bridge called several times to tell us to commence smoking, but try as he did, he couldn't produce any. He tried the opposite to everything he had been taught at Sheepshead Bay on how to prevent smoking, but to no avail.

When the submarine alert passed, the commodore issued orders to cease smoking. But at this point the fireman had just caught onto the technique for producing it and we began to belch heavy clouds of it from our stack. We got messages from the bridge to stop it.

Finally, everything was restored to normal. I told the fireman, "My watch has been catching hell from everyone since the trip began for smoking and now that we have to produce it, you can't!"

The convoy split up into smaller groups, with each group diverted to various ports in the British Isles, as we approached the English Channel.. We were ordered to Swansea, in Wales. While maneuvering the engine to pick up our pilot to enter port, the first assistant engineer was handling the engine throttle, I was logging the bells from the bridge, and the chief engineer was walking around the engine room observing.

As we approached the pier, we began receiving several telegraph bells in rapid succession including one stop bell which caused all of us to age ten years. During the stopped period, we heard a clatter behind us and turned around to see my oiler climbing out of the crank pit, his arms loaded with oil cans. He had dumped one batch onto the steel floorplates which had caused the clatter and returned for a second load. With a big grin, he said, "Hey, Mr. Murphy, I got all those oil cans I dropped during the trip across!"

The chief grabbed his forehead and just shook his head in disbelief while the rest of us stood there with our mouths open. The clearances between the sides and bottom of the crank pit and the throw of the crankshaft was only a few inches. If we had answered a bell from the bridge while he was in there, he would have been crushed in one revolution of the engine!

When the chief recovered from this shock, he lit into the oiler and gave him the worst chewing out I had heard in a long time. I think the chief used this opportunity to get a lot of things that happened on my watch off his chest—losing all those oil cans, smoking problems, and especially the glob of warm oil hitting him in the chest.

When the *Clara Barton* arrived in Swansea, our first British port, a doctor came aboard to check the crew for any signs of venereal disease. Although the captain explained to him we had just arrived from the States and no one had had an opportunity to contract any diseases, the doctor told him that their laws prohibited anyone from having shore liberty until they had been examined.

The captain then told the doctor to use the officers' dining room for the examination and if he wished, he could have breakfast there. I entered a few minutes later and saw the doctor seated at the next table and assumed he was there for breakfast.

The boatswain appeared in doorway and the doctor asked his name. "John Doe, boatswain," the boatswain replied.

The medic looked at his copy of our crew list, made a check mark on it, and then said, "All right, young man, drop your dungarees and undershorts for me."

Just then the messman brought in my scrambled eggs and bacon and placed them in front of me. I stared at them and then at the half-naked boatswain and said, "What the hell is going on here?"

The doctor said, "I have to examine each crew member for VD before there can be any shore liberty."

"In the dining room during breakfast?" I asked.

"The captain said to do the examination here, and also told me I could have breakfast while I was in here."

"I don't think the captain realized what the examination consisted of, Doctor. I suggest you have your breakfast first and then do your examining elsewhere."

He agreed. The boatswain pulled up his drawers and dungarees and left, and the doctor ordered breakfast. Later he did his examining in the ship's hospital.

When the *Clara Barton* returned to the States after our first trip, we anchored in Boston about 7:00 P.M. awaiting docking orders. The anchorage was crowded, but the pilot selected an area clear of all other ships, at least for the time being.

After port officials cleared us, the skipper began to use up some of the remaining whiskey he had purchased in Europe. Jason was standing an anchor watch on the bridge taking routine anchor bearings. The second assistant engineer was on watch below and began pumping fuel from one of the ship's deep tanks to the starboard settling tank located in the engine room.

About 10:00 P.M. a large tanker dropped anchor nearby. This caused Jason to become concerned because if it had swung on its anchor, we would be in danger of him striking us. So Jason called the captain who by now was pretty well inebriated.

The captain arrived on the bridge and realized Jason was not only correct, but the tanker had already begun to swing toward us. He called the chief mate to go to the bow and begin heaving in the anchor and then rang "slow ahead" on the engine room telegraph.

When our ship had anchored earlier, the chief engineer had asked the captain if it would be necessary to keep steam on the main engine for an emergency. The engineer was told it was not necessary because this was considered a "safe anchorage." Thus steam was secured to the engine and "finished with engines" rang on the telegraph.

The normal procedure when getting underway is to have a couple of hours notice in order to put steam on the engine and warm it up slowly before committing the engine to a state of readiness. Once the bridge is notified by the engine room that the engine is ready, standby is rung on the telegraph, and from that point on, we may maneuver the engine as required.

The second was attending the fuel pump at the time the telegraph was rung to slow ahead, but he ignored it, assuming someone on the bridge had bumped against it. When he didn't return the signal to the bridge, the captain rang it again with repeated swings on the handle, causing it to jingle continuously in the engine room.

The second called the bridge and the captain answered, telling him he required instant maneuvering. The second told him it was impossible because steam was off the engine, the main valves closed, and he had just rung the telegraph from finished with engines to slow ahead, bypassing the standby signal.

This infuriated the captain, so he called the chief engineer and first assistant who rushed to the engine room to get the engine ready. I was in bed at the time, but the first stuck his head in my room and called me to get below. As I entered the engine room from the refrigeration flat, which was one level down from main deck, the second passed me rushing up the engine room ladder with the captain in hot pursuit.

I went below where the chief and first were opening the valves to ready the engine. The telegraph signals came fast and furious as we shifted the ship to a new location in the anchorage. During the maneuvering we felt a slight bump. The tanker had struck us during its slow swing, but caused only minor damage to our starboard lifeboat davit.

Just before we began receiving telegraph signals from the bridge, the fireman walked to where we were standing and dropped three or four pieces of broken teeth onto the log desk. He told us they came from the second's mouth when the captain slugged him in the fireroom!

While maneuvering the engine, we suddenly found ourselves sticking to the steel floorplates and looked down to find us standing in a puddle of black, viscous fuel. The settling tank had overflowed through its open sounding tube which was located on the top of the tank. The hot fuel poured out the top, down the sides of the tank, onto the floorplates, and into the bilges. We had been so consumed by the rush of activities to get the engine ready for maneuvering that none of us realized the fuel transfer pump was in operation.

We secured the pump and continued answering bells while standing in the fuel. When the ship was finally secured at its new anchorage, the chief went to the bridge to inform the captain of the fuel spill. The chief and captain went to the second's room to speak to him, but he had barricaded himself in there and would not come out. The captain went below to the engine room to view the spill and then ordered all hands, including the cooks and deck department personnel, to the engine room to commence cleaning operations.

This massive effort continued throughout the night, but by morning it appeared nothing had been cleaned.

The ship shifted to the pier at 0700 and at 0900 a U.S. Coast Guard inspector arrived on board, apparently called by the second assistant. He interviewed the captain, chief engineer, second, Jason, the fireman on watch, and me and then went below to view the mess.

Shore cleaners were hired but there was still plenty of evidence for the inspector to see. After a second "consultation" with the captain, he issued a requirement to "clean traces of fuel from engine room tanktops!"

End of investigation. I don't know just what the captain said or did for the inspector, but somehow he got to him.

The second quit that morning, threatening to sue the captain, but out of all this confusion, I was promoted to "acting second assistant engineer." Acting, because I didn't possess a second's license yet. Several months later, I was questioned by our U.S. Lines attorneys and gave a deposition about the incident, but never learned the outcome of the second's case.

CHAPTER FOUR

SS *CLARA BARTON* VOYAGE #2

Jason and I were somewhat discouraged at the end of our first trip, mostly because of the antics of the captain. We talked it over and decided if we were to make another trip and if it lasted as long as the previous one, we would have enough time to sit for our next license so we signed on.

I had really wanted to make the next trip because of the opportunity to sail as second assistant engineer. I was happy that the chief engineer and first assistant had the confidence in me to promote me. The U.S. Coast Guard issued a waiver for me the next day and I signed on as second.

Most of the engine department was staying on because the first assistant was like a father to all of us. He was like the chief who had answered his country's call to return to the sea in spite of his age. Both of these men could have been working ashore in a defense plant or shipyard earning more money and in comparative safety, so they had the respect of all hands.

In a few days we were loaded with vehicles in the holds and planes on deck that were carried on a type of temporary framework welded to our decks. Like the previous trip, we joined a convoy off Halifax and were on our way.

On the third day at sea, some of the armed guard sailors came into the engine room on my watch to ask for some one-eighth-inch pipe. They said they needed the pipe to make repairs to the hydraulic system on their equipment. They had the required measurements of the pipe, so I cut it to length and they left the engine room.

The following day was extremely windy and the convoy was proceeding without incident when we received an urgent message from the convoy commodore, "Lower that kite, or leave the convoy!" Jason, who was on the bridge, called the captain because he didn't know what the message meant. When he arrived on the bridge, they looked aft and there saw what the message referred to.

The gunners had constructed a massive kite about twelve feet long and eight feet wide from the pipe I had given them. They used cloth from our rag bin sewn over the frame. The wind was so strong and blustery that just as soon as they released it from the after gun turret, it lifted itself into the sky and kept climbing as fast as they could pay out the line.

The captain called the gunnery officer who went aft and told his sailors to reel it in as fast as possible. It now seemed to be a hundred feet up in the sky. As they began to haul it in, the line broke and the kite began diving and pitching all over the sky behind us.

It took one final plunge and landed in the forward gun tub of the Liberty behind us. The gunners on watch there, who had been watching us since the episode began, leaped from the tub to the deck to avoid being injured by the crazily tumbling missile.

A few days later, some of the gunners came into the engine room to request some copper tubing, again to make repairs to the hydraulic systems. I said, "No more kites!"

They laughed and said, "No, Second, this time we are legitimate," but I had my doubts.

Like many Libertys, the *Clara Barton* spent many days in British ports awaiting orders to join a convoy and head for the invasion which everyone knew was imminent. After loading some cargo for a few days, we would shift to an anchorage to allow another ship to use our berth to load a special type of cargo and then shift back again to the pier for more specialized cargo.

Another Liberty was always nearby—the SS *Charles Morgan*. Our two ships had come to England months before in the same Atlantic convoy. Wherever we were sent in Great Britain, whether Southampton, Belfast, or Glasgow, or Swansea or Newport in Wales, she was always with us. Our gunners became friendly with theirs, meeting ashore as well as on board each others' vessel.

One morning while at anchor, we noticed a boatswain's chair suspended from the bow of the *Morgan*, its occupant a sailor from its gun crew. He was sketching with chalk an outline of what appeared to be a naked woman on the hull below the anchor. The following morning another sailor began painting in the chalk figure with a homemade mixture of flesh colored paint. Late that afternoon there she was in all her glory, a real blonde beauty about twelve feet tall! In the next few days another appeared on the other bow, this time a brunette.

As they later told our gun crew, "If the Army Air Corps can have naked women painted on their planes, we should be able to have them on our ships!"

This started a rush of bow paintings among the many Libertys in British ports, and soon the ships became competitive in their art work. Aboard the *Clara Barton*, the gunners painted a lovely voluptuous blonde on one side and a redhead on the other.

Our skipper even stood on the pier one day to observe ours and act as an art critic, advising the sailor to make her legs longer, add more blonde hair, raise her arms, etc. Whenever two ships passed or entered another port, one would signal over to the other commenting on the art work. The gunners even carried their art work into their gun tubs and onto the flak shields of their guns.

This type of amusement was short lived, however, because War Shipping Administration officials soon learned of it and told all the ships to paint over the girls and restore the hulls to their wartime gray. Some of the gunners argued saying this was a carryover from sailing ship days when ships had figureheads, but this argument fell on deaf ears.

WSA reasoned that if we weren't permitted to have the ship's name boards or the name of the ship painted on the hull, it would be stupid to allow us to keep the girls there. The enemy could easily track a ship's movements by knowing which girls were where at any given time. In any event WSA won and all the girls were soon gone. Well, almost all of them!

The two beauties on the *Clara Barton* were first painted over with three coats of clear marine varnish and when dry covered with a light coat of gray paint. Whenever the gray appeared to be wearing off in some areas, the boatswain would send a man over the side to touch it up.

Someone likened the paintings to works of great masters which had been deliberately painted over to await a finer day. Months later when the *Clara Barton* returned to New York, the heavy seas of the North Atlantic had washed away the gray and we steamed into the harbor with our two girls standing out in all their glory. Passing ships and tugs even sounded their whistles at us, or rather at them!

Meanwhile back in Europe, all the Libertys had painted over their beauties, and the hulls were once again their drab wartime gray. A couple of weeks later aboard two ships at anchor, deck crews were working overboard from boatswains' chairs touching up some rusted areas on the hulls with red lead. After these men returned aboard their vessels, there in five-foot-high letters was a sign on one ship which read, "NMU"—the initials for the labor union representing the crew on board. On the other hull was another sign, same size, which read "HUNGRY!"

Whether this was a message announcing a food shortage or a reflection on the culinary skills of the cooks, I never found out. But once again the WSA visited the ships and told them to paint over the signs, explaining that these were still a means of identification for the enemy.

Liberty launches were making regularly scheduled trips to the ships anchored in Southampton harbor. The captain and chief mate went ashore nearly every night to frequent many of the after-hours bars which could be found in most English cities. Access to these establishments was routinely offered to most anyone after the owners determined one could be trusted to keep its location a secret. Many of these became a base of operations for "ladies of the evening," who after all, were the drawing card for most of the sailors.

The problem the captain and mate faced was the expense of going ashore every night. So one evening they asked two of the girls if they would be interested in joining them aboard the *Clara Barton* and living aboard as "housekeepers" while the ship was at anchor. They accepted and came aboard that night. At breakfast the next morning they were introduced to the officers and assigned seats in the officers' dining saloon.

The captain's "housekeeper" seemed to have a sense of loyalty to him, but the mate's had a roving eye and apparently could see a lucrative potential for making a great deal of money while on board. After a few days the mate awoke to find his girl missing from his room, so he dressed quickly and went down two decks to the main deck where the crew lived. He quietly walked through the area hiding in open doorways when he heard a door open. In a few moments he spotted her leaving an oiler's room and immediately entering the next room, that of a wiper. He waited a few minutes, then knocked on the door and opened it to find her naked as a jaybird in the upper bunk with the wiper. She was sent ashore on the next launch, most likely much richer than when she came aboard a few days earlier!

The captain's girl, named Elsie, remained on board for a few more days, until one evening when the young lady's world seemed to come to an embarrassing end.

I had left my room to go to the head, and while standing at the urinal, heard her voice behind me, "Hi, Second." I turned and saw her standing in the doorway to the head. We were chatting when the captain came to the top of the stairway next to the head and shouted for her to go to the mate's room, and stop talking to the engineers.

She left and went to the chief mate's room which was forward on the same deck and slightly off the center of the passageway on the starboard side. I watched her as she wiggled her way up the passage, and then I stood in the doorway to the head where I could see into the mate's room.

The next room inboard to the mate's was the room of the first assistant engineer. There was a common bulkhead separating them and their two bunks were secured to each side of this bulkhead. At bunk level in the center was a loosely fitted kickout panel for escape to the next room should the vessel be torpedoed and the door to one's room jammed closed.

Elsie was wearing a riding habit; blouse, riding breeches, and boots for some reason. (Some wag would probably say it was appropriate.) She went to the mate's room and the captain came in shortly after. They sat on his settee and offered the mate a drink, but he refused, telling them he wasn't feeling good. He said he was hungover, and asked them to leave so he could get rid of his headache.

They laughed at him, and then the captain said, "Elsie, take off your clothes and jump into the bunk with him and show him a good time!"

When I heard this I repositioned myself in the doorway to get a better look, and moments later she was undressed and in the bunk. He pleaded with her to leave him alone, but she said, "I've been given an order by the captain, I can't disobey him," and they began wrestling while the old man roared with laughter on the settee!

Somehow, her rear end got between the mate and the bulkhead when the mate gave her a shove with his knee. Her fat, bare behind knocked in the kickout panel onto the legs of the first assistant engineer who was asleep in the next room! He awakened, turned on the light over his bunk, and sat bolt upright just staring at the big ass staring back at him from the bulkhead!

The door to this room was hooked back in the fully open position so I had a good view of both rooms, especially now that he had turned on his light. He looked up, spotted me down the passageway nearly doubled over with laughter, and began to laugh himself. He spit on his hands, rubbed them together, and began to spank her rear end while she was screaming in the mate's room to pull her free. The captain and mate pulled her loose like pulling a cork from a bottle. The first assistant stuck his head through the hole and said, "Good Evening, something wrong?"

Everyone was laughing, everyone that is except Elsie. Her pride was hurt more than anything, and she became furious at them for laughing, so she packed her belongings and left the ship on the next launch.

The following morning I was in the first's room laughing about the incident when the ship's carpenter appeared in the doorway. "Kickout panel loose in here, First? Mate told me it fell in during the night." Little did he know!

CHAPTER FIVE

NORMANDY

We didn't know where or when the invasion would take place, but rumors were circulating about maybe the south of France, the west coast of France, or somewhere near Holland. Whenever rumors are about a ship, the ship's cooks seem to have the inside information, but in this case they didn't seem to have any insight.

Whether the cooks have inside information because they feed some of the shore people working aboard and are told in confidence, or whether it's just a reputation they have acquired over the years, the galley is the place to go for up-to-date information on sailings and destinations.

Two Royal Air Force observers had come aboard in Southampton with all their gear and reported to the captain and U.S. Army security officer aboard. They were to live on the ship, but that was all the information they would leak. Each day they would conduct a drill between them by holding up flash cards similar to those we used in early school days to learn our arithmetic.

Their cards pictured silhouette views of Allied and enemy aircraft in various forms, such as front views, side views, top views, etc. They would stand apart at a given distance, one holding the cards, the other with binoculars. The cardholder would expose a view for a fraction of a second and then cover it, while the other would shout out its identity.

The role they were to play in the invasion was obvious and we marveled at their expertise. During the actual invasion they would wear headphones matched to those of our gunners and call out "friendly or enemy." Presumably, the gunners would only fire at the enemy, but sadly though, this was not always the case.

During the actual invasion whenever a plane appeared out of cloud cover, even if only for a moment, the nervous gunners began firing without waiting for the word. Also with the loud noise from the rapid firing of the 20-mms the gunners could not always hear through their headphones.

Moving into Utah beach on D day, the sky was filled with Allied and Axis planes. It looked like a huge fireworks display with the tracer bullets from over two hundred ships filling the blue sky. The battleship USS *Texas* was at the beachhead and a reassuring sight for us with our small eight 20 mms, one 3 inch 50-mm, and one 5 inch 50-mm guns.

When all the ships began firing wildly at any plane in sight, the admiral in command of the *Texas* sent word out quickly that he would remove the protection of the *Texas* if the gunners didn't wait for the signal to fire from the spotters. This warning seemed to settle everyone down somewhat and the war became a little more orderly. Shortly after, the next waves of Allied planes to fly over had three newly painted stripes on the under sides of their wings for identification. This saved many pilots.

Each of our 20-mm guns had a steel protective shield around it in the form of a tub to protect the gunners from shrapnel. They also had a round-shaped iron bar welded to the top of the shield to interrupt the gun barrel as it swung through its arc while the gunner was tracking a plane in his sights. This prevented him from sweeping across our bridge with a hail of bullets!

When a gunner is tracking a plane he is so intent on following it, he doesn't have time to think where the shells are landing, especially if it is a low flying plane. These protective bars worked well for our ship, but there was nothing preventing the gunners on other ships from strafing us, or us shooting at them. Many ships suffered losses in this manner.

Each of the Liberty ships at Normandy carried a barrage balloon tethered to a special winch mounted on the fore deck. Upon our arrival at the beachhead, the balloon was inflated from a helium bottle on board and sent aloft several hundred feet to ward off any low flying enemy planes. The theory being that the plane would collide with the steel tether wire and it would slice through its wings, causing a crash.

While an Army stevedore battalion was discharging our cargo of vehicles, the gunners of a Liberty next to ours inadvertently shot some 20-mm shells through our balloon, causing the huge, floppy monster of rubberized fabric to deflate instantly and come lumbering down. It draped itself over the running rigging and mast of our jumbo boom!

This caused cargo operations to cease at two holds, so the call went out to all hands, "Anyone with boatswain's chair experience please report to the fore deck!" Jake and I went forward and, recalling our experience in that gymnasium a few months earlier, assisted in releasing the balloon. My thoughts went back to those academy days when I asked, "Why in the world am I being taught how to rig a boatswain's chair?"

Barrage balloons were to be found all over the British Isles during the war, and unquestionably served a useful purpose in keeping enemy planes high. By keeping them high they became good targets for the British searchlights and anti-aircraft batteries. A popular joke during those days between British girls and our GIs was that the Germans could never sink the British Isles because they would stay afloat on the balloons!

In June of 1993, my class from Massachusetts Maritime Academy held its fiftieth-year reunion and I was telling the story of our barrage balloon being shot down that day over Normandy. Almost unbelievably, one of my classmates remarked that his ship at the same beachhead had shot down a balloon from the Liberty ship next to theirs. We had to assume it was the one from the *Clara Barton* because no other balloons were shot down during that time.

About 500 GIs boarded the *Clara Barton* in Southampton on June 5, 1944, the eve of the invasion of Normandy. Some slept in temporary bunks set up in the cargo holds while others slept out on deck. I use the word "slept," however I'm sure none of them did, anticipating what lay ahead for them the next morning.

Each GI wore a collapsible life belt around his waist made of a rubberized fabric snapped together in the front. It had a fold in it which was also snapped closed for keeping it close to his body. To inflate it the GI merely had to squeeze the area behind the front snaps, causing two sharp points to pierce the caps of two small CO_2 cylinders within the belt. During inflation the fold also unsnapped to allow the belt to completely surround his body snugly. Each belt also had two hoses fitted by which he could inflate it by mouth if necessary.

During the crossing of the English Channel, one GI was lying on #4 hatch trying to sleep in the darkness of early morning when another GI attempted to step over him to go to the latrine. The heel of his boot scuffed the belt in the area of the CO_2 cylinders causing the life belt to quickly inflate!

The GI wearing the belt awoke, startled as his belt tightened around his midsection, grabbed his rifle, and went into a prone position for firing! The soldier who had caused the scare shouted to him that everything was OK, and they both had a laugh over it, but it showed the tension they were under.

Upon our early morning arrival at Utah Beach, scramble nets were rigged over the sides to allow the soldiers to climb down to waiting landing craft alongside. One GI could not locate his rifle when he was awakened and reported it to his sergeant. The supply sergeant issued another immediately and he was on his way. His rifle had been next to him all through the night, so no one could understand how it could be missing. Another GI fell through an open hatch cover and landed on the hood of a truck below and suffered a broken leg. His war service ended right there. After the GIs were off the ship, we had to wait to received wounded men aboard where a mini-hospital was set up in the officers' dining room to treat them.

In the meantime we conducted a ship search for the missing rifle, but couldn't find it in any public spaces or areas where the soldiers had been billeted. We then conducted a search of all crew and officers' rooms and found it in a wiper's room hidden beneath his mattress. He claimed he had gone out on deck during the night and "found" it lying on the deck, so he just picked it up. The gun was returned to the Army security officer on board, and the captain logged the wiper.

After a few days we returned to Southampton for another load of vehicles and GIs. While there the wiper quit to join a pool of American merchant seamen waiting to fill in on any American ship where a shortage existed. I believe he quit for his own safety aboard the *Clara Barton* because he was taking a lot of verbal abuse and threats from his union brothers. They looked upon the incident the same way the rest of us did; a guy has to be a lousy bastard to steal a soldier's gun just before he goes into battle!

The fireman/watertender on my watch, Red Bengston, about forty years old, was designated as the merchant crew substitute "hot shell-man" for our 3 inch 50-mm gun on the bow. On the night of June 6, 1944, our Navy hot shell-man got burned from a hot shell casing when the gun's ejection mechanism jammed. The gunners corrected it and called the engine room to have Red go forward to fill in. When he left the engine room he was wearing only a tee shirt and dungarees. Arriving at the bow in the dark, he put on the long heavy gauntlets used by the hot shell-man and took his place in the gun tub.

Up to this point Red's only training had consisted of handling a dummy shell, cool to the touch and light in weight, in daylight on a make-believe gun! During his training the dummy shell was shoved into the breech, the breech closed, and "firing" simulated. After firing the breech was opened by hand, a pawl caught the flange of the shell casing and extracted it about two inches where the hot shell-man would grasp it and remove the dummy shell clear of the breech.

Now he was confronted with the moment of truth, the real thing! At night, in a blackout! His eyes, not yet accustomed to the darkness, could not make out much when he felt a long, heavy shell thrust at him by one of the gunners passing ammunition. He took the shell from him, much heavier than in practice, and groping in the dark, managed to get it into the breech.

Before he could turn his head away from the gun, the gunner fired the shell. Almost immediately the breech opened, a huge bright flame from the breech blinded Red, and the red-hot shell casing came back at him like a projectile!

The casing struck him in the belly with a loud, sickening sizzle as it disintegrated his tee shirt and seared his stomach. He collapsed in the gun tub and had to be removed by the gunners and treated by the medics on board.

Earlier when Red had been drilling on the dummy gun, no one had told him to shield his eyes, turn his head, and stand aside the breech. Also, while the time in training, performing the duties of a hot shell-man took from ten to twenty seconds for each round, the real thing was instantaneous. Thus he wasn't really properly trained for that position. He was off duty for several days, but his burn healed and he was soon back standing his watch.

Discharging of our military vehicles by the Army stevedores was going on night and day. Many of the stevedores slept aboard, while others relieved them for short spells, thus there was no delay in changing of the shifts.

The discharging went sporadically because each time enemy planes came overhead everyone was under orders to take cover. Some of the planes seemed to be observing the scene below, but others would come in on a bombing mission at high level. Although the discharging went on into the night, the same conditions existed with planes, except that the Germans would drop brilliant flares to illuminate the entire area and then drop bombs. With the planes flying higher than the flares, they were difficult for our gunners to pick up in their sights.

The ships were blacked out with special screens fitted into the portholes which allowed ventilation, but prevented light from the quarters leaking out. The doors leading to the deck were fitted with two blackout curtains draped in a staggering fashion inside each entrance. When anyone had to go out on deck, it would be necessary for him to first pass through one curtain, then the next, and finally open the watertight door.

The chief mate was about to go out on deck one evening to view the cargo operations. In a drunken stupor, he swung the first blackout curtain aside without making sure it was returned to its proper position, then swung the second to the opposite side in the same manner, and then opened the watertight door allowing a bright shaft of light to shine out on the stevedores on the after deck.

Immediately, several GIs shouted, "Shut that damn door, light is leaking out!" The mate shouted back, "Who in hell do you think you're talking to? I'm the chief mate on here; only one man can tell me what to do, he's the captain!" With those words he shone his flashlight up into the night sky shouting, "You don't want light, how's this?"

In a flash, several GIs jumped on him from the boat deck and pummeled him into unconsciousness. He was rescued by other GIs but not before he had suffered several cuts and bruises! Moments later, one of the planes made a diving run toward the ships and dropped a bomb which landed between us and the Liberty on our port side. The chief mate was treated on board by the purser, but he didn't dare go out on deck again to view the cargo operations.

A few days later (on June 10) still at Utah Beach, I had just gone below to stand my 4-8 watch when I heard and felt a tremendous explosion. My oiler came over to me with a cup of coffee, which was spilling out of the mug from his shaking hand. I could hardly take it from him because my hand also was shaking badly. I sent him up on deck to find out what had happened. I gave him orders to be sure to return below and let us in on it, just in case we had been hit! I didn't want him running for his lifeboat and forgetting us down there!

He returned in a few minutes to tell me the *Charles Morgan* just got hit in the after hold and was sinking slowly. I felt a lump in

my throat because the *Morgan* and our ship had been through so
much together. A small crew of GIs had been cleaning the hold
after discharging its cargo and had been in the hold when the bomb
landed. All of them lost their lives.

The *Charles Morgan*, a Liberty like ours, and the *Clara Barton*
had left England together in the same convoy to join the invasion
fleet. We even anchored next to each other at Utah. Often in bars
one crew would kid the other about making a "romance" between
Charles and Clara. And now, sadly, Charles was gone.

Upon our arrival at Normandy we anchored. After our troops
left the ship aboard landing craft for the beach, we began discharging our cargo into amphibious vehicles called "Ducks," but offi-
cially designated DUKWs. These were a rather small land and
seacraft capable of carrying one or two sling loads in their cargo
area and operated by a single driver. There were literally hundreds
of them carrying the cargoes from a multitude of ships laying off the
beachhead.

They were unique in their design, capable of lumbering awk-
wardly through the water pushed by their propeller until they struck
the sandy beach and then with a shift of gears, the craft's wheels
took over for driving on land. After talking to one of the drivers
about their operation, I was told their biggest complaint was keeping the after compartment dry, where the propeller shaft went through
the body. The driver told me the shaft packing arrangement left a
lot to be desired because the packing wasn't holding up. It was
being ground to a powder by a mixture of sand and gravel whenever
they climbed up onto the beach.

I asked if there was anything we could do aboard the ship to
assist him because we had a pretty good variety of packing in our
storeroom. I showed him some of our packing and he finally settled
on a piece of our flax-stern tube packing which was saturated with
tallow. What he required was only about 3/8 inches in diameter and

the piece he took from me was one inch in diameter and four feet long.

"It'll never fit," I said.

"Don't worry about that," he said. "The other drivers and I will unweave it and make it work. It's better than the junk we have now." I saw him the following day and he said our packing was working very well and holding up much better than theirs.

I felt good about being able to help these guys out. My GI buddy told me if there was anything he could do for me to just let him know. The battalion of these GIs worked night and day, ship after ship, through bombing attacks, shore batteries firing down on the beaches, and enemy strafings.

The radio operator and I had been on our ship's bridge earlier that day watching the activity ashore and he said to me at that time how he'd like to sneak ashore to see the action firsthand. I told him I would also and then later it came to me—my buddy the driver—I'll bet he'd give us a lift to the beachhead.

It was 2000 hours and I was due to go on watch at midnight. We had four hours, so I contacted Sparks and we decided this would be the night if he would take us. We met the driver a half hour later and he said he'd be glad to drop us off at the beach.

This was a hair-brained idea, but we thought we'd have one up on the rest of the gang on the ship if we could pull it off! We changed into khaki clothes, grabbed our flat, World War I helmets and a fistful of cigars for "piece-offs" and climbed down a Jacob's ladder into the driver's compartment of the DUKW.

As soon as he had his two sling loads in the cargo compartment, we left the ship's side and headed in to the beach. We had plenty of time, it was only nine thirty when we crawled out of the DUKW in France, and we expected to be there only a half hour and we would start back. We gave our driver a few cigars and he thanked us. Then we talked to the truck driver who was receiving our cargo and he asked us if we wanted a ride into town where he would deliver his cargo. This wasn't part of our plan, but we thought what the hell, we'd never have this chance again so we said OK.

We rode through darkened roads between hedgerows and could see signs in the dim light, "AREA NOT CLEARED OF MINES" on each side of the road. Suddenly, this brought the war right to us. We arrived at the center of a small town which appeared to be a marshaling area where many trucks and tanks and GIs were assembled. Everyone was staring at us in our khakis and World War I helmets, so we thought we had better get back to the beach, and soon! We stood out like Laurel and Hardy!

We gave our driver some cigars and grabbed another truck back to the beach. Once there we felt somewhat relieved, except that now our only problem was to find a DUKW driver to take us to our ship. None of the hundreds of ships in the bay had names painted on them for security reasons, but each was assigned a location number for the beachhead and, of course in our brilliance, we couldn't be expected to think of getting the number before we left the ship!

While standing there on the beach an air raid alert sounded and everyone on the beach lay down flat, including Sparks and me, holding tightly to our pancake helmet. The "All Clear" sounded in a few minutes and we began questioning DUKW drivers if they knew which ship was the *Clara Barton*.

We asked everyone, "Do you know the position number?" Of course we felt foolish saying we didn't, so the GI couldn't help us. After spending what seemed hours on the beach asking various drivers if they knew where our ship was, we finally lucked out. We found our buddy who brought us ashore. He brought us out to our ship and we climbed aboard. It was now 1:00 A.M.

When we got to the main deck, we were greeted by the drunken captain, the chief mate, the chief engineer, first assistant, and several others who had been searching for us. They had started their ship search at the 11:30 watch call that night when I couldn't be located to go on watch at midnight.

The captain threatened to log me for not being there to go on watch, but I think the chief and first talked him out of it because the following day nothing was said. I think they were envious of me because they kept asking me questions about our visit to France.

For the first few days at the beachhead our 20-mms, 3-inch and 5-inch guns were in almost continuous use, day and night. After the enemy was forced to retreat because of the constant pounding by our land, air, and sea forces, our gunners were able to relax somewhat and take a much needed breather. The action after that was mostly only at night, primarily shooting at planes which were foolish enough to venture toward the beach.

During the daylight hours, the gunners would clean their equipment, gather up all the empty brass shell casings littering the decks and gun turrets, and place them in bags to be collected by the Army at a later time. At least that was the plan, but both gunners and crew were collecting as many for themselves to make ash trays, lighters, lamps, and whatever else they could dream up. No one really minded because it was something to give them a little relaxation and helped to keep their minds off the war around us. The only problem was some weren't satisfied to use spent shell casings and began dismantling live 20-mm and 40-mm shells in their rooms!

They soon learned how to work the projectile end from the crimping of the brass casing, empty the powder overboard, and dismantle the projectile. Removing the primer from the casing was another story, however. The gunnery officer was constantly lecturing everyone about the dangers involved in this practice, but some still persisted.

The purser attempted to dismantle a 20-mm primer in his room under the "protection" of handling it underwater in his sink! It blew up and shattered his porcelain sink into hundreds of pieces, but luckily missed injuring him. The engine utility removed a similar primer and left it on his fold-down desk in his room.

He left the room for a moment, the primer rolled off, and blew a hole in the cement deck beneath his desk about ten inches in diameter! This explosion could be heard all through the midship house. So all hands rushed to the area to see what had caused the loud noise, but could barely see into his room due to the heavy smoke. When it cleared, he was standing there like a little kid who had just been caught with his hand in the cookie jar.

After these episodes, a ship search was conducted of all rooms, storerooms, and work spaces and several more live shells found. They were turned over to the gunnery officer and to the Army security officer aboard.

The day following D day, I was in our wheelhouse watching the scene on Utah Beach with a pair of binoculars. The third assistant came to tell me a story he had just heard from a warrant officer who was being interrogated by senior Army officers in our saloon a few minutes earlier.

The warrant was a glider pilot with the airborne and had landed his glider with a dozen airborne troops just before "H" hour on D day in an orchard behind the German lines. His troops were immediately surrounded by Germans, lined up, and shot. But the pilot, who had been knocked semiconscious from the crash landing, was spared because he kept muttering "American officer." He was taken by the Germans to a farmhouse which was apparently local headquarters for the area. He had been searched by them at the glider and his sidearm confiscated, but they had overlooked a single hand grenade concealed on his person.

While being questioned in the farmhouse, an open touring car drove up outside, apparently carrying a high ranking officer. The interrogators left the warrant to go outside to greet the officer and while outside, the warrant seized the opportunity and lobbed the grenade into the midst of the group.

During the ensuing confusion, he dashed out of the farmhouse, grabbed a German's automatic rifle and binoculars, jumped onto a motorcycle, and sped off down the road! He eventually made his way back through the lines to the beachhead and boarded a landing craft which was returning to our ship for another load.

The third assistant then said, "Boy, I find this hard to believe, it's something right out of the movies!"

At that moment, an Army officer standing nearby came over to us and said to him, "Here, take a look at the beachhead through these binoculars, you'll get a better idea about what's going on ashore!"

He accepted the binoculars and, as he brought them up to his eyes, he noticed am emblem—an eagle with a swastika beneath it! "Hey, these are German binoculars!"

"Yeah, and this is the automatic rifle. Now do you believe the story? I'm the guy you're talking about, any questions? If you think that story came out of Hollywood, you'd better smarten up mister, this war is for real!"

The third assistant apologized to him and felt quite humble after that.

The warrant's story stayed with me all through the war. I thought about him often and still do from time to time. I often wonder if his luck stayed with him until it was over and if he made it home safely.

Listening to that young warrant on the bridge suddenly brought the realities of war to me. I couldn't get him out of my mind after that. Thinking of how frightened I was during our slow movement toward the beach that morning, I wondered how he could think clearly enough to attempt that brave effort to escape.

It was brought home to me again a short while later when one of our fighter planes appeared out of the clouds, smoke trailing from his engine while he desperately tried to maneuver toward the beach to be over 'safe' territory before bailing out. After assuring himself he would land in friendly waters, he bailed out while one of his pilot buddies who had been escorting him circled him during his slow downward flight, suspended from his parachute. He hardly got his feet wet because he was surrounded by friendly landing craft of all kinds at the moment he landed and was swooped out of the sea to safety. His buddy flew in low over the landing craft, dipped his wings, and went on his way.

In contrast to this example of camaraderie, later that day an enemy plane appeared alone out of the cloud cover and one could almost read the pilot's mind at that instant. There stretched out below him was an armada of hundreds of ships all with their antiaircraft guns swinging toward him. Almost at once he was identified as enemy and the guns opened up.

With every fifth shell a tracer, the sky made it appear as though we were in the bottom of a huge birdcage looking upward with the tracers lighting up the sky, looking like the wire sides of the birdcage.

He tried desperately to come about and run for cloud cover, but his doom was sealed. His plane was hit with hundreds of shells and literally disintegrated. I felt a strong gut ache when I saw this. There was a human being in that plane, and he went to his maker at that point; he didn't even have a chance to bail out. I felt sorry for him in a way even if he was the enemy. Then I began to sense what courage it must take to face the enemy and have a showdown—him or me. I gained a new insight into war that day and a renewed respect for all those courageous guys who went ashore at Normandy.

After two days at the beachhead, our cargo at #4 hatch was discharged, and the chief engineer told me to sound the fuel oil deep tanks located in #4 lower cargo hold. The sounding tubes were located on the main deck just aft of the midship house, so after lunch I stepped out on deck to start.

I had just dropped the fifty-foot-long sounding tape down through the deck opening when I heard a loud, piercing, whistling noise overhead. I continued with the sounding when another similar noise was heard. Just at that moment the chief engineer ran out onto the boat deck and shouted, "Murphy, forget the soundings, get your ass down below and help the first put steam on the engine!"

"I had better wind up this tape first, Chief; I don't want to leave it in the sounding tube," I said.

"To hell with the tape, don't you hear those shells screaming overhead, a German gun battery has a bead on us!"

Now realizing that was the screaming sound I had heard, I saw a burst in the water a hundred yards away off our starboard side and the next about the same distance off our port side. My gunnery course at Massachusetts Maritime suddenly took over, "They're bridging us," was my next thought. Bridging was a method of shooting where shells would land alternately on each side of a target with each shell landing closer to the target until it was destroyed.

I grabbed my World War I helmet and quickly put it on. It looked like a pancake sitting on my head, but it gave me a certain assurance and it was better than nothing.

When I arrived below, the first had already put steam on the engine and was rocking it to warm it up. We called the bridge to let them know we were ready and immediately started taking bells to maneuver out of there.

When the captain rang up "full ahead," we felt a bumping sensation in the engine room, a sure indication we were aground. Then the telegraph rang "full ahead" again and we poured the steam to it and the bumping worsened.

The captain called down to tell us we were aground, but maybe we could free ourselves off the sandy bottom with the engine. By alternating the ahead and astern throttles, we literally rocked the ship off the sandbar and got loose! After leaving that anchorage and proceeding into deeper water about a mile out, two U.S. Navy destroyers moved to our previous position and began lobbing shells in the direction of the German gun. Suddenly the shelling stopped. They scored a bull's-eye and our ship blinked over a "thank-you" to them.

After making several shuttle trips to Omaha and Utah beaches from various ports in England, the Allies had liberated Cherbourg, so on our next trip over we were scheduled to dock there. After tying up, we were lectured by the Army about going ashore. We were told not to pick up souvenirs, to stay within mine-cleared areas, obey the curfew, beware of booby traps, etc. So by the time the lecture was finished, most of us were almost afraid to venture off the ship.

Overlooking the pier area was a high hill which we were told was "off limits." That was all some of our guys, including me, had to hear! We walked up the hill and found it filled with tunnels and cave openings in which the Germans had mounted several 88-mm gun emplacements.

Nearby in neat stacks, were many shells still packed in their protective shipping cylinders, each about five feet long and six inches in diameter. The ship's carpenter picked up one of them to take back to the ship to make it into a lamp, stating he would figure out how to disarm it after he got it aboard! He threw it over his shoulder and headed back toward the ship. When he arrived at the pier, he found the tide had gone out and the main deck of the ship was about five feet below the pier, so he heaved it off his shoulder and let it land on deck. It hit with a thud on one end, bounced up in the air and landed again on the other end, and continued in this manner until it settled onto the steel deck!

Several crew members witnessed this and took off in all directions, scrambling from what could have been a disaster! The shell wasn't armed, but Chips didn't know that and it could have been intentionally armed by retreating Germans in the event some crazy American might want to make a lamp from it! Arming many potential souvenirs with mines was a favorite trick of the enemy, knowing the souvenir happy Americans.

The captain and mate soon found out about the live shell and under the direction of our gunnery officer, it was turned over to the military for disposal.

Nearby was the wreckage of a German fighter plane from which the pilot had parachuted when it was shot down several days earlier. Other crew members had hiked over to view it, again against military orders. The engine utility, sensing a potential source of souvenirs, carried a hacksaw with him ready to dismember any part he might think would look good at home and he could tell his grandchildren about fifty years from then.

The plane was badly wrecked, but one blade of its aluminum propeller was in good condition, so he began sawing it at the hub.

The hub was about six inches thick, but he knew it would saw quickly because it was soft metal. When he was about one inch into it, his saw blade broke! Although he had the foresight to bring the hacksaw with him, for which I had congratulated him, he didn't have enough common sense to bring spare blades!

Standing just a few feet away was an AB, holding a hacksaw, and his fist full of spare blades! He was like a lion waiting to pounce once the engine utility abandoned the propeller. The utility asked if he could borrow a blade, but of course, the answer was a resounding "NO."

"How about selling one to me?" the utility asked.

"Nope!" said the AB.

The utility then began attempting to wiggle the partly severed blade back and forth in an attempt to break it off at the hub, but he hadn't cut through enough of it at that point. He finally gave up on it, and in moved the AB.

Ironically, the AB finished cutting through the propeller using only one blade, the one fitted in the saw, and never had to use a spare!

I had only a pair of pliers with me and I only had them because I always carried them in my dungarees pocket. But I managed to remove the cotter pins from the joy stick in the cockpit and took it back with me.

A few minutes later, some MPs saw us and told us to "get the hell away from that plane, it hasn't been cleared for booby traps!" Once again, like our trip ashore at Normandy beach in the amphibious DUKW, our naiveté could have been fatal.

After the initial invasion of Normandy, many of the participating ships returned to England to begin a shuttle service to the beachheads from various British ports.

The *Clara Barton* was tied up in Southampton, had just completed its loading, and was to leave in the morning on its first shuttle trip. It would join other ships and proceed across the English Channel to "Utah Beach" in a small convoy.

The captain and chief mate had been on a drinking bout since dinner that last night in port and decided to go ashore to further their binge after they discovered they were out of whiskey. They called for a cab, a rarity in those days, and soon found there were none available. Taxis were used sparingly in those days due to the fuel shortage. Some even operated on charcoal burned in a small trailer towed behind the cab, while others used a combustible gas carried in a large canvas tent-like structure mounted on the cab roof. I was in one of the latter one time and was asked by the driver to please get out and walk up a steep grade because his gas pressure wasn't enough to carry the two of us. I rejoined him at the top. He had picked me up as a fare because I was headed in the same direction he was going to refill his gas container.

The mate and captain were not about to walk the two miles to town, so they turned on the steam to the deck winches for #3 hatch and removed a few hatch covers and the hatch beam. The last vehicle which had been loaded still had the wire slings beneath its wheels and was directly under the booms, so as to be the first discharged at the beachhead. It happened to be a personnel carrier and the ignition keys were in it. They hooked onto it, removed it from the hold, and deposited it on the pier. The mate climbed into driver's seat and the captain rode next to him. They drove it out of the pier area and into the city where they parked it in front of a bar which they had frequented before.

After several drinks, they got into some sort of altercation and were thrown out when the police were called. They left by the side door, and couldn't recall which vehicle they had used for their ride ashore. There was a jeep parked where they were standing, with the keys in it, so they thought that had to be the vehicle they used. They climbed aboard, drove it back to the ship, and loaded it in the space where the personnel carrier had been removed.

Bills of lading, cargo plans, and documentation were not a worry when we arrived at the beachhead, so all our cargo was discharged without incident! Of course, we never learned how some GI explained the missing jeep, or if he drove the personnel carrier back to his base!

After completing a few shuttle trips to the beachheads the *Clara Barton* was anchored in the harbor of Southampton one evening awaiting a berth. It was a warm summer night and the porthole over my bunk was open for ventilation.

I was suddenly awakened by the loud sputtering of what sounded like an aircraft nearby whose engine was failing. I sat up in my bunk and looked out the porthole and could see what appeared to be a single engine plane losing altitude rapidly as it passed close to us.

I had a sinking feeling in my stomach, thinking it could be some RAF pilot or U.S. Army Air Corps pilot struggling to make it to his base. I said a silent prayer for him that he would make it or at least have bailed out in time.

It crashed in a field nearby in a tremendous fireball which lit up the sky and caused a rush of air which blew by my face as I stared at it. I couldn't get to sleep that night thinking about the pilot.

The next morning at breakfast, we were listening to the BBC news. We heard the Germans had just launched a new weapon, an unmanned missile called a V-I, at a number of cities in Great Britain, and that one had landed close to Southampton! I felt relieved that at least it was not an Allied plane as I had suspected.

The V-Is were soon followed by a more sophisticated rocket named a V-II, but fortunately, the war ended before the Germans could perfect it to be guided accurately.

The chief cook aboard the *Clara Barton* was a former fishing boat cook from the New England area. Although his primary job aboard a fishing boat out of Boston was to cook for the crew, he also took his turn at hauling nets and other chores necessary aboard a boat with a small crew.

He was an agreeable type, a good shipmate and was well liked by the crew, something that could not always be said of a ship's cook! He had been telling some of the crew members of his fishing boat experiences, and how he held the speed record aboard his boat for filleting a fish. His boat had been a factory ship on a small scale, where the catch was immediately filleted, flash frozen, wrapped, and ready for delivery to a wholesaler upon the boat's arrival at the pier.

At anchor one day, one of our crew was fishing over the side, something often done by crew members to while away the hours off watch, and he caught a number of fish. He decided to call the cook's bluff about his ability to filet a fish in record time, so he challenged him. Five dollars if he could filet the fish in less than a half minute.

The cook accepted the challenge and everyone gathered to witness his skill. The cook played up his part like an actor on Broadway. He broke out his best knife, brought along a sharpening stone, and with a flourish, sharpened it, then tested it on the hair on his arm, sharpened it again, tested it, and carried on like a real ham. When satisfied it was suitable for the job at hand he asked a crew member to have a stopwatch ready. The crew member told him to never mind the theatrics, just get on with it.

The cook took a fish in one hand, knife in the other, and in a flash of shiny steel almost impossible to follow with your eye, had two filets of fish laying in front of him, with the head, tail, and bones at his feet!

The doubting crew member had turned his head for a moment just as he started and missed the entire performance. He asked the cook to repeat it and he refused, picked up the money, and walked off to the galley!

One of the reasons the cook was so well liked was because he would gladly filet and cook any fish the crew would catch as a favor to them.

The cook was missing the middle finger of his right hand, the result of a previous torpedoing of his ship. When the torpedo struck, the abandon ship signal was sounded, and the ship began to sink quickly with only enough time to launch one lifeboat. The cook donned his life jacket and rubber survival suit and made his way to the fore deck where he jumped overboard. He landed close to a life raft, which had just been launched by the gunners from its gravity platform on the fore deck, and swam for it.

When he came alongside, he attempted to climb aboard, but it was already occupied by several members from the gun crew. As he tried to board, he was shoved backward into the water by one of the gun crew who told him the rafts were for the Navy, the lifeboats were for the crew, and to swim for one of them.

Realizing he had no chance to make it to the only lifeboat, he grabbed a lifeline attached to the raft and pulled himself alongside until he reached the opposite end where other gunners pulled him on board. The raft was pitching heavily in the mountainous sea and was still quite close to the hull of their sinking ship.

Suddenly, the raft turned completely around as it rode the top of a swell, and a gunner tumbled overboard, landing in the water between the raft and ship. The cook was at that end of the raft and spotted the sailor whose head was about to be crushed between the raft and the ship. The cook reached down and dunked the sailor down into the water with all his strength. The raft landed heavily against the hull with a thud, smashing the cook's hand before he could withdraw it from the water. His hand was badly mangled, but he held it there until the raft bounced away from the hull. Then he reached down into the water and pulled the sailor up out of the water and into the raft!

When the cook looked at the gunner, he saw it was the same man who had pushed him from the raft a few minutes earlier! When they were eventually rescued, his hand was in poor shape, but the medics were able to save it. He did, however, lose his finger.

After several trips across the English Channel ferrying troops and vehicles from Southampton, Swansea, Newport, and other British ports, we were departing Cherbourg one afternoon in a small convoy en route to England for another load. The commodore was aboard our ship and we were in the lead column of ships. Apparently it was the duty of each convoy commodore to check on the buoys at the beachhead, and in the channels leading out of France as well as those in the English ports. So our commodore ordered the helmsman to approach one buoy rather close for examination.

The ship got so close that we collided with it and it seemed to cling to our starboard side as we slid along. He quickly rang stop on our telegraph, but I didn't have time to shut off the steam to the main engine when the engine came to a screeching stop by itself. The boiler safety valves popped off because the fireman couldn't react in time to secure the fires, and then the cylinder head relief valves began to pop off. Steam was blowing and filling the engine room with hot, wet steam and the noise was unbearable until the fireman could shut off the fires in the boilers. When I finally managed to shut off the throttle, the relief valves stopped, and it was quiet.

The chief and first came dashing down to assist me. They told me we had struck the buoy and it was apparently jammed in our propeller. With the steam shut off, the chief had me put the jacking gear in and we attempted to jack over the engine using the small reciprocating engine connected to the jacking gear. We tried it in the ahead and astern directions, but it would only move a few degrees and stop.

The jacking gear is a worm-type gear which is normally stowed on a rack near the jacking gear engine. When used, it is removed from the rack and inserted in a small cavity where it is meshed with a large round ring gear mounted on the crankshaft. When in place, a long square key is dropped into its center to keep it centered. Its purpose is to slowly rotate the engine when setting the piston valves, or making other repairs such as to bearings or crossheads.

While attempting to jack the engine, the resistance to the turning shaft was so great that the worm gear literally wore down to a knife-edge. The chief notified the bridge that it was useless to attempt to free the buoy in this manner, so the commodore told the captain to drop our anchor and he would send help. He and his entourage of British signalmen and sailors then left us to board another ship in the convoy and resume their trip to England while we sat there!

We waited through the next day expecting some help in the form of a towboat, or Salvage ship with a diver to cut the buoy loose, but no one showed up. The next day passed and still no help. After the third day with no help, a group of crew members lowered a life raft overboard, and without telling the captain or anyone else, attempted to hacksaw the buoy loose. When the captain found out about it, he blew his top and ordered the men to bring the raft aboard and wait for help. Everyone thought it was a futile effort on their part, but when we awoke the next morning, the buoy had disappeared! We believe the buoy sank by itself as a result of slamming into the propeller blade tips and having its skin pierced. The anchor chain of the buoy was still wrapped around our propeller, but at least the buoy was gone. Now with renewed encouragement, and believing they were responsible for its sinking, the crew members appealed to the captain to let them try again, but he refused fearing injuries.

I remarked to the chief engineer that it was too bad about the propeller, but he quietly told me, "Cheer up, that propeller is our ticket back to the States." I began to think about that and thought maybe he was right. In a few more hours a Salvage boat appeared alongside with a diver. He had an underwater acetylene burning rig on board and in a few hours had the chain cut loose. His examination revealed that all four of our propeller blades had been bent, twisted, and curled over in many directions, so any hope of making any reasonable speed was out of the question.

We limped into Southampton where another diver surveyed it and reported the same condition. There were no dry docks available or spare Liberty ship propellers in the area so the WSA official said, "Send them home!" It was the best news we had heard in the nine months we had been gone.

In a few more days the captain and gunnery officer were to report to a convoy conference in Southampton where they would be told our position in the convoy and other necessary details. They were also told that this convoy would be made up of a group of ships whose speed was not the fastest on the seas, and that we were to do our best to stay with them. In other words, everyone is on his own once we leave the comparative safety of the British Isles if we can't keep up. The following night we sailed for Belfast where we would meet the other ships, and in another day or two, all the ships were assembled.

Some of the ships were in tough shape and many were extremely old, but somehow they had survived the war and probably many had already served a useful life. Our fastest speed was only five and half knots and we were in a six-knot convoy, but off we sailed, home-ward bound, one way or another.

Two days out of Belfast our engine and propeller shaft began vibrating so badly that we had to inform the commodore we could not keep up the pace. He gave us a choice, either turn around and head back to England or proceed toward the States on our own. Some choice.

The captain and chief put their heads together and made the decision to keep going, after all it was November and Christmas wasn't too far off. If we returned to England, who knows when we would have the chance to head home again.

We waved good-bye to the convoy. It was a lonesome night, knowing we would be all alone in the Atlantic. In the morning the convoy was out of sight and it really hit home.

We hadn't taken any fuel in England; the chief was sure he had enough to make it, but I had no idea because I hadn't taken any fuel soundings for a couple of months. I supposed he was going by our daily consumption being in port for so long, and doing little steaming except for the twenty-plus miles each way crossing the channel, so I didn't give it another thought.

Our progress was very slow, keeping the engine RPMs to make the best speed without excessive vibration. The following day heavy weather set in and we began bouncing all over the ocean. The ship was empty of cargo, had little fuel for weight, and the weather threatened to get worse before it got better.

The next day was a repeat of the previous one—worse weather, the ship standing on its beams end at times, and many men seasick. In the mountainous seas, we slowed down even more to prevent the vessel from pounding itself to pieces. Stories began to circulate about some Libertys which broke into two sections while in heavy weather. One day we made a forward progress of only ten miles and the following day we lost them and twenty more while hove to.

As second assistant in charge of fuel transferring, I began to worry about our supply, but the chief kept telling me where to transfer each days supply to the settler tanks, those tanks which have heating coils and from which each day's steaming is taken. I began having weird dreams at night about the old man screaming at the chief because he had to call for a towboat, when we would run out of fuel. It would be understandable if we were in short supply but getting closer to the States each day, but we weren't. We were still struggling to make a hundred miles every twenty-four hours.

The chief would keep subtracting the amount of fuel we consumed each day from the previous day's supply and record it in the engine department logbook. Finally, the day of reckoning came, we were showing 0 barrels of fuel remaining on board in the log, but we kept on steaming!

I asked him where the fuel was coming from and he smiled and said, "Don't worry, Second, we'll be OK." This was my first experience with what is known as "having fuel up your sleeve." For the next five days we steamed on "sleeve fuel." He had slowly over the past several months managed to conceal the extra fuel from the authorities and gained a few barrels each week.

The total passage from England lasted twenty-six days, twenty-four of them alone. Eight days out of New York, the steward reported to the captain that he only had one day's supply of food left! Luckily, the last group of GIs we had carried in our holds had left several cartons of "C" and "K" rations on board. They were removed from the hold and turned over to the steward who was given the duty of distributing them at each mealtime.

Each package of rations contained two cigarettes and two pieces of candy in addition to the usual "main course." I struck a deal with the first assistant, his candy for my cigarettes. I didn't smoke so I did OK., but it was a swap looked forward to each day. The crew was extremely irritated over running out of food, tempers were short, and rumors began circulating about perhaps running out of fuel as well.

The captain had heard through the grapevine that some crew members had been sending routine reports to the USCG back in the States about his conduct during the trip. They reported his drunkenness, the removal of the vehicle from the cargo hold in Southampton, the women aboard during wartime in spite of the tight security measures, and other events, so he summoned the crew delegates from each department to his office one day.

He told them he wanted to make a deal, "If the weather holds out, we could make New York by Christmas Eve," he said. "However because of the food shortage and limited fuel supply, we should divert the ship to Halifax. This would mean that we couldn't be home for Christmas and New Year's Eve could be questionable also."

The captain also told them if they wanted him to continue to New York and be home for the Christmas holidays, it would have to be on the condition that none of them would testify against him at any hearing that might be held!

The delegates told him they couldn't speak for the rest of the crew, but that they would talk to them and ask for their opinions. Their answer, "Get us into New York for Christmas and we will forget everything that happened on the trip!"

With assurance from the crew that they would not testify at any hearing that might be held, the captain became almost civil. Of course, he had only the word of the ship's crew, not the gunners or ship's officers. We plodded onward, "enjoying" our "K" and "C" rations, steaming slowly, but headed for New York and home.

I pumped up the two settling tanks from the double bottom tanks which the chief told me held our last remaining fuel, and just as the settlers were nearly full, I lost suction on the pump. I switched to every other tank, opening and closing valves one after the other trying to pick up a suction, but to no avail. We were empty. I thought at least the settlers are full, so we're good for a couple of days.

Two days later on Dec. 24, Christmas Eve, we arrived at the Quarantine Station off Staten Island. We made it! After twenty-six days alone in the North Atlantic. Fortunately we had not encountered any submarines, but by now the American and British Navies had blown most of them out of the ocean.

From then on we were within towboat range. After a short stay to clear quarantine, we heaved up our anchor and proceeded to a remote pier on the New Jersey side of the Hudson River in Guttenburg, New Jersey.

I told the chief I would gladly take all the port watches so the other engineers could go home because I planned on getting off after the holiday to raise my license. The only thing I wanted to do was to go ashore, kiss the ground, and call my mother and father and tell them I was OK.

The first was happy to be going to Boston for the holiday and the two thirds were off to New York where they lived. The chief was from the West Coast, so he stayed on board with me. The captain told all the mates to go home and he would take the deck watches over the holiday, after he went ashore to enter the ship at the customs house. Although I was on watch, I was allowed to sleep during the night, leaving orders in the engine room with the oiler and fireman to call me if anything unusual were to happen. Actually, they could probably have handled any emergency that might arise because they learned much during the voyage and really became very proficient at their work. I told both of them they would be welcome aboard any ship I would ever sail on in the future. Ten months earlier, I didn't think so!

Christmas morning I was in the saloon, enjoying a cup of coffee with the chief, when the captain entered and poured a cup. We wished him a Merry Christmas, but all we got in return was a growl. The chief and I were relaxed, no worries about fuel, food, or submarines. We could hear Christmas Carols playing over the loudspeaker from the crew mess room, life seemed pretty good after all!

The captain spoke up, but seemed to be looking right through the chief and me, and started ranting, "I'd like to get the Coast Guard and stomp on them!"

The chief signaled to me to get out and he followed me. I went to the engine room while he went to his room and locked his door. Apparently the old man had picked up some liquor while he was ashore the day before and had been hitting it all throughout the night.

The captain left the saloon to locate the source of the music and stopped at the door of the crew mess where the two members of the gun crew who had the security watch were having coffee.

"Merry Christmas, Captain," said the gun crew.

"What are you doing in the crew's mess room, this is for my crew. Get next door to your own area!"

"But Captain, there is no radio speaker in there and we are only listening to Christmas Carols."

"We'll see!" he growled, and disappeared up the ladder leading to his room.

He returned a few minutes later with a gun in his hand and pointed it in the direction of the two Navy boys. They fled, one running by him and out the door, and the other out through the pantry. He fired twice! One bullet tore through the pantry sink and the other ripped a furrow in the tile in the deck.

Luckily, neither young man was hit. One made it up to the boat deck, where he hid in a lifeboat under the seats, and the other jumped overboard onto a float acting as a fender between the ship and pier.

He managed to climb from the float to the horizontal beams between the pilings, and made his way slowly to the head of the pier, crawling from beam to beam!

He notified the U.S. Coast Guard sentry on duty who informed his officer and others and a squad was organized and rushed to the ship. Heavily armed, they proceeded cautiously and made their way to the captain's room. His door was open.

He was found in his bunk, gun still in his hand, and a heavy froth covering his entire lower face. The officer carefully removed the gun from his hand and they lifted him from his bunk. He awakened for a moment, but his eyes rolled upward and he fell into unconsciousness. They carried him from the ship in a stokes stretcher, placed him into an ambulance which took him to the marine hospital.

The day after Christmas we paid off, said our good-byes and each had to be interviewed by the Coast Guard where statements were taken from all hands. I never learned of the outcome of any hearings, if ever there were any held.

One July morning in 1944 Ken Levi, a new man in U.S. Lines, came to the marine superintendent's office to fill out an application for a job. Although he held a chief mate's license, the only opening that day was for a second mate's position, so Levi said he would take it. He was told to report the following day for his assignment letter and be prepared to leave for the West Coast. He went home happy to be with the company.

That afternoon another man, David R. Parsons, a graduate of Massachusetts Maritime Academy a year earlier, came to the office seeking a job, having just passed the test for his second mate's license. At this point fate was about to change the entire scene.

While Parsons was in the office, a call came from our office in Norfolk that the chief mate on a Liberty ship at a pier there had just quit and the ship would require a chief mate. The marine superintendent then told Parsons to report to him the next morning. Thus when Levi came to the office the following day, he was appointed chief mate to the Norfolk ship and was on his way. Later when Parsons reported, he was given the second mate's job on the West Coast ship, a brand-new vessel which was on the loading berth for its first voyage. It should have worked out nicely, but sadly, it didn't.

The West Coast ship was named the SS *Quinault Victory* and was tied up behind the Liberty ship *E.A. Bryan* in Port Chicago, an ammunition depot north of San Francisco. As Parsons was boarding the *Quinault Victory*, a tremendous explosion occurred causing both ships to disintegrate with a loss of all hands on each ship, including the gun crews from each. It was one of the most devastating explosions to take place during the entire war, completely wiping out the town of Port Chicago. Today one can still make out the sidewalks and streets of the town, but it was never rebuilt.

Today Parsons name is engraved on the Merchant Marine Memorial dedicated to those who perished in World War II, which stands in front of the administration building at Massachusetts Maritime Academy.

In 1978 and 1979, U.S. Lines began sending its engineers to the United States Merchant Marine Academy at Kings Point, New York, to attend diesel engineering courses to prepare them for billets in our new Econ ships under construction at Daewoo Shipbuilding and Heavy Machinery Ltd., at Okpo in South Korea.

Not only were U.S. Lines engineers in attendance, but several American shipyards also sent some of their machinists and supervisory personnel to give them a working knowledge of the main engines being installed in the ships.

The shipyard could then advertise that their men were trained by factory personnel to encourage U. S. Lines to use their yard for future overhauls. Most of the instructors were factory representatives.

The course lasted for two weeks so many of the students were assigned rooms at the academy because they were from a long distance away. This gave ample time to tell sea stories, particularly after dinner each evening.

I told some fellows one night about an incident that occurred during World War II, and like so many others who served in that war, I referred to it as "World War II, the big one!"

Before I could say another word, a young machinist from a Florida shipyard challenged me with anger in his voice. He shouted, "What the hell are you talking about, 'the big one.' Vietnam was the big one. We lost more Marines than any other fighting force, etc."

I asked if he had served in the marines in Vietnam and he replied, "You bet your ass I did and I'm proud of it!" It took me a few minutes to quiet him down, and with the help of others, we were able to convince him the expression, "The Big One," was only an expression, and no harm was intended, but it did make me think about the pride of some of those Vietnam veterans.

Prior to the invasion of Normandy, one of the short shuttle trips we were to make took us from Southampton to Oran, Algeria, in North Africa, carrying Army vehicles. After discharging our cargo, we shifted the ship to an anchorage just off shore from the ill-famed caves of Oran. Several other Libertys were anchored there with us, all waiting to return to England in convoy.

The caves were located along the beach at Oran and housed Oran's prostitutes. The mate on watch discovered, while scanning the beach with binoculars, that he had an excellent view of the activities going on in the caves! Our gunners soon learned of this, so they took turns sitting in the saddles of the three-and five-inch guns on our bow and stern, training the gun sights on the caves and watching the performances through the magnified sights!

Word spread quickly among the other ships via our Navy signalmen, and in almost no time all the Libertys had their gun sights trained on the caves. They slowly rotated the gun as necessary to keep up with the swinging of the ship as it turned with the tide! In

the meantime, the young ladies in the caves thought they were plying their trade in the solitude of the abandoned beach!

CHAPTER SIX

SS *DEFENDER*

I left the *Clara Barton* after shifting the ship to the shipyard to renew the propeller. I had a month leave coming so I attended a refresher course in Boston and then sat for my second assistant engineer's license. After receiving it, I called U.S. Lines and asked for a new assignment as second assistant if a berth was available. There were plenty of jobs because the war was still on but in its waning months in Europe.

I was assigned to the SS *Henry W. Longfellow*, another Liberty about which I will write later. The war in Europe ended while I was aboard the *Longfellow*, but I had spent enough time there as second to gain the sea time needed to sit for my first assistant engineer's license.

Once again I attended upgrade school in Boston and then passed the license examination. Anxious to get off the low-pressure ships and onto the higher-pressure jobs, I called the company again and asked for one of the new C-2 Class ships which were being delivered from Wilmington Shipyard in North Carolina.

I was assigned to the SS *American Traveler*, making its first voyage. I had the lofty position of licensed junior engineer, which was all I wanted at the time to give me a chance to get accustomed to the turbine-driven machinery and high-boiler pressures.

After one trip to Europe, I was called to the office of Superintendent Engineer, Joe Cragin, who wanted to interview me for some reason. After spending about ten minutes with him, he asked if I would like a first assistant's job on a similar C-2. I told him if he had the faith in me to ask me, I would certainly try it.

I asked him what run it was on, and quickly emphasized that it didn't matter, lest he think I might not accept the promotion if it was on a long run.

His reply, "I'm Shanghaiing you, Heh, Heh, Heh!"

"Shanghai?" I asked trying to keep my composure.

"Yes, you leave tomorrow morning at 0600 hours. Transfer your gear from the *Traveler* to the SS *Defender* this afternoon and then come to the office for a letter so you can rush to the shipping commissioner's office to sign on."

Things then happened so quickly I barely had time to call my folks and say good-bye. About 3:30 the following morning, I awakened to go below to the engine room of the *Defender* and, consulting the notes I had taken aboard the *Traveler,* began raising vacuum to prepare the plant for sea.

My new chief, George Grover, came below and introduced himself, and assisted me in warming up the plant. He was a nice man and apparently he and Cragin had talked prior to my appointment as first, so he knew I was completely new at the first's job. The reason I got the job was because the other first assistant had taken ill just a day before and would not be able to make the trip. I was the only man on the piers at the time with a first's license. Cragin told this to me during our interview and admitted he was going out on a limb to appoint me.

I could only assure him I would do my best. Chief Grover was a tremendous help, and a man with infinite patience! Our trip took us to Shanghai, and then to Australia, on to Trinidad, then to Canada, and finally New York after five months.

Upon our arrival in New York from Australia, George Grover signed off the ship. He had been suffering chest pains during the voyage, but said nothing to anyone until we had tied up. He had written to the superintendent engineer from an outport regarding his condition to enable him to have time to obtain a relief, but didn't want anyone on board to know about it.

After securing the main engine and cutting out one boiler, I received a call from the chief's office to please come topside when I finished below. I went up to his office and there met the new chief, a man I had never met nor heard about in the company.

In a company which operates a large number of ships, the word soon gets around among the fleet as to who is where and on what run. But this man was a new name to me. For obvious reasons, I prefer not to mention his name. The retiring chief had, during the previous two voyages, studied the plant and come up with some modifications in the piping systems to conserve fuel and water. He had me make the changes and after a few weeks in use, if we saw room for additional improvements, they were made also. This was standard practice aboard most new ships. When the improvements showed merit, they were exchanged throughout the fleet in that class of ship, so the entire fleet profited.

As an anecdote to this, one engineer, Bill Van Cott, second assistant on the *American Scout,* thought it was a waste of fuel to keep the ship's steam whistle warm by constantly circulating steam through its jacket, even though the whistle wasn't in use at the time. So he secured the 125-pound steam line supplying steam to it and supplied it using the same pressure through extraction steam from the main high-pressure steam turbine.

This worked well as far as conserving fuel, but was only effective while the main engine was in use at full speed. The first time the ship entered a fog bank, the captain slowed the ship, and thus the extraction steam pressure dropped off. At the same time he attempted to sound the whistle and only got a puff of steam with a low, long groan.

He immediately called the engine room to inform them of no whistle, and the engineer quickly turned on the live steam feeding it and they were back in business. The chief and second decided that it was bordering on false economy not to have the whistle readily available, especially if in traffic, so they restored the piping as designed.

While his relief was in his office, the chief offered to take the new chief to the engine room to show these changes to him, but he said not to bother. He said if the first assistant was aware of them, that would be good enough for him.

I said good-bye to the old chief, wished him well, and thanked him for tolerating me since this had been my first job as first assistant. Subsequently he was found "Unfit for duty" after a series of tests and had to take early retirement.

The following day while still in New York, the new chief told me he would leave the day-to-day operations of the engine department to me. The day before, when I was introduced to him, the other chief told him I had done a good job, but the new chief commented, "He'll have to prove himself to me!" So now I was somewhat puzzled. I soon learned he had no desire to go below to the engine room, except in an emergency. I would have preferred a chief who would at least visit there daily and talk over any problems with me and the other assistant engineers, but that was not meant to be.

Now ready to sail from New York, I had the main engine ready for sea, gear tested, and reported to the chief that all engine department personnel were aboard and we were ready to leave. He said, "OK, First, you go below and handle the main engine throttles. I always make it a point to go to the bridge leaving and entering port." I wasn't sure I had heard correctly, but I said, "OK, Chief, I'll know where you are if I need you." He continued, "Yes, I go to the bridge so I can I can be right there in case of a steering gear failure or problem with the telemotor."

My immediate thought was that if he was concerned about a steering failure, he should station himself in the steering gear room back aft. That's where the bulk of the steering machinery is located. My next thought was, "How will the captain take to this?" It wasn't too long before I found out!

After dropping the pilot, we were in a moderate amount of traffic, nothing unusual for that area near the pilot boat. We were proceeding at sixty revolutions per minute (full ahead on the telegraph, but below our normal full speed at sea), when a ship a few miles away changed course. His new course put him on a potential collision course with us if both ships were to maintain their speed and headings.

Calmly, the captain rang "half ahead" on the telegraph to reduce our speed slightly. I was at the throttle and slowed the engine accordingly. Moments later, he rang "slow ahead" and I again slowed the turbines. This was soon followed by a "stop bell," so I closed the ahead throttle and opened the astern to brake the ahead turbine and bring the engines to a complete stop.

A few minutes later, he rang "slow astern," followed soon after by "half astern," and finally, "full astern," with each command having been spaced about a half minute apart. When the telegraph order came for "full astern," the telephone also rang at the maneuvering platform. I reached for it and answered, "Engine room, First Assistant."

I heard the chief engineer's voice on the other end shouting, "Murphy, give it everything you got astern, hurry up!"

At that moment the telegraph rang "full ahead!" I was now momentarily confused, the chief telling me to give it everything astern, and the telegraph ordering me to give it everything ahead!

Instinct and common sense told me to obey the telegraph, which is what I did. We proceeded at full ahead for about a half hour and then the bridge rang up departure, the official time for leaving the port for logbook purposes, and marking the beginning of the sea passage. A few minutes later we had orders from the bridge to speed up to our normal sea speed. After securing the auxiliary machinery, machinery which is not needed while the main engine is in use, and assuring myself that the plant was settled down, I went to the chief's office to confront him.

I roared into his office and asked what the hell went on up there on the bridge—him telling me to give it everything astern and the telegraph ordering full ahead! "Who the hell am I supposed to obey?" I asked.

He replied, "The captain realized he could go around behind the ship crossing in front of us, instead of backing down, so that's when he changed his mind."

Doubting this story, and knowing the type of shiphandler the captain was, I went to the mate for his version. He said, "All that time we were maneuvering, leaving New York, the captain kept staring over at the chief. I could tell he was slowly becoming peeved at him because he was there instead of being down below, but when the chief grabbed the phone and called you to tell you to give it everything astern. He decided to go around the other ship, just to let the chief know who is conning the ship! He had everything under control and at no time was the ship in jeopardy!"

He continued, "The captain then turned to the chief and told him, 'Leave the navigation to me Chief.'" Embarrassed, the chief left the bridge and never returned.

CHAPTER SEVEN

SS *AMERICAN JURIST*

The SS *American Jurist* was renamed from the SS *Parkersburg Victory*, one of eight Victory-type vessels purchased by the company from the United States Maritime Commission after World War II. These ships inaugurated a new service from the East Coast of the United States to Antwerp, Amsterdam, and Rotterdam.

I reported to the engineering personnel office one morning and was told by Duke Dwyer, personnel manager, that I was being assigned to the *Jurist* as first assistant engineer. This assignment, he assured me was only temporary until we took delivery of our new C-2 Class ships from a shipyard in Wilmington, Delaware.

This "temporary" position lasted from 1947 until 1954! The chief engineer was William McAfee, a graduate of Massachusetts Nautical School, later Massachusetts Maritime Academy. William R. Gretcher was the master. These two men, highest ranking officers aboard, did not have anything in common except their first name, and became foes almost as soon as they were introduced.

Captain Gretcher, with all his shortcomings, was a fine sailor, excellent navigator, and must have been a fine chief mate in his day, but he was a perfectionist and expected all his mates to be the same. As a result he went through a total of twenty-three mates from chief mate to third mate in the first year of operation!

Eventually, it became a feather in the cap of any mate who quit or was fired by him and he was usually rewarded with a promotion aboard another ship if a position was open. By contrast, Gretcher took a liking to the ship's engineers, all but the chief, much to the chief's chagrin. This put us in the uncomfortable position of keeping to the middle of the road so as not to offend either. As first assistant engineer I got along with both.

Gretcher's pet peeve was a noisy ship. He enjoyed an after-noon nap and retired early nearly every evening. All hands having any need to come on "his deck," as he referred to it, were to be as quiet as possible. This included mates, quartermasters, and ABs who had to use the stairway outside his room to get to the bridge. Although he referred to it as his deck, there were two other resi-dents on that deck, the radio operator and purser.

The purser's room was on the starboard side, just aft of the captain's. His door was fitted with a hook about eight inches long used to keep his door open slightly for ventilation. Next to his door over a desk was a shelf which held his radio. Whenever the radio was playing, no matter how softly, Gretcher would storm into his room complaining about the loud racket from it.

A favorite trick of the mates was to quietly walk by the purser's room late at night and while the purser was asleep, reach in, turn the radio on to full volume, and disappear. The radio, being a tube-type, took about a half minute to warm up before blasting forth, giving the perpetrator ample time to be long gone. By the time the radio was up to full volume, the purser was just awakening and Gretcher was already at his door! In spite of the purser's claim to innocence, the captain refused to believe him.

One early evening while the purser was lying in his bunk listen-ing to soft radio music, Gretcher came storming in again to com-plain. This time the purser, in his pajamas, climbed out of his bunk and told Gretcher to follow him. He marched out of his room, up the passageway, and into Gretcher's bedroom. He climbed into the old man's bunk, pulled the covers over himself, and then sat up exclaiming, "I can't hear a damn thing, Captain!" Gretcher was speechless to think he would take such liberties with a captain, but he never bothered him again about the noise!

The purser seemed to be one step ahead of him all the time. One afternoon the two were heading for the U.S. Customs House to enter the ship in a port and were walking up the pier to catch a cab. The captain was carrying a briefcase containing the ship's pa-pers, while the purser was empty handed. The captain, realizing he shouldn't be carrying it, told the purser to hold the briefcase while he adjusted his necktie. In a few minutes, the purser looked over at the captain and seeing he was finished, said, "Here Captain, you carry the briefcase now, while I adjust mine!" He handed the bag to Gretcher who then carried it the rest of the way to the cab stand.

Captain Gretcher was very insistent about being referred to as the "Captain." Once while tied up in New York, we were having lunch when someone entered the dining saloon and asked if the master was aboard. He set the man straight, telling him he was the "Captain," not the master. On another occasion, I showed him a news clipping which mentioned a ship was "skippered" by John Doe. He became upset over this as well, saying, "I hate that expression, 'skipper,' the man was a Captain!"

Usually McAfee would pick up on these petty remarks, but didn't on either of these occasions. So I later asked McAfee why he hadn't, and he said he didn't want to antagonize the captain further.

The feud between them was ongoing day in and day out. Whenever the *Jurist* was in a bad North Atlantic storm, with ship rolling heavily, the saloon messman would place thick mats, made from old blankets, on the dining tables and place the tablecloths over these. He would then dampen them with water and this would keep the dinner plates and glasses from sliding off the table.

The officers' saloon was located on the starboard side on the boat deck and was fitted with three tables holding four people each, mounted fore and aft, and one athwartships. A settee was mounted on the bulkhead behind the three tables. The captain sat at the center table on the settee; beside him sat the chief engineer. The chief mate and I sat on pedestal chairs opposite them.

In spite of the precautions taken to prevent things from sliding off the table, in an extremely heavy roll some would go flying. We could usually anticipate this, so each one would reach out across the table to hold anything which might get away, such as ketchup, a milk carton, or jar of pickles.

One evening the messman had just served Gretcher a pot of hot tea and placed the pitcher directly in front of him with the spout pointing toward him. Just at that moment, the ship began what we could anticipate would be a long, heavy roll to starboard, so each of us, Gretcher included, reached out to hold something. As the ship continued its roll, hot tea began to pour out of the spout and was landing in Gretcher's lap!

He released his hold on the ketchup and mustard and started to let out a low groan which soon developed into a scream. He tried to stand up to give the spilling tea a place to land, but it followed him as he stood up! While he was partly suspended between the back of the settee and table, the tea continued pouring onto the seat. When the roll subsided, he flopped down onto the settee and sat in the puddle of tea.

His khaki uniform was now soaked, front and rear, so he excused himself from the table and dashed out of the saloon. No one dared laugh until he left, but then everyone broke out in gales of laughter! Although the teapot was out of my reach, I asked the chief engineer and chief mate why they didn't reach across the table to move the teapot, but neither one offered any reason, so I assumed they were glad it happened to him.

I thought that attitude was uncalled for, but said nothing. I later asked the captain if he had been burned and he said, "No, but it could have done a lot of damage!" I agreed with him.

A few days later McAfee and I were in the saloon pantry making a cup of tea. He opened a cabinet door looking for tea bags and found the captain's teapot. It had "Captain" painted on its side and was the third one used by him that trip.

The two previous ones, also with "Captain" painted on them, had "fallen" from the shelf and broken when they landed on the tile deck. After that he left orders with the messman to hide it after each meal.

McAfee removed it from its hiding place and turned toward me with it held high in the air and then dropped it saying, "Oops!" It smashed into several pieces and he stood there laughing. He didn't have the last laugh, however, because the steward broke out another one the next day, telling anyone who would listen that he had a whole case of teapots in his storeroom, which the captain had told him to order in New York.

Captain Gretcher eventually had a falling out with his principals in the office and probably realized he was not to be employed too much longer, at least as master. On our next trip, we sailed from the New York/Chelsea piers one afternoon an hour or so earlier than the time posted on the sailing board. The captain told the chief mate to single up the lines after lunch and be ready to leave soon after. The mate did not realize he wanted to leave before the posted time, but Gretcher had said he wanted to make the pilot station at our next coastwise port during daylight hours.

Our undocking pilot arrived aboard at lunch so the captain invited him to eat, and told him he wanted to leave the pier as soon as he was finished, providing the tugboats were alongside. They arrived shortly, so he ordered the gangway lifted and told the mates to take in the remaining lines. As we were being breasted away from the pier, Captain John Green, port captain, and later marine superintendent, arrived on the pier to come aboard to talk to the captain. At that moment, a crew member arrived at the pier also to come aboard. Green ordered Gretcher to redock the ship to allow this man to board, saying he had every right to board because it was more than one hour before the scheduled sailing time, the required time for all crew to report aboard.

The ship was now about a hundred yards off the pier and being swung to head downriver by the tugs. Gretcher, using a megaphone, shouted back, "Tell him to take a train to the next port. I'm not docking this ship again." He didn't know that Green also wanted to board.

Green, now livid, shouted back, "This is your last trip, Gretcher. You're fired when you return to New York!"

When the *Jurist* returned to the company piers a week later, after a short coastwise trip, Gretcher told our docking pilot to put the ship into the pier stern first, which was opposite to the customary method of docking at these piers. He told the pilot the company had some specialized cargo which had to be stowed on the port side of the ship, and bringing it in stern first would put the cargo hatches under the house blocks in just the right position for loading it.

This sounded reasonable to the pilot, so he directed the tugs accordingly and the ship approached the pier stern in. Just at this point someone in the marine department happened to look out the window, saw the ship heading in backwards, and called to Green. He rushed to the pier to tell the pilot to bring the ship out into the stream, turn it around, and dock it the proper way.

After it was redocked properly, Green stormed onto the ship to confront Gretcher, asking what was the meaning of this display of seamanship, docking the ship backwards.

Gretcher replied, "I knew I was getting fired, so you can not only kiss my ass, but you can kiss my ship's ass as well!"

Shortly after, he left the ship with his suitcase and never said good-bye to anyone, not even McAfee!

Captain Gretcher probably got the idea of docking the ship backwards from an earlier incident in which another master succeeded in having his ship tied up to the Chelsea piers upon learning he was about to be fired also. Only that time the ship was completely secured to the pier before the mistake was discovered.

Soon after World War II ended, the *American Jurist* made a trip to Germany carrying a full load of potatoes to Hamburg. During the crossing, one of the main boiler feed pumps developed a problem so it was secured and the other main pump put on the line. An inspection of the faulty pump revealed its piston valve to be broken. We could not repair it on board because we were not allowed to have any welding equipment aboard, a silly rule of the United States Coast Guard.

After docking in Hamburg, I asked our agent if he could have it repaired, but he said, "We have no shipyards left, you people bombed them all out of existence. But I know of an elderly man who has some equipment in his home, maybe he could help you."

When the man came aboard to pick up the valve, I asked him how I could pay for the repair but he said not to worry about payment until he brought the valve back. He returned in a few hours with the repair completed so I asked if he wanted cigarettes as payment, I had no German marks.

"I don't want cigarettes, but I am embarrassed to ask for what my family could really use. My grandchildren live with my wife and me and have never eaten chicken. My son has not yet returned from the German Army and all the chickens raised in Germany were given to the military. I would gladly accept a chicken from your refrigerator as payment."

I told him I was sure I could arrange it and had him accompany me to the ship's meat box. Much to the anger of many chief stewards, most chief engineers and first assistant engineers had keys to the ship's refrigerators so they could enter them to check on the frosting up of the coils as well as check on the diffuser fans in each. The stewards never took to this too kindly because they always believed that we would help ourselves to a can of chilled juice or a box of ice cream, which, of course, was out of the question.

We entered the box and found a cardboard carton containing several frozen chickens. I opened it and grabbed one chicken by the leg, but five more chickens came with it, all frozen together. I handed them to the old man and said, "Here you are, one chicken."

Shaking his head, he said, "No, no, this is many chickens!"

"It's only one as far as I'm concerned. Take it; and when you get home, tell your grandchildren they came from an American."

Tears welled up in his eyes and he shook my hand warmly. I felt good after that, even though a few months earlier I had been fighting them, but now things seemed different.

After we left Hamburg, I installed the valve and tested the pump. It operated about ten minutes and then began acting as before so I secured it and upon examination found the valve broken in the exact same area he had repaired!. When we returned to New York, I ordered a new valve from the manufacturer, but still felt good about the chicken(s).

CHAPTER EIGHT

DECK VS ENGINE

Chief Engineer William McAfee and Captain William R. Gretcher were always arguing about their licenses and responsibilities. Gretcher maintained he had the complete ship on his shoulders, McAfee would counter with, "Everything except the engine room."

The argument would continue with the chief adding, "Your responsibility is practically nothing when the ship ties up to the pier, while mine is increased ten fold. Although the main engine is shut down, I have another generator in operation for the cargo winches, always with the threat of a breakdown and a detention; plus sometimes hydraulic hatch covers, plus the machinery for the hotel services provided. That's why I make more money than you do!"

These last few words usually upset Gretcher more than anything. The company had a policy where the chief would earn an extra five dollars a month longevity for each year's time as chief after the first three years. Gretcher did not have as much time as the chief, therefore his pay was less. The company soon corrected this situation, after a complaint made through the Masters' Guild, an organization made up of U.S. Lines masters, but in reality a company union. The new rule was that the master would have to earn at least as much as the chief engineer, but McAfee held this over Gretcher when their arguments got heated.

Later on while sailing with Captain J. A. F. Knowlton, I would occasionally get a dig from him about how the MEBA was bossing us around, especially at contract time. I would usually counter with, "Why don't you masters get on the ball and ask for a raise through your union, the Masters Guild." He would get furious and reply: "The Masters Guild is not a union, it's an association of company shipmasters who get together to talk over various conditions as to the operations on our ships, such as improvements to make them more efficient and profitable."

I would reply, "But when we get an increase in pay and better living conditions through the union, the masters follow suit, so anything we gain, you gain."

The MEBA union contract would be nearing its termination date about the middle of June. Negotiations would usually commence a few months prior to that, so that the new contract would be signed by that date, thus assuring the continuity of operations and schedules. The masters, mates, and pilots contracts would be due also. They would always wait until they saw what the engineers gained and then request the same increases, so they became known as the "Me, too union."

Eventually, the Masters' Guild fell by the wayside and the masters joined the Masters, Mates and Pilots Union.

This rivalry between deck and engine wasn't anything new. It had been in effect for years before I ever came along. It probably began when Robert Fulton first operated a steamboat on the Hudson, and I'm sure was evident during the first steam crossing of the Atlantic on the *Savannah.*

When I entered the Maritime Academy we were confronted with it from almost the first day. A condition of admission was to be interviewed by one of the academy's instructors. We were asked why we wished to attend such a school and whether we wished to be enrolled as a deck or engine cadet. I had already made up my mind because my older brother, Bill, had just graduated as an engineer and he advised me to have nothing to do with the deck group because of their instructors. He said the engineering instructors were much better guys.

As my luck would have it, my interview had to be with one of the deck instructors, a Lt. Connors, who I later learned had the affectionate nickname "The Bum." He asked me why I wanted to attend the academy and I told him my brother had just graduated as an engineer and I would like to follow in his footsteps.

He asked his name and I replied, "William R. Murphy."

"Oh yeah, I remember him. Well it's a good thing for you that you want to be an engineer cadet," Connors said.

I later asked my brother what he meant, but Bill just said, "He and I didn't get along too well!"

Lt. Connors turned out to be a pretty good guy in spite of his reputation although I didn't have any subjects with him.

Today some cadets are graduating from the Merchant Marine Academy at Kings Point with dual licenses, third mate and third assistant engineer. If they follow the sea very long, they'll have to decide which department they would like to settle into to continue their careers. If they want to stay clean, they go on deck; if they aren't afraid to get their hands dirty, they go engine. About the only problem I ever had with Lt. Connors happened during a liberty formation one Friday afternoon. Dress blues were the uniform of the day, with a white cover on our "high-pressure" hats. We had to stand in formation to be inspected by the officer of the deck, Lt. Connors, for cleanliness prior to being released for weekend liberty.

If he found something wrong, such as unshined shoes, lint on our blues or a dirty white shirt, (cadets were notorious for trying to squeeze too many wearings between washings in the days before wash and wear materials), we were sent to our rooms to correct the problem. In the meantime, the others who passed were free to head home for the weekend. Those who failed would have a half hour to correct the problem and report later to "late liberty formation" for a second inspection.

The white covers for our hats were made of a cotton material and were a magnet to dirt. Each cadet carried a stick of white chalk in his pocket for a last minute touchup before taking his place in formation.

Lt. Connors was wise to this trick, having been a cadet himself several years earlier. So on that particular afternoon he must have suspected I had chalked my hat cover because he asked to examine it. I removed it and handed it to him. He looked at it closely and then without warning, slapped it against my blue uniform jacket, causing clouds of white chalk to fly off in all directions and leaving a white streak on my uniform.

"Nice try, Murphy, you're excused from formation, see you in a half hour!"

Because of this, I missed the last train from Hyannis to Boston, and had to thumb my way home for the weekend.

Everyone who graduated from the Maritime Academy in my class was sworn in as an ensign in the Naval Reserve, and most who opted to serve in the Merchant Marine during the war maintained their reserve status after the war. This was accomplished through correspondence courses or by being a member of a reserve unit aboard ship.

I maintained my rank so that in the event of another war if I were called to active duty, I would have accumulated the maximum number of points, called fogies for the rank I held, thus giving me the maximum amount of pay for that rank. Although this may seem less than patriotic, I had to consider the support of my family. The extra sixty or seventy dollars a month that I would receive would come in handy.

After the war, U.S. Lines applied to our government for an operating differential subsidy for some of its trade routes. One of the conditions for granting the subsidy was that at least fifty percent of the ship's officers be in the reserve. This was another reason for maintaining my commission.

Not all the officers on board every ship were reservists, however, so the company began a recruiting program aboard each vessel on routes for which they had applied for subsidy. Aboard the *American Jurist*, a Navy captain and commander addressed the officers to explain the advantages of joining. We reservists were invited to sit in on the talks, probably to encourage the others. After giving their canned speech, they invited questions from the group. One officer asked what rank he could expect if he joined and was told that would be commensurate with his position aboard, license held, time served on his license, as well as his education, age, and physical condition.

The commander then attempted to give an outlandish example of the type of person they would not be interested in. He said they could not honor an application from an individual sailing as a third assistant engineer with six issues of a third's license, in advanced years, and extremely overweight. In other words, "The Navy doesn't want any sixty-year-old ensigns," he said.

With this, Willie Meier, our third assistant engineer, spoke up with wrath in his voice, "What the hell is wrong with a sixty-year-old engineer with a third's license?"

The commander was taken aback, asking Willie if he held a third's license and was sixty. "Yes, I am, with six issues, so what?" replied Willie.

The commander apologized to him and Willie stormed out of the meeting. Later, the commander told us he had tried to create the most ridiculous case as an example, but he hit Willie right on the button. At least he said nothing about Willie's fifty-five-inch waistline!

Whenever a ship approaches a pier to tie up, not only are there line handlers present to take the mooring lines, longshoremen waiting to board to start cargo operations, company and boarding officials awaiting its arrival, but all sorts of tradesmen ready to do business. Some of them would have a pass from the company; others, after making a deal with the gangway watchman, would be allowed aboard providing the individual paid him off. The watchman was usually a local from a watchman's service retained by the company.

It was possible for a crew member to buy liquor out of bond from a bonded ship's chandler at a tremendous saving because it was tax free. He could also get a haircut; have his shoes repaired; send his laundry and dry cleaning ashore; buy souvenirs, clothes, tulip bulbs, candy, food, furniture, and cigars; and in some ports enjoy the pleasures of a "fille de joie." Mostly, these commodities were cheaper than ashore, and if paid for with cigarettes purchased from the ship's slop chest, even cheaper. Doing business in this manner also had its advantages because the crew member didn't take the risk of smuggling the cigarettes ashore. That was up to the vendor and more than likely he was taking care of the custom guards at the gate.

I recall one time when a tailor came aboard the *American Jurist* selling suits. He showed me his materials and promised a good fitting suit for forty-five dollars, and five dollars more for an extra pair of trousers. While measuring me, Willie Meier entered my office and inquired about the suits. He looked through the material and found one he liked and told the tailor to measure him.

When he measured Willie's waist, he told him the trousers would cost an additional five dollars because his waist measurement exceeded the fifty-inch maximum. This infuriated Willie, so he inhaled heavily, drawing in his waist and holding his breath, grunted, "Measure me now!"

The new measurement was under the extra five dollar limit, so Willie told him to use that measurement. I told him he was foolish, the pants will never fit, but he said, "Go ahead, Tailor, make the suit!"

When our suits arrived three days later, mine fit well, but Willie couldn't zip up the fly on his trousers. He accepted the suit, in spite of it, wore the jacket as a sport coat, and used the trousers, with the fly unzipped, for work pants in the engine room.

I asked him why he did such a foolish thing. He said the tailor made him angry with his remark, but it was obvious he didn't wish to discuss it with me anymore and he walked away.

Willie hailed from Baltimore and had served aboard the *American Jurist* for two years while I was first assistant engineer, but we didn't get along too well. The chief engineer was Norman Jones, also from Baltimore, and he had known Willie for many years. So I didn't complain about Willie to him, but I was always settling disagreements between him and the other engineers.

On one occasion, I found it necessary to renew the bottom head gasket of the steam reciprocating lubricating oil pump, so I assigned the task to Willie. It wasn't a difficult job, but required one to work below the engine room floorplates in a confined space. He attempted to climb down into the area, but couldn't because of his obesity and the congestion of piping and floorplates supports in the area.

I told him I could squeeze into the space, and he could stay above me handing tools to me. Before I could begin the work, however, it was necessary to drain the lubricating oil from the pump. I removed the drain plug, and was able to place a small tuna fish can beneath it to catch the oil. When the can filled, I held my finger over the hole and handed the can over my head to Willie who was to empty it into a large one gallon can and hand the small can back to me for refilling.

Twice I tried to hand the full can up to him, but he didn't take it from me. I turned around and found him dozing. He had been ashore the previous night in Antwerp and came aboard the ship about 5:00 A.M. when the bars closed, so he wasn't only tired, he was hungover as well.

I yelled at him to stay awake and told him that I was in an extremely uncomfortable position, while all he had to do was stay alert to receive the full cans. The pump cylinder was nearly drained and I was filling the last can, when I felt something warm land on the back of my neck!

I swung around and found he had fallen asleep while kneeling above me and spilled the entire gallon of oil all over me! He awakened at once and got out of there fast! When I caught up with him, I told him he had better get off the ship when we arrived in New York. He said, "We'll see about that," with a mild reference to Norman Jones.

When we arrived in New York, the superintendent engineer, Joe Cragin, came aboard to ask Norman if he would be interested in taking a port engineer's job for the company in Baltimore. Norman wasted no time in telling him how much he would like that. He liked the chance to be home more often while his kids were growing up, so he accepted the offer. Cragin then turned to me and said, "Mr. Murphy, you're the new chief!"

In a few minutes the word passed and not long after that Willie went to the personnel office to ask Mr. Tanghe, engineering department personnel manager, for a transfer to a company ship on the German run. Willie, being German, told him he wished to be transferred to enable him to visit relatives there. He was transferred the following day, and finally out of my hair.

The next day, a new third reported aboard. I removed the key to his room from my key cabinet and escorted him to his room, the room vacated by Willie the previous day. Upon entering the room, a large colony of cockroaches scattered in different directions. I closed the door and told the new third to use a spare room until we could have the other room cleaned up. Willie had never allowed the bedroom steward to enter his room to make the bed or clean the room, a routine performed daily for the officers and crew.

Whenever the ship was tied up in Antwerp, Amsterdam, or Rotterdam, Willie always went ashore to locate a street vendor selling smoked eels. He would buy a couple of dozen at a time, wrapped in newspaper, return to the ship and seclude himself in his room, eating them like an ear of corn. I looked in on him one evening and found him sitting with his wastebasket between his knees, gnawing on the eels, and spitting out the skins, aiming at the wastebasket, but not always hitting it.

I called the chief steward to ask him to have the bedroom steward begin cleaning up. The first thing he was to do was to release a few canisters of insect repellent in the closed room. A short while later, the roaches were seen scurrying out from under his door and through the joints of the bulkheads into each adjoining room. The engineers occupying these rooms came dashing out to complain about the invasion, so we released canisters in their rooms also.

Willie's mattress had a large hole burned in it, apparently from smoking in bed, but we never knew it. In a few days the room had been freed of roaches, cleaned and painted, and a new mattress fitted so it was finally inhabitable. The *Jurist* had always been roach free, probably because there were enough food scraps in Willie's room to keep them confined there.

I felt good about making my first trip as chief. The second assistant engineer had been promoted to first, and the other third promoted to second. The only new man among the engineers was the new third, and he soon proved to fit right into the system.

We completed the trip to Belgium and Holland without incident. The ship was to remain in New York for the weekend upon our return, so I had a chance to go home to Massachusetts to visit my parents. When I returned to the ship Monday morning, Captain Jim Knowlton, master of the ship, asked what kind of reception I received when I arrived home.

I said, "I gave my mother a hug and kiss, and hugged my father like I always did, why?"

He said, "Didn't they hold a party for you or any type of celebration?"

"No, why should they?"

"Because you made your first trip as chief engineer. When I made my first trip as captain, my folks held a garden party for me with all the neighbors present!" Knowlton said.

"My father asked how everything went and I said everything went well. Then he said, 'Glad to hear it.' As far as my mother was concerned, I don't think she really knew the difference between a chief engineer and a third assistant engineer anyway." I said.

I then added, "About all most parents know about the work their kids do is what the kids have told them, especially when it comes to the importance of it!" With that, he walked away.

One afternoon aboard the *American Jurist*, we were cruising along at fifteen knots in the North Sea en route to Rotterdam, when Captain Jim Knowlton came to my office to tell me about a Norwegian ship off our starboard beam. I stepped out on deck with him and asked what was so special about the ship, which was about two miles off. He explained he had just heard on our radio an arrival message which the Norwegian had sent to their office estimating their time at the Rotterdam pilot boat at the same time we were planning to pick up our pilot. Captain Knowlton asked if I could speed up our engines slightly so we might arrive at the pilot station ahead of them because he feared there might not be enough pilots that late in the afternoon to man all the ships headed for the port.

Company regulations governed the speed and horsepower for our normal cruising speed, and this speed was not to be changed except in an emergency, such as a rescue, longshoremen awaiting our arrival, heavy weather, etc. The rules also stated if an increase in speed was necessary the captain was to give the chief engineer the speed-up orders in writing. The reason for this was fuel conservation as well as to prevent us from arbitrarily speeding up to get into port earlier.

He knew this clearly was not an emergency and didn't want to put it in writing. He asked if it was possible by using up some of the fuel which I had "up my sleeve." It was the practice of most chief engineers to keep a couple hundred barrels in reserve just for such use, or in the event of a fuel spill which had not been recorded.

At this time we were about sixty miles from the pilot boat. So I went below to the engine room and opened up three more nozzles on the turbine which increased our speed slightly. We slowly pulled away from the Norwegian and in a few hours, arrived at the pilot boat where our pilot boarded. The Norwegian also picked up his pilot and proceeded up the river behind us to Rotterdam.

After an uneventful trip up the river, we tied up to our pier and shortly after the company agent boarded. The captain, agent, and I were having a drink in the captain's office when the agent said, "It's too bad you arrived in Rotterdam ahead of that Norwegian tonight, Captain. He became the five-hundredth ship to enter the port this year so the mayor and city council are throwing a party for the officers and crew tonight at city hall. They're having a buffet and open bar and each man in the crew will receive a wristwatch, a gift from the people of Rotterdam!"

I glared at the captain and he said, "My gosh, Chief, don't tell the crew!" I said, "Don't tell the crew, hell, you owe me a dinner and a wristwatch!" I never received either from that cheapskate!

CHAPTER NINE

CAPTAINS

No book written by a marine engineer would be complete without a word on captains. U.S. Lines, like most major steamship companies, had many extremely capable shipmasters, partially because the fleet was large enough to have time to train junior officers, promote them within the company on various types of ships, and evaluate them prior to any advancement in rank. The same held true for its engineers.

Like any large group of men of responsibility, the captains displayed many personalities; some mild mannered, some short tempered, some humorous, others serious, but for the most part, a group of men of class.

However, we also had other types. Othello is rumored to have said, "We cannot all be masters." He should also have said, "Thank goodness we have engineers!"

There is a difference between a shipmaster and a captain of a ship. To begin with, the license issued by the United States Coast Guard is made out as "Master," not "Captain." U.S. Lines rarely used the word "captain" in any of its correspondence to its vessels. Instead official letters were addressed to the "Commander, SS Whatever."

I recall on one ship I served, Jones F. Devlin, U.S. Lines vice president of operations, and a former shipmaster, boarded to talk to the master prior to sailing. Not long after, an office boy came aboard to give Devlin a message and addressed him as "Captain Devlin." Devlin quickly told him, "Don't call me captain, I'm not the master aboard this ship. That man over there is the captain," pointing to the man at the desk. There can be only one captain on a ship and he is called captain only while he is assigned to a ship. I am to be addressed as Mr. Devlin, young man!" Thus said Jones F. Devlin, a man not too many people, especially captains, would care to use as an authority.

Some have referred to themselves as "master mariners," another misnomer as far as I can determine. During my cadet days, we heard the expression used occasionally and asked one of our instructors, himself a former shipmaster, its meaning. He said it was a term frequently used to designate a mariner who held a license as sailing master and had subsequently been endorsed as a powered vessel master. And even then, there were few of those individuals still around in 1942. During World War II, the USCG reduced the required sailing time between license examinations from one year to six months in order to fill more licensed billets sooner. Thus some mates and engineers had sufficient time to qualify for dual deck and engineer's licenses. Under these conditions any individual obtaining both a master's and chief engineer's license was then often referred to as a master mariner.

In Great Britain a master's license is written as a master mariner. Today in the United States, captain is a titular name used honorifically, such as "Kentucky Colonel." One engineer I know always said the word "captain" was used as a nickname.

Captain James Knowlton always wore his service ribbons with his dress blue uniform aboard ship. Most of the other officers wore khaki uniforms; jacket, shirt, tie, and trousers without any ribbons. Knowlton could not remove his ribbons because they were sewn to his jacket above the pocket.

Seated next to Knowlton at mealtimes was the radio operator, Jack Conroy. Jack was a graduate of Adelphi University. He previously taught English in a New York high school, but had gone back to sea for the higher pay.

Whenever any discussions were held during mealtimes, Conroy seemed to be one jump ahead of the skipper, whether the conversation was about women, politics, or General MacArthur, one of Knowlton's favorite people. He also had a good command of the English language and often threw a curve to the old man by using a word that was unfamiliar to him, and at other times seemed to bait the unsuspecting captain.

One lunch hour Conroy asked Knowlton what all the ribbons represented. He took great delight in explaining their meaning; European Theater of Operations, Naval Reserve, Victory Medal, Pacific Theater of Operations, etc.

Conroy asked, "Do you have medals for all the ribbons?" Knowlton replied, "No, some of them are not represented by medals, but the Victory and Naval Reserve ribbons do have medals."

"Why don't you wear the medals sometimes, Captain?"

"It would be foolish to wear them always, they'd be getting caught on everything. Besides they're only worn for formal occasions. By the way, Sparks, you were in World War II; don't you have any ribbons or medals?"

"Yeah, I have the Victory Medal." Conroy said.

"Then why in hell don't you wear it?"

Conroy replied, "I do," and lifted up his necktie to reveal his medal pinned to his shirt.

Everyone in the dining room burst into laughter; Knowlton said, "You bastard, Sparks, you conned me, I'll get you yet!" Conroy had brought the medal from home weeks earlier and just waited for the appropriate time to zing Knowlton.

Fred Collison was another one of our class captains, but he seemed to have tough luck following him for a long time. He was younger than many captains, and often would just about unpack his seabag when he would be bumped by a senior skipper.

He was finally assigned to the *Pioneer Ming* where I was serving as chief engineer. I was glad to have him aboard because we had been friends for many years and he and my brother Howard had been shipmates for a long time. After completing one Far East voyage, he was called to the company office where he was informed by the marine superintendent that he was again being bumped.

Captain Knowlton, who was now aboard the *Pioneer Mist*, had been talking to an old friend, Captain John Hart, and telling him all about the mariner ships; their fast speed, excellent accommodations, easy riding, and good trade route.

Hart wasted no time in convincing his boss the *Pioneer Ming* should be his because of his seniority. He reported aboard, I said Good-bye to Collison and greeted Hart. We left shortly after he boarded for another trip.

Homeward bound while transiting the Panama Canal, our canal pilot was a classmate of mine, Bill Hopkins, so while we were in Gatun Lake, in the midpoint of the transit, I went to the bridge to say hello to him. He received a message on his walkie-talkie, telling him another U.S. Lines ship named the *Pioneer Main* was coming into the lake from the other direction. Captain Hart, standing nearby, asked, "Who's on there, Chief, do you happen to know?"

I replied, "Pat Price."

"I've never heard of any Captain Price."

"He's not the captain," I said, "He's the chief engineer."

"I don't care who the chief engineer is. When I ask who is on there, I naturally mean the captain," Hart said.

"When you men talk, you are referring to your own. When we talk, we are referring to our guys," I said.

"Stop the ass dragging, Chief, who's the captain?"

"Fred Collison," I replied.

"Isn't he that young fellow I bumped off here?"

"Yes, he's the one."

"Well, I imagine he'll probably sound his whistle as a salute to me, being senior, so I'll just position myself by the whistle switch," Hart said.

Hart stood there with his hand on the switch as the two ships passed within a hundred feet of each other, port to port. I looked over at the *Pioneer Main* as we passed and could see Collison standing in the wheelhouse looking straight ahead, never casting a glance toward us. After we had passed, Hart removed his hand from the switch, saying, "Well, it looks like he's not going to sound the whistle to me!"

"It sure doesn't look like it, Captain, he's a hundred yards astern of us now!" I said.

Several months later I met Collison and we were discussing the incident and he said, "I'll be damned if I would salute the guy that bumped me off one of the best ships I ever served in."

Some of our shipmasters were prima donnas. One tore up a letter addressed to "Capt. Blank" because the purser who typed it had not spelled out the word captain in its entirety. The purser was instructed to retype it.

Another incident I recall occurred while I was chief engineer aboard the *American Jurist*. It was February and we were on our way up the Hudson River to Albany to load grain for Europe. Just ahead of us, heading for the same grain pier, was another U.S. Lines ship. The weather was freezing, the river filled with ice flows, and it was blowing an icy gale. We were struggling in the engine room using our steam-out valves to keep our sea chest strainers from icing over, which would destroy our vacuum and consequently result in our slowing and sometimes stopping our main engine because of the lack of cooling water.

The captain and pilot couldn't tolerate the vessel standing still for any length of time, lest the ice freeze in around us and trap us.

It was a long, tiring day, but we finally arrived at the grain pier about 6:00 P.M. I had heard we were to be in Albany for the weekend so I rushed out to the pier telephone to call American Airlines for a reservation to Boston. The ticket agent said the flight was full, but I could go on stand by. While returning to the ship to change clothes, a man walking toward me asked if the phone was working. I said it was and continued trudging through the snow.

After changing clothes, I called a cab and left for the Ten Eyck Hotel where an airport limo would pick me up for the trip to the airport. The limo driver arrived and called out two names, mine and another. The two of us were seated in the limo when the other man asked what flight I was booked on. I told him I wasn't booked but was on the standby list for American to Boston. He replied, "That's the flight I'm trying to make; I'm also on standby." He then added, "I wonder if you're ahead or behind me on the list."

I replied, "I don't really know, but we'll find out when we get to the airport." He then said, "It's extremely important that I get to Boston tonight, I'm a ship's captain!" I said, "I'm a ship's chief engineer, so what?" He then backed off, somewhat embarrassed, realizing he was on even turf. He had no idea up to that point that I was in the same industry as he. It turned out that he was the same man who had asked me if the phone was working, and he was the skipper aboard the other U.S. Lines ship. There were plenty of seats on the flight so we rode to Boston together. It turned out he was a graduate of Massachusetts Maritime Academy about ten years before I graduated.

I could picture him as an upperclassman. I'm sure he would have fit the category of those graduates under the signal flags in Faneuil Hall!

After World War II, U.S. Lines established a system on each of its cargo vessels whereby the chief mate was required to hold a master's license, and each of the other mates to hold the next higher license to the position he held. This set up was established to enable each deck officer to advance one rank aboard the ship when the master took his vacation. This system was good in theory because it would ensure continuity of the routine maintenance aboard. The only drawback was several of the masters did not think their chief mate was worthy to hold that exalted position. The same system was adopted in the engine department and many chiefs had the same attitude as the master about their reliefs.

Both the master and chief engineer soon changed their attitudes, however, when informed by the office there would be no reliefs for their vacations if they didn't accept this system.

There was a period in the company, just prior to World War II, when some of the company ships were placed under the Belgian flag for Neutrality Act reasons. At that time many of the masters, mates, and engineers who were naval reservists were advised to request active duty with the Navy temporarily until it was determined which direction the country, and thus the company, was headed because of the impending war.

When we entered the war these men were well established in the Navy and many rose in rank and responsibility aboard Navy vessels. At the end of the war, the company was operating ships under bareboat charter to the government, but soon purchased many new vessels in addition to some former Navy cargo ships which had been converted for merchant use. These new vessels would be needed for the company's anticipated new trade routes in addition to those which had previously been served by its prewar vessels. Of course it would follow also that the more vessels in use, the more jobs that would be available. For one example, the company took delivery at frequent intervals of nineteen new C-2-type freighters from one shipyard in Wilmington, North Carolina, in addition to other deliveries from yards on the West Coast.

This new influx of vessels meant several masters and chief engineers, as well as other positions, would be required almost instantly. A problem arose, however, because when those men who had gone on active duty returned to the company, many held only third's or second 's licenses both on deck and in the engine room. Because of their time, experience, and responsibilities in the Navy, they were permitted to sit for their master's and chief engineer's licenses thus skipping licenses normally worked toward by experience and time served in those in-between ratings.

The company installed these newly licensed masters and chief engineers aboard the new vessels, though some had not held a position aboard a cargo vessel higher than third mate or engineer prior to the war. These men relied heavily on their assistant engineers and mates. Some of the new masters never had any cargo experience, which would have been gained by rising through the ranks. The chief mate is considered the cargo mate. He must assure not only that the cargo is stowed efficiently and safely, but also that the ship's stability is not jeopardized, that the cargo is not overstowed by its discharge port, and that it is not mixed with other types of goods which could damage either one.

As an example, on the *American Jurist*, animal hides were once stowed in the upper tween deck next to sanitary napkins. Needless to say, the consignee of the napkins filed an exception upon their delivery because of the odor.

In another instance, in Honolulu while the *Pioneer Ming* was loading cargo on the fore deck, the captain was observing the loading from his office porthole. The chief mate was overseeing the stowage when the captain opened his porthole and shouted to him, "Mate, make sure they don't exceed the safe working limit for that section of deck!" The longshoremen in the area heard this and looked toward the mate for his reply. He shouted back, "Yes sir, Captain!" A moment later he shouted, "By the way, Captain, what is the safe working limit?" The captain became flustered and mumbled, "Just a minute, I'll check on it." The chief mate shouted back to him, "Don't bother, I already looked it up before we began loading, it's two hundred pounds per foot!" With that, the captain closed his porthole and disappeared.

I made a relief trip aboard one of our C-2 Class ships many years ago, the captain of which had a reputation of being hard to get along with, even for a chief engineer. I won't mention his name for obvious reasons.

C-2's were designed for 15 knots, powered by a 6000 HP turbine fed by boilers steaming at 450 pounds. This was considered high pressure compared with the Libertys, but they still had one thing in common with them; their electric power was direct current. This meant all the electric motors on board were fitted with commutators and brushes, which could be a constant source of trouble in our maintenance schedule. The ships were not outfitted with air conditioning either, so each room had at least one wall fan mounted on the bulkhead.

A few days out of New York heading for Europe, the captain called me on the phone to tell me the fan would not operate in his bedroom. Suspecting it might need brushes, I told the electrician to check it out.

The electrician returned to my office a few minutes later, furious, and calling the captain all sorts of names. He said, "I'm not going back up there, Chief, he can cook in that room as far as I'm concerned!"

I calmed him down and asked what happened. He told me the captain was drunk when he arrived in his room and showed him the fan.

"I found the plug partly out of the receptacle, but was being held in place by the ground wire. I merely plugged it into the receptacle and the fan started up. I told him there was nothing wrong with the fan and showed him what I did to start it and he blew his top at me!"

The captain yelled at me, "Are you trying to embarrass me, mister? Don't you think I know when something is wrong with a fan?" With that, the electrician said the captain grabbed the fan by its wire guard and tugged on it so that the guard became distorted and was now striking the blade.

"I immediately turned it off so it wouldn't burn out the motor and walked out. I don't know how he didn't cut his fingers grabbing the guard while it was running."

"I don't blame you, don't go back there. I'll handle it from here."

I went to see him and he told me to fire the electrician when we got back to New York. I told him I wouldn't and furthermore, I had given him orders not to work on his fan.

The following day he had sobered up and asked if I would fix the fan and I still refused. Later I noticed that he had a fan in operation in his room. I refused to ask where he got it, but found out the chief mate had removed the fan from the ship's hospital and installed it in his room.

This is another episode concerning an electrician, a fan, and a man with a different personality. Compare the two.

President Harry S. Truman was traveling to Europe aboard our SS *America* many years ago. The *America*, our largest and newest passenger ship at the time, was a deluxe liner for its time, but its electrical power plant was also direct current and, like the cargo ship in the previous story, it was not air conditioned.

The wall fan in the President's stateroom was acting up, so he reported it to one of his staff, who in turn reported it to the steward and eventually to the chief engineer. The chief told the electrician to examine it, but to go through the proper procedure for performing work in a passenger's room.

The steward waited until the President left his room to go out on deck, then notified the electrician so he could enter to fix it. They also assured themselves that a member of the President's staff would be present.

He determined that it needed new brushes, which he had brought with him in his tool kit. While working on it Truman returned to his room. The electrician told him he would leave at once and complete the repairs later so as not to bother him.

"We are not permitted to be in a passenger's room while the passengers are present," he said. "It's against company regulations, sir."

The President replied, "I have fresh coffee ready, would you care for a cup. You can continue your work at the same time. I'm sure if you told your superiors that the President of the United States invited you to have coffee with him, they wouldn't object, do you?"

He smiled and said, "Sir, it would be an honor!" He finished the job with the President looking on, then sat down for a few minutes with him while he finished his coffee.

Two fan stories, two electricians, two entirely different personalities.

Now back to that C-2. We were headed for Liverpool and due to pick up the pilot in the early evening. At dinner that evening the main course was veal cutlet, mashed potato, and a side dish of red cabbage.

U.S. Lines would always get the same pilot at Liverpool on each of its ships, as was the custom in many European ports. Thus our captains were familiar with these men and many friendships grew from the associations.

Whenever the pilot would board the SS *America* or *United States* in Cobb, or Southampton, to take the ship out of port, it was not unusual for him to bring along a fully packed suitcase, and upon arriving at the pilot boat, find the weather "too severe" to disembark the pilot. He would be "forced" to remain aboard and make the trip to the United States. Of course, this was never planned, but how would they account for the fact that he would appear in the first-class dining room each evening in a tuxedo.

When the pilot boarded a couple of hours later, he reported to the bridge. The captain, after greeting him, told the AB to go to the officers' pantry and get the pilot's dinner for him. He returned in a few minutes with a tray containing the dinner covered with a napkin and handed it to the captain who placed it on a foldout table. With a flourish, he removed the napkin, and said, "Pilot, be my guest!"

The pilot took one look at the plate and said, "Captain, I don't think this is one bit funny!"

Someone had removed the cutlet, dumped the red cabbage into the mashed potatoes, and mixed it into a purple, sloppy mess! When the captain saw this, he became furious and headed for my office, so I was told, but I wasn't there. I was in the engine room maneuvering the engines after picking up the pilot.

Later on after tying up to the pier, he came back to my room, screaming, "One of your men stole the pilot's cutlet, I think it was that electrician!"

"I don't even know what the hell you are talking about. I just came up from below," I said. He stormed out of my office in a rage.

A few hours later I learned that the second mate had been the culprit. He had been chewed out by the old man earlier that day and apparently this was his way of payback! When I next saw the skipper, I told him I had learned who was responsible, but would not tell him, except to say that it wasn't one of my men.

When we returned to New York, the regular chief came back from vacation and I was relieved in more ways than one. And the electrician wasn't fired!

On another occasion aboard the SS *American Jurist*, two crew members started an argument in the crew mess room over an incident that occurred during World War II. The unlicensed electrician, who had been a GI fighting the Battle of the Bulge, accused the messman, who had also been a GI and whose unit was supposed to relieve the messman's, of failing to fulfill his mission of relief, thus causing the loss of many lives.

It was New Year's eve and the crew was having a party where the liquor was flowing freely. We were at mid-Atlantic at the time in the middle of a gale. The argument got worse and the two started slugging it out, but the crew broke it up. So the two retreated to the laundry room, closed and locked the door from the inside, and started fighting again.

At this point the boatswain decided he had better call the chief mate. He notified the mate, who then called me because one of the engine department men was involved. He and I decided we had better let the captain know also, so the mate roused him from bed. He climbed out of bed, still in his pajamas, and the three of us started down the four decks to where the laundry was located. With only one more deck to go, the captain said, "Just a minute, wait right here, I'll be right back."

We waited and he returned a couple of minutes later, but now he was not only in his pajamas, he had gone back to his room to put on his hat with the scrambled eggs on the visor. He said, "This is so they'll know who I am." This on a small freighter with a crew of thirty-six men!

We arrived at the door to the laundry, found it locked, and yelled at the men inside to open up, but there was no sound. I rushed into the machine shop for a crowbar and jimmied the steel door open. We found the two lying locked together on the deck. The electrician had the messman's cheek of his rear end between his teeth biting as hard as he could, and the messman had the electrician's middle finger in his mouth, also in a death grip with his teeth. This was the reason they didn't answer our calls.

We separated them, put them in irons for the night to keep them separated, and released them the next morning. The messman's rear end healed, but the electrician's finger developed blood poison which eventually turned gangrenous and began to travel up his arm.

We still had three days steaming before our arrival in New York, so the captain radioed for emergency assistance from the marine hospital in New York. There were no ships in the vicinity with a doctor aboard, so the purser had to treat it with the facilities on board, being guided by radio from the marine hospital doctors. Treatment on board consisted of continuous soaking of his arm in a saline solution and medication applied periodically. Whenever his arm was lifted from the saline solution, it was necessary to open all the passageway doors on that deck because of the foul odor of the gangrene.

We were met at the pilot station by a USCG launch which rushed him to the marine hospital on Staten Island for treatment. The doctors there managed to save his arm but found it necessary to amputate the finger.

I always wondered if the captain had not delayed us while he went to find his hat, if those couple of minutes would have made any difference in the outcome.

Before the blood poison had set in, the electrician told me the reason he was biting the messman in the rear end was because the messman had bitten him there first! After separating the two, the purser had examined each for injuries, and while checking the electrician's rear end, he began to laugh and called the mate and me to assist in the examination.

We couldn't imagine why he would want us in on it, except perhaps as witnesses, so we went to the ship's hospital where he lay. He had sobered up by that time and was proud to show his backside.

There, on each cheek, was tattooed a propeller! He laughed while he explained that he had it done as a gag so he could go into a house of ill repute and tell the girls he was known as a "Twin Screw!"

One of our more outspoken captains was having a discussion with the chief engineer of one ship about who had the greater responsibility. He told the chief that being a chief was nothing spectacular, there were several other chiefs aboard most ships.

"Whatta you mean, several?"

"You got the chief engineer, chief mate, chief steward, chief cook, chief electrician and, sometimes, the chief reefer," the old man said with a chuckle.

He then added, "Beside that, once a captain, always a captain! He will retain that title throughout his lifetime, even in retirement, but you won't!"

By now the chief was doing a slow burn, so he came back with, "How about when he can't find a master's job and has to sail as third mate to make a living. Do you think the ship's captain is going to tolerate four mates, all with master's licenses, being called captain? Like Hell he would!"

"Also, how about when you read in the union newspaper, Captain John Doe is sailing as third mate for MSC or Captain Joe Blow is working as a second mate for the XYZ Company? That sounds stupid!"

"And one more thing, Captain, always remember 'there are two professions in this world with titles. One which vainly attempts to retain it for life, and the other desperately tries to lose it. The first is a captain, and the other is a whore!'"

At this point the discussion became quite heated so they parted and went their separate ways for the time being, but the following day the argument resumed.

Later on, I boarded the ship and the captain told me about their discussion, so I naturally stood up for the chief. The captain then told me he had been checking the payroll for the voyage just completed and found he was the fourth highest paid man on the ship because of overtime.

"Who was before you?"

"The chief engineer, then the chief mate, and after him the first assistant, and finally me!"

"Well, you know the answer to that, don't you?"

"No, what?"

"Resign, reapply for Kings Point, and take up the engineering course. When you graduate you can get a job as an engineer and work your way up to chief!"

"Remember, Captain, there is no one out here on these ships just for the sheer enjoyment of it, they are all here to make a living and that's all. They want to make as much as they can to make up for the sacrifice of leaving their families for long periods of time, so more power to them!"

"Yeah, I guess you're right, George, but I have a right to bitch about it, don't I? Anyway, the regular master is due back tomorrow and I'll revert back to mate. I won't be so bad off."

I had to agree with him.

It was common practice for one company ship to sound its whistle to another, when passing, in a sort of greeting. Another custom was to dip the American flag to an American warship, or in some cases to a warship of a friendly nation.

On one U.S. Lines vessel, the captain made it a habit of dipping the American flag when his ship passed the headquarters building of U.S. Lines at One Broadway in lower Manhattan.

It has been told that he instructed the Kings Point cadet assigned to his ship to dip the flag when passing the building and the cadet refused, informing him that the American flag is only dipped to a ship of war.

An issue was made of it, the cadet refusing an order from the captain, but the cadet proved to be correct. From that point on, the U.S. Lines house flag was dipped instead.

As mentioned earlier, many years after graduation from Massachusetts Maritime Academy most of us were still in the Naval Reserve, although some of us had never had any active duty. In order to maintain active status in the reserve, the Navy required us to complete correspondence courses while at sea in the Merchant Marine.

One course I selected was seamanship. At dinner one evening after leaving New York for the long trip to the Far East, I mentioned this fact to Captain Hart and the chief mate, Bill Atterbury. The captain said, "Ha! You've finally wised up and want to learn what the deck department is all about, huh? Well, I hope you don't intend to try to get my job. Right, Mr. Atterbury?"

He replied, "Yeah, Captain, and I hope mine is safe, too!" But both then added, "If there is anything we can help you with let us know, we'll be glad to answer any questions when you get stuck!" I said, "Go ahead and drag ass, both of you. It'll be a cold day in hell when I give either of you the satisfaction of helping me."

Two days later they started in again at dinner, "Are you stuck on anything the captain and I can help you with, Chief? Anything you need to know, just ask us, HO HO HO."

A few days later the harpoon was again aimed at me. When I returned to my room, I looked in the back of the seamanship textbook and found a glossary of old nautical terms. One was "Hearst folding bed," and another, "gilligan hitch." I wrote down the definitions to these two expressions and gave one to the second assistant engineer, Walter Wood, and the other to the purser, Joe Flynn.

A few days later, when everyone was present at dinner, I said, "I hate to admit this, but I'm stuck on a couple of words used in the text of my seamanship book." Captain Hart said, "Ha Ha, I knew you'd be coming to us sooner or later. What's the problem?"

"I don't know what a Hearst folding bed is." He stared at me, bewildered, "A Hearst folding bed?" he asked.

"Yeah, a Hearst folding bed."

He stared at Atterbury, "Do you know, Mr. Atterbury?" Atterbury shook his head, but just at that moment, the purser turned in his seat and said to us, "Hell, Chief, I haven't heard that expression for years. A Hearst folding bed was named for anytime crew members on sailing ships carrying newsprint for cargo had to chink any leaks in the wooden hulls so they grabbed some of the cargo, rolled it up into tight rolls, and pounded it into the cracks between planks."

I said, "Joe you must be correct because the chapter I'm studying is all about damage control, thanks!"

Captain Hart said, "That's one I never heard of before." I then spoke up and asked if they knew what a gilligan hitch was.

"A gilligan hitch?," asked Atterbury, "Do you know, Captain?" Neither of them knew, so I asked the purser if he was familiar with it as long as he knew the other expression. But he replied he didn't. Then the second assistant engineer spoke up and said, "I know what that is. It's a name given to any unnatural knot that will not hold anything tight."

I said, "You must be right, Woody, because of the way it is used in the text, thanks."

Then with a smug look on my face, I turned to Hart and Atterbury, "So much for you two whiz kids. When I'm stuck again I'll ask the second assistant engineer or the purser; thanks for nothing!"

Later on, I overheard Hart talking to Atterbury and he said, "You know, I think Murphy set us up!" Atterbury agreed.

U.S. Lines had its share of characters for captains. One who comes to mind is Captain Fletcher, of the "Infamous Four," Fletcher, Gretcher, Johnson, and Wight. Fletcher was a competent master, but often behaved like a child, on and off the bridge.

When his ship arrived in Manila one time, he knew from experience the first officials to board after tying up at the pier were the Philippine customs. It was their procedure to board before anyone else was allowed, and go directly to the captain's office to receive their payoff, a few cartons of cigarettes. After this transaction was completed, they would collect the crew list and cargo manifests and then get on with their next order of business, the officers' dining room for breakfast, lunch, or dinner, depending on the time of arrival at the pier.

The customs entourage usually consisted of a lieutenant and at least seven assistants, or put another way, two seatings at the dining room table.

On this particular arrival day, Captain Fletcher rushed down one deck from the bridge to his office as soon as the ship was secure at the pier. He quickly inserted a large funnel into the front of his trousers and stood in his office awaiting the knock on his door from the customs. Moments later, the knock came and he placed a coin on his forehead and shouted, "Come in."

In trooped the eight customs men, led by their lieutenant. While they stared open mouthed at Fletcher, he tilted his head forward and the coin dropped into the funnel. He once again placed the coin on his forehead and said, "Just a minute, gentlemen." Again he attempted to drop the coin into the funnel, but this time he purposely missed. He removed the funnel and said, "This is a new game they play in the States, see how many times you can drop the coin into the funnel without missing!"

The captain asked the lieutenant if he would care to try it. The lieutenant, seeing how simple it was and probably thinking here was an opportunity to shine in front of his men, agreed to it. Fletcher inserted the funnel into the front of the lieutenant's freshly starched khakis, and told him to tilt his head way back so he could place the coin on his forehead.

While his head was tilted, Fletcher reached for a glass of water which he had earlier placed nearby and poured it into the funnel! The lieutenant let out a scream and became furious and belligerent at this lack of respect for a customs official. The front of his trousers had a large wet spot in an embarrassing place, not to mention his humiliation in front of his men.

He stormed out of the office and off the ship, followed by his men. He refused to allow anyone from ashore to board the ship to start cargo operations, or to let any crew members ashore for liberty until the captain issued a formal, written apology.

On another occasion while Fletcher was master aboard a ship on the Antwerp/Rotterdam run, he arrived at the pier in Antwerp at 0200 hours one morning. The office clerk, a Belgian, boarded to deliver Belgian francs for a crew advance and to pick up the cargo manifests. He was to bring the manifests to the office to prepare for an eight o'clock start by the longshoremen. In those days in contrast to today, the crew advance was given out in local currency due to restrictions on bringing in U.S. dollars. The francs were in small denomination bills wrapped in small paper straps.

Antwerp, like so many European ports, was a good Liberty port, with its bars open until 0600, at which time they closed only to sweep up and reopen. For this reason, the crew lined up early outside the master's office to receive their draw.

The newspaper-sized manifests were stacked on Fletcher's desk when the clerk entered his office and asked for them. With a flourish, Fletcher swooped them up from the desk and threw them into the air, saying, "Catch!" He laughed as they scattered about the room, and laughed even more when the clerk had to get down on his knees to gather them up. Needless to say, the clerk was fuming!

After gathering up all the papers, he said, "I have the money for the crew advance, Captain, do you want it now?" The captain replied, "Yes, the sooner the better, so I can get the crew off my ass and get some sleep." The clerk reached into his briefcase and quickly tore the small paper straps binding the stacks of bills together. He gathered the entire five thousand in his hands and with a flourish, said, "Here you are, Captain," and threw all the money into the air, saying, "Count it!" Fletcher stood there with his mouth open, not believing what he had just witnessed, as 50 and 100 franc notes fluttered to the deck around him!

Fletcher quickly closed his office door to prevent any of the money from blowing out into the passageway, but the clerk just as quickly opened it and said, "Goodnight, Captain, see you at eight o'clock, have a nice night!"

Fletcher never seemed to wise up enough to realize that most of his practical jokes backfired on him. Such as the time he appeared in the darkened wheelhouse of his ship one evening about 1:00 A.M. while at sea, without announcing his presence to the third mate who was on watch. He donned a Frankenstein mask and quietly crept up behind the mate in the dim blue light shining from the chart room.

He tapped the young mate on the shoulder from behind. When the fellow turned around, Fletcher shouted, "BOOOOOO!"

The mate startled, turned, and seeing Frankenstein, swung a left hook that caught Fletcher square on the jaw and knocked him sprawling across the wheelhouse! The captain quickly removed the mask, picked himself up, and shouted, "You fool, it's me, the captain!"

I don't believe the mate's reply was recorded, but I'm sure it wasn't, "I'm sorry!"

On still another occasion, his ship was making a pilot pickup in the North Sea at 2:00 A.M. en route to Rotterdam. After stopping at the pilot station, he watched over the side from the bridge wing to be sure the pilot boarded his ship safely and that the pilot boat got away from the ship's side en route to the mother ship.

He then rushed back into the darkened wheelhouse, rang full ahead on the engine room telegraph, and told the mate to set the automatic steering on the course for entering Rotterdam. He then instructed the mate and helmsman to go to their predetermined hiding places on the bridge.

In a few moments the wheelhouse door opened and the pilot entered. In the darkness he said, "Captain, pilot here." There was no response so he said, "Mate, pilot here." Still no answer. Then he observed the RPM indicator and found the vessel making sixty-five RPM, about twelve knots, and the gyro compass indicated the vessel to be on a steady course for Rotterdam. All this was taking place in busy North Sea traffic, so he began to think he had boarded a ghost ship with no one on the bridge!

Suddenly, Fletcher jumped from his hiding place and shouted, "Surprise, Pilot!" and then the mate and helmsman appeared. The pilot was now fuming at this complete disregard for good seamanship and told Fletcher he would have to file a report of the incident to the proper authorities in Rotterdam.

I never found out the outcome of this escapade, or whether the pilot actually reported it or not. The people in U.S. Lines were reluctant to discuss it.

Captain Fletcher was prohibited from entering some ports because of his practical jokes, so the company had to watch which ships he would be assigned. Many agency and port officials did not consider his sense of humor very funny.

On one voyage to Australia, our U.S. Lines agency in Sydney, Wilhelmsen Line, catered a shippers' party aboard his ship. The shippers were prominent wool merchants in Australia, and had requested the Wilhelmsen officials to hold a get-together on one of the American ships. They wanted to tour the ship and meet the officers, the people who would be carrying their product to the United States. Wilhelmsen Line, a Norwegian shipping company, also carried wool for these same people to Northern Europe, so they wanted this party to be a success.

Everything was going well for awhile; the deck officers answered their questions and gave tours of the bridge, while the engineering officers gave tours of the engineering spaces. And then Captain Fletcher appeared on the scene. He casually removed a foil-covered book from his jacket pocket and left it in a prominent place in the officers' dining room, where the reception was being held. Soon one of the staid, dignified shippers picked up the book and reading its title, *Secret Pictures From A Nudist Camp*, turned his back to the others to take a peek inside. When he opened it, he found it was not a book at all, but a battery loaded device which gave him a severe shock! He let out a yell, and dropped the book. One of his friends picked it up and he too received a shock! Both men were humiliated.

Not long after, one of them sat on a whoopee cushion which Fletcher had placed discreetly beneath a cushion on his chair! This was the final straw for these men and they stormed off the ship!

Later that same day, the vice president of Wilhelmsen Line called Fletcher to his office on the pier to discuss the embarrassing incidents which took place earlier that day. He said, "I have no choice, but to notify your principals in New York of your conduct and request that you not be allowed in this country again in any U.S. Lines ship! I regret having to talk to you like this because you're the captain, but these men are our bread and butter. I hope there are no hard feelings between you and me, but that's the way it is."

Fletcher apologized and reached out to shake hands with the vice president. As they shook, the vice president jumped back; Fletcher had hidden a joy buzzer in his hand which sent a buzzing, irritating sensation in the VP's hand. Needless to say, he never returned to Australia!

CHAPTER TEN

CHIEF ENGINEERS

While I have written much about some of our masters and mates, I would be negligent if I didn't mention some of our chief engineers and assistants.

For instance, there was an old grouchy chief named Tiffany who was constantly misplacing his dentures when he turned in at night. Each morning the search would begin to find them. Sometimes he'd find only the uppers and at other times the lowers, and on a rare occasion he'd find them together.

He finally came up with a solution. When he sat on the edge of his bunk at night, he would remove his left shoe and then remove the uppers and place them in the toe of his shoe with the sock stuffed in behind them! The same procedure was followed for the lowers. In the morning, upon getting dressed, he put the socks on, removed the teeth, inserted them in his mouth, and put the shoes on. He never lost them again!

And then there was a chief named Joe Perry, with whom I sailed in the Liberty ship SS *Henry W. Longfellow*. For many years after the war Perry served as chief engineer on many ships of all types. He was chief engineer aboard the SS *Pioneer Main* which had just returned from a trip to the Far East and was tied up to a pier in Staten Island. I was handling the ship as port engineer and had called for a surveyor from the American Bureau of Shipping to conduct a load line survey on his ship.

The surveyor assigned to the job was a crusty old veteran of many year's experience at sea, Harry Dumbleton. When he and Perry saw each other, their eyes lit up, they broke into smiles, and shook hands. They had been shipmates aboard a tanker many years ago and hadn't seen each other since.

The only problem I could foresee was that Harry had brought his son with him. The boy had recently graduated from New York State Maritime Academy at Fort Schuyler, and was tagging along with his dad to observe the workings of a bureau surveyor while waiting for a seagoing job. Knowing Perry as well as I did, I was afraid he would say something to embarrass the boy's father.

Harry took a fast turn around the ship for survey purposes and then returned to the chief's room to settle down and talk over old times with Perry. With the son present their conversation was quite respectable and Perry's demeanor beyond question. I marveled at this, and eventually Harry said he had to leave for another job. The two old shipmates shook hands and said their good-byes while I breathed a sigh of relief.

The chief and I walked out onto the boat deck to wave good-bye again as they stepped off the foot of the gangway. Suddenly Perry shouted, "Hey, Harry, come aboard again when we're in port. Only next time don't bring your kid along and we'll talk about that time you had to jump out of the second-story window of that whorehouse in Le Havre!" I should have known his silence was too good to last!

Perry never changed. When we were together in the *Longfellow*, it was wartime, in convoy in the winter North Atlantic. I was second assistant engineer, standing the 12-4 watch; and Perry was first, standing the 4-8 watch.

He dreaded that watch, and rightfully so, because most of the torpedoing occurred during those hours. A Nazi sub could position itself between the convoy and the rising or setting sun and be difficult to spot by our lookouts against the bright sun low in the sky.

After being in convoy for a week, Perry began to relieve me a little later each morning. I suspected why, of course, and I didn't enjoy being down there during the torpedo hours any more than he did.

One morning when he hadn't relieved me by 4:15 A.M., I sent the oiler to his room to call him. When he finally appeared on the floorplates, I showed him an extension cord about fifteen feet long I had made up. It had a plug on one end and the other ends of the two wires were stripped of their insulation for six inches.

"What the hell is that for?" Perry asked.

"The next time you're late for this watch, I'm calling the chief to relieve me while I go to your room, walk in quietly while you're still asleep, and place one of these bare wires in one hand and the other on your cock, and plug it in!"

"You could kill a man doing that" he said.

"Yeah, and I could get killed down here standing your lousy watch," I shouted.

He was never late again.

CHAPTER ELEVEN

PASSENGER SHIPS

United States Lines operated many passenger ships over the years, the SS *California,* SS *Virginia,* SS *Manhattan,* SS *Washington,* SS *America,* SS *United States,* and the MV *John Erickson,* to name a few. There were many stories to be told about life aboard these floating cities, about their crews, officers, and passengers. Following are some I have heard over the years, but first I would like to relate an incident that occurred leaving Newport News' Patrick Henry Airport.

As a port engineer I had just completed the dry-docking of one of our container ships in Newport News Shipyard and was flying home to Newark Airport aboard a Boeing 737. I had a window seat on the right side of the plane and was leaning with my face against the window watching the sights below as we climbed.

A lady seated next to me was attempting to look over my shoulder and was leaning closer to me as we gained altitude.

"What can you see down there?" she asked.

"Well, that's Hampton, Virginia, over there," I said, pointing to the horizon. "And that's Newport News in that direction," pointing again. "And the *United States* is directly below us."

"Well, I know that," she said with a touch of sarcasm in her voice.

I wondered why the sarcasm for a moment and then began laughing. I said, "I'm talking about the SS *United States,* not the country!"

"Oh, I'm sorry, I thought you were being facetious!" she replied.

I enjoyed her company after that and we made pleasant conversation all the way to Newark.

After World War II U.S. Lines operated the passenger ship, MV *John Erickson* to carry war brides to the States from Europe under charter to the U.S. Government. The ship was tied up in Cherbourg and had just completed loading its human cargo of young French girls and some children, many enthusiastic to leave for a new life. It was bittersweet for others, however, because they were leaving behind families and the only homeland they knew, but they were still looking forward to what lay ahead in their new world.

The ship was nearly ready to depart, the pier was filled with parents, relatives, and friends, and the ship's rails lined with young women waving handkerchiefs and tears flowing.

Earlier one of the ships' crew members had gone ashore for a last fling in a house of ill repute and fallen asleep in one of the rooms. He was awakened by the piercing wail of the siren of a French police car and pounding on his room door. Quickly realizing the house was being raided, he climbed out the rear window. After looking at his watch he found he had overslept and could barely make the ship's sailing if he could find a cab.

His only problem—he was wearing no clothes! He had forgotten where he left them in the room when he checked in, but was not about to go back for them now. He quickly found a cab and told the driver where the ship was located.

He told the driver he would be amply paid if he got him to the ship before it sailed, but the driver questioned how he could pay him. If he had no clothes, obviously he had no money. The crew member quickly assured him he had money on board the ship and to please hurry.

The cabby delivered him to shipside, but looking out at the crowd of people present, both on the pier and lining the rails, he had second thoughts about getting out of the cab naked. He called to a gendarme nearby who came to the cab, and he told him of his problem. The cop removed his cape from around his neck. He told the crew member to secure it around himself, make a dash for it, go to his room, put on some pants, and return to the deck and drop the cape down to him.

He put the cape on and rushed to the gangway. The only problem—he was wearing the cape around his neck, just as it was meant to be worn, and it only came to his waist!

He rushed up the gangway to the cheers of all the young ladies as well as the people on the pier! He made it to his room, changed into a pair of trousers, picked up some money, and lowered both money and cape on a rope to the pier where the gendarme and driver were waiting. The two walked away from the ship side to more cheers from the crowd.

Needless to say, the he was fired upon the ship's return to New York.

One of the many colorful characters in U.S. Lines was a chief engineer named Paddy Brennan. He was a massive hulk of a man, towering over most of his assistant engineers so he held their respect, if not for his rank, then for his size.

He served as chief engineer on most of the early passenger ships in the company, the SS *Manhattan, Washington,* and *America.* I never learned of his serving in any capacity except chief, though I expect he did, so no stories have surfaced of those years. But many stand out from his chief's days.

I had the pleasure of meeting him once early in my career in U.S. Lines. He shook hands with me when another port engineer, Leo Van Damme, introduced us on Pier 62 and it felt as though his hand was wrapped completely around mine as he shook it!

He was good for the passenger ships because he was a charmer when it came to entertaining the passengers, especially those of the cloth. It is told he was holding forth one time with a group of nuns en route to the United States from Europe. He had so impressed them that they came aboard the next time the ship returned to New York just to visit with him.

As they approached the gangway they heard someone shouting extremely foul language, so they backed off and stayed ashore until the person let up. When they decided it was safe to board, they hustled to Paddy's room and told him of the awful vulgarities being shouted as they attempted to board. Of course it was Paddy chewing out one of his assistants, but he sanctimoniously said, "My dear Sisters, I'll find out just who that was and see that he is properly chastised! Now, how about a little taste of wine?"

Another story was told to me by a man named George Grover, who served as Paddy's second assistant engineer. Their ship had changed its boilers from coal burning to firing with fuel oil. The uptakes of the boilers, where the smoke and residual flame meet the lower end of the smokestacks, contained heavy steel dampers, previously used while burning coal but no longer needed for fuel oil. These dampers were so heavy they had to be cranked open through a series of gears and then a bolt inserted to keep them in the open position.

While in port and with one boiler shut down, Paddy wanted to examine the firesides of this boiler. He wanted to see how much soot had built up since its last cleaning, so he had the crew open an access door into the firebox for the examination. The access door was only about eighteen inches in diameter, so Paddy climbed through it first, and when he was completely in the firebox, Grover started through.

Grover was only half way into the access, when some crew member, hiding in the upper engine room and watching the scene below, pulled the bolt out of the damper. The heavy steel door crashed down onto its landing with a loud booming noise and shook the entire boiler.

This shock caused most of the dirt and soot to be loosened and come pouring down onto Paddy in the blackness of the firebox! Grover being half in and half out of the access acted as a plug in the opening so no light could reach the interior until he eased his way out. After he backed out Paddy could see the opening and he climbed out. When he emerged he was covered with soot and as black as midnight. He then went into a rage. He rushed to the upper engine room in an effort to find the culprit, but he was long gone!

One of Paddy's idiosyncrasies was that he didn't permit smoking in the engine room by anyone. The engine room gang soon discovered a way to get around this by always leaving the engine room elevator in its lowest position at the floorplate level. Whenever one of them noticed the elevator start to rise without an occupant, they knew it was the chief calling for it to come below to the engine room. This gave the men time to hide the ash trays and extinguish their cigarettes. They maintain he never wised up to them!

Another passenger ship engineer comes to mind, a man named Joe Bruno. Bruno was a perennial second assistant engineer on passenger ships, never raised his license beyond that rating, and never had any desire to do so. He served aboard the SS *United States* under Chief Engineer Bill Kaiser and also John Logue, after Kaiser retired.

Passengers were not permitted to tour the engine room due to national defense features of the engine room power plant. But one time Bill Kaiser made an exception when the Duke of Windsor asked for a tour. Kaiser couldn't conduct the tour personally for some reason so he called the engine room to tell the second to show him around.

When he talked to Bruno, he told him the Duke of Windsor was on his way to the engine room via the elevator, and to give him a quick tour of the machinery space.

"Who is it, Chief?" asked Bruno.

"The Duke of Windsor."

"Oh Duke? OK Chief."

When the elevator arrived at floorplate level, Bruno greeted him, "Are you Duke?"

He apparently didn't realize who the Duke of Windsor was, and was under the impression his name was Duke Windsor. If the company had ever realized one of their most highly valued passengers was being treated as a mere peon, they would have probably reduced Bruno to the Far East run as a third assistant, but the Duke didn't seem to be bothered by the familiarity.

"Come on, Duke, I'll show you the boilers. Over here we have the fuel pumps, and over there, Duke, are the generators," and so it went.

At the conclusion of the brief tour the Duke left the engine room via the elevator, and apparently enjoyed the visit because he never complained of the lack of decorum to which he was accustomed.

Another story was told about the British movie actor, Monty Wooley. He was making a trip aboard the *United States* and was seated in the first class ballroom one evening. During a lull in the festivities, he stood up and apparently his suspenders broke allowing his tuxedo trousers to drop to the ballroom floor.

Unruffled, he remained in his standing position until he caught the eye of a busboy and signaled him to come forth. When the busboy approached, he pointed to his trousers at his ankles. The busboy dutifully hoisted them up to the waiting hands of Monty who then strode off the dance floor with his British dignity intact, and to the applause of all present!

Apparently Paddy Brennan, for all his toughness and seriousness, was also a practical joker at times. On one of the early passenger ships in which he served he had the engineers construct a dummy of old clothes; trousers, shirt, hat, etc. and stuffed with newspaper. The dummy was hidden in a coal bunker out of sight, until one day while Paddy was conducting a tour of the engine room with a group of passengers in tow. One of the engineers in on the joke approached him to tell him one of the coal passers had been hit on the head with a shovel and they thought he might be dead.

Paddy said, "Don't take any chances, we could be sued, throw him into the furnace!"

With this they opened the access door to the firebox, quickly grabbed the dummy, and threw it into the furnace! The passengers stood there aghast at this until Paddy put their minds at ease and explained it was only a joke they sometimes pull on passengers.

Life aboard the *United States* for some engineers was not always dull, even though their work hours were four hours on and eight off, day after day. For the refrigeration engineer, it had its pleasant moments and bad ones as well.

At sea it was his duty to routinely check the temperatures in the air conditioning ducts at various points in the system, particularly in the passenger and public spaces. One evening he was making his rounds and climbed onto a grating in the void space over the first-class ballroom to read a thermometer. While standing there he took advantage of one of the perks of the job; he could see down into the first-class ballroom through the ventilator outlet and the indirect lighting, and watch the people dance. He leaned over the railing to get a better view when his pipe fell out of his shirt pocket and landed on ceiling tile below him. He reached further to retrieve it and lost his footing. To save himself, he stepped onto the ceiling!

His foot broke through, throwing debris down onto the people below in their evening gowns and tuxedos! He quickly withdrew his foot, but made the fatal mistake of peering down through the hole just as the chief engineer, who was in the ballroom, looked upward.

The chief recognized him as one of his men and the engineer was fired upon the ship's arrival in New York.

Paddy Brennan had a reputation of never having refused to "go out on the pier" to settle a dispute. I don't know of anyone who ever challenged him because he was certainly no one to fool with in his prime! Paddy was killed in an automobile accident shortly after he retired and one man said at the time, "That's the only way Paddy could ever die, by being killed. He was just too mean and tough to simply lay down and go naturally!"

One of the more tragic incidents told to me by an old timer took place aboard one of our early passenger ships in the 1920s. The ship was fitted with deluxe accommodations for first class, comfortable quarters and spaces for cabin, or second class, and a third class which was not nearly as plush as the others. Sometimes another class was carried called steerage which was made up mostly of immigrants who were quite poor and had probably saved for years to buy passage to their new homeland where they hoped to start life over.

The people were separated in steerage with men and women sleeping in separate compartments, a condition which was tolerated even by families in order to get passage to the United States. Young children usually stayed with the mother.

The sanitary facilities in steerage consisted of group toilets and showers, again separated by sexes and which, in this particular ship, were on the other side of a steel bulkhead separating them from the crew quarters. The ship was of riveted construction, having been built before the advent of welding, so the bulkhead had several rows of rivets where the overlapping plates were pieced together.

Several women were showering one evening when one of them noticed a rivet missing from a row about waist high. She kept observing it and could see light coming through it for a few moments and then it would darken for a short period and then show light again.

Suspecting someone on the other side of the bulkhead was using it as a peep hole, she slipped out of the shower, went to her locker where she picked up a hat pin, and returned to the shower room where she moved along the bulkhead until she was just beside the hole.

With the hat pin poised just above the opening, she told one of the women to signal her when the hole became dark, and at that moment she thrust the hat pin through the hole! The crew member on the other side who was spying on them lost the sight of his eye, but during a subsequent investigation no one in steerage would come forth to tell who had done it.

From that point on, rivet inspections were held prior to boarding passengers, and any found missing were promptly replaced. In

addition, periodic inspections were held in the crew areas when the
vessel was underway.

   One of the many stories told in the company concerned Rita
Hayworth who was a passenger aboard the SS *United States* during
one of the vessel's eastbound crossings. After she had been aboard
a day or so, some of the more mischievous engineers thought it
would be unique to have a piece of her toilet seat as a souvenir.
   On the selected day, with a deck steward acting as lookout, the
steward signaled the engineers when he saw her leave her stateroom
for a stroll on deck. They entered her room, which had been opened
for them by the steward, removed the seat, and were about to replace it with a spare they had drawn from the storeroom when the
steward signaled them that she was returning to her room.
   They quickly left the area taking her seat and the replacement
with them. When she arrived in her room, she reported the seat
missing to the steward who promptly notified the chief engineer,
who then assigned the plumber to replace it with another from the
storeroom.
   In the meantime, her original seat was placed in a vise in the
ship's machine shop and sawed into small cubes. A hole was drilled
through one corner of each cube and a tag attached which read,
"Part of the toilet seat used by Rita Hayworth, Voyage #17,
Eastbound, SS *UNITED STATES.*"
   I never saw any of them, but I have been assured they are out
there somewhere!

   On another occasion aboard a passenger ship, one of the engineers was romancing a ship's nurse. While their time together aboard
was strictly business, they had their romantic moments ashore in
various foreign ports.
   Prior to the ship's arrival in Southampton, the enginer informed
the nurse that he would not be able to accompany her ashore in that

port because he wished to go to a tailor shop to be measured for a new suit which he would then pick up the following trip about four weeks later.

Whether he ever made it to the tailor shop is not known, but at some point during his shore leave, he stopped in a British pub and met a young English girl. They were sitting in the rear of the pub in an isolated booth when the nurse and a few other crew members stopped in for a beer before returning to the ship.

The nurse spotted him, but he apparently didn't see her and she soon returned to the ship with the others. Several days later while at sea, the engineer was taking a noontime nap on the settee in his room with his head nearest the door which was hooked open about ten inches.

The nurse happened to walk by his room and saw him asleep with his mouth open so she quickly went to the ship's hospital where she picked up a bottle of acid, returned to his room, reached through the open door, and poured the acid into his mouth!

The man awoke screaming, but the nurse was nowhere to be found. He was rushed to the ship's hospital where he soon died. She eventually admitted to the act when confronted by authorities and was held for trial ashore.

The individual who related this to me never heard the outcome of it. Strangely, after hearing this story many years ago, I asked my boss who had served on those ships if he had ever heard of this happening, He became furious with me and told me never to repeat the story again, which then made me even more curious!

During prohibition after one of our passenger ships had tied up at its terminal in New York, a third assistant engineer was leaving the ship via the crew gangway carrying a suitcase. He was intercepted by a customs officer who asked to examine the contents of the suitcase.

The inspector informed him that due to prohibition some people were attempting to smuggle European liquor, such as Cognac from

France and Scotch from England, to be sold here for a tremendous profit. He explained this to the young engineer in order to allow him to return to the ship with the suitcase in the event he was carrying liquor. The engineer explained that the suitcase contained the ship's cat and he was taking it to a veterinarian for its annual checkup and shots.

He also said that if the cat escaped while the suitcase was open, it would probably dash up the gangway and hide in the vastness of the ship and he would have trouble finding it again.

The inspector insisted, however, so the engineer pointed the suitcase toward the gangway and opened it with a sudden, fast motion. This frightened the cat and it leaped from the suitcase and dashed up the gangway. The inspector saw this and felt somewhat guilty about doubting the engineer and apologized, "I really didn't think you had a cat in the suitcase, I'm sorry!"

The engineer returned to the ship, waited about fifteen minutes, and then returned to the gangway with the suitcase. He told the inspector he was lucky to find the cat which he said was in the ship's galley, the cat's favorite hangout.

He then asked the inspector if he wished to examine the suitcase again and the inspector said, "Hell no, I don't want to put you through that again, go ahead!"

The engineer paraded out through the gate, hailed a cab, and took the suitcase home full of Cognac!

While most of the company ships lowered the company house flag when passing our headquarters building at Number One Broadway, some also sounded their whistles as they passed the Battery in New York harbor in a salute to the office.

Number One Broadway housed many of the departments needed to operate a large steamship company, but the operations department was located at the foot of Twenty-third Street on the North River. Although it was referred to as the North River on the company letterhead, it was really the Hudson. The river was named the

North River years ago, while the Delaware was referred to as the South River and the East River retained its name. I have never been able to find much more information than that.

Directly opposite Twenty-third Street, across the North River on the New Jersey waterfront was the Bethlehem Steel Shipyard and next to it was Todd Shipyard. Bethlehem and Todd were each allotted a certain group of freight ships on which to perform voyage repairs, and Beth was also assigned the SS *United States* and Todd, the SS *America.*

One day just before noon, the SS *United States* was moving slowly up the river, en route to Pier 86. As it passed our operations office at Twenty-third Street, it sounded its deep-throated whistle several times as another salute to the company.

Across the river in the general manager's office of Bethlehem Steel, a shipyard supervisor, Cliff Bryn, was talking to the shipyard manager, Doug Manzell. Cliff handled all the repairs on U.S. Lines ships for Bethlehem and did a good job, but was sometimes concerned as to what his boss thought of his work.

When the ship sounded its whistle, the loud blasts could be heard up and down the river, and Manzell, looking out his office window wondered aloud, "Why are they blowing their whistle around here, I don't see any river traffic in the area?"

Bryn, seeing an opportunity to gain favor with his boss, replied, "Oh that, Mr. Manzell. They're blowing it as a salutation to me as they pass by the yard; they do it every time they go by. It's a sort of courtesy gesture!"

Manzell gave the appearance to Bryn of having been impressed by this, but then he wondered, "Would they really do that?" Bryn never offered any other explanation.

CHAPTER TWELVE

PASSENGERS

Most U.S. Lines cargo ships had accommodations for carrying twelve passengers. Twelve was the maximum allowed by U.S. law on any vessel without a doctor aboard, or a continuous radio watch, which would require hiring two more radio operators. The accommodations on some ships were similar to first class on a passenger ship, but on other ships the accommodations could be compared virtually to steerage. The passengers ate their meals with the officers' dining room, often called the saloon, and were permitted to use the officers' lounge for any recreation they could manage to create for themselves, such as playing cards, checkers, darts, etc.

On a short trip to Europe it was quite tolerable for passengers, but on an extended trip, such as to Australia, it was very boring. After clearing the last lock of the Panama Canal and dropping off the pilot, passengers faced twenty-three days at sea before a landfall at Brisbane. Such a long trip for the crew was routine, people were on watch, day workers put in their eight hours each day, so there was really no boredom for the crew.

For the passengers, however, after six or seven days, they began to get on each others nerves. Tempers were short at times, and their sleeping hours were being turned upside down due to time changes every other night. We tried to divert their attention by giving tours of the bridge and engine room and by inviting them for coffee or tea with us after dinner in the saloon.

Often movies would be shown if the ship had a projector and a few films. This diversion was welcome each time they were shown, even if the passengers had seen the film five or six times. On later vessels when VCRs were put aboard, the passengers had a much larger variety of movies.

One morning aboard the *Pioneer Star* en route to Australia, after a week at sea, I entered the saloon and found all the passengers in there eating breakfast. Seeing their bored faces, I remarked, "Land is only three miles away." They dropped their knives and forks and rushed to the portholes to view it, but of course, it wasn't in sight. They asked where it was, and I pointed downward, under the ship. That didn't exactly make a hit with them so early in the morning.

On another voyage aboard the SS *Pioneer Star*, we were bound for Australia with a stopover in Papeete, Tahiti. Papeete had no navigation lights to light the short channel run from the pilot station to the cargo pier, so a daylight arrival and departure was necessary. Since the ship carried only enough cargo for a four-hour stay, it was almost mandatory to adjust speed a few days away to make an early evening arrival, lest we miss a night in port. While well-planned, the company must have realized it was prearranged because every ship on the schedule always managed to arrive in early evening.

To make an early morning arrival and leave four hours later, after ten days at sea, would be almost unforgivable. On board were twelve passengers, one of whom was a minister returning to his flock in Melbourne after completing a course of postgraduate studies in the States.

The ship tied up at the pier, which was located in the center of Papeete, about 5:00 P.M., just the right time to be "forced" to remain in port for the night. Just about every crew member left the ship shortly after docking for shore leave, some to see the sights, others to stretch their legs and just get off the ship for awhile.

The minister was one of the first passengers to leave. A few hours later while some of us were standing on the boat deck observing the stevedoring operations, an open touring car with no roof arrived alongside the ship. In the back seat, sitting between two Tahitian beauties and wearing a carnation behind his right ear, sat the reverend.

When the vehicle came to a stop, he leaped from the rear of the car, over the door, and onto the pier. He rushed up the gangway, acknowledging us with a wave and saying, "I came back to get more money!" Moments later he left the ship, leaped aboard the car landing in the seat between the two girls, and they sped off.

Papeete has a rule regarding shore leave for crew and passengers from any ship in port for cargo purposes. When cargo operations are completed and the ship secured for sea, all hands must be aboard or the ship doesn't leave. No beachcombers tolerated! The only exception is if a man is hospitalized.

The following morning with cargo operations finished and the ship ready to leave, the officers, crew, and passengers had to line up on the main deck while the chief of police personally assured himself that all were aboard. He held a crew list and passenger list and checked everyone off.

Earlier the department heads had conducted a preliminary crew check and determined several to be missing. Two from the steward's department, three from the engine department, and two from the deck department, and one passenger, the minister.

The captain informed the police chief of this beforehand, so he advised us to sound the ship's whistle a few times. Being a small city the whistle could be heard throughout. This worked because in a few minutes several people returned. We informed the chief that only the boatswain and minister were now missing. The chief took off on his bicycle and headed toward a known house of ill repute, and soon returned with the boatswain. He was drunk and the chief, riding a bicycle, was prodding him along with the front wheel while riding slowly.

While the chief was explaining to the captain that we couldn't leave without our passenger, we heard a screech of brakes. Everyone rushed out on deck in time to see the minister climb from the rear of the open car, alone, and race up the gangway. As he passed us, we saw the results of his night in Tahiti—his left eye was nearly closed in the early stages of one of the finest black eyes I would see in a long time.

We left Tahiti that morning with all hands aboard, but the minister stayed in his room in seclusion, having his meals brought in by the steward for several days.

Prior to our arrival in Tahiti he had been holding Sunday services in the officers' dining room, but after his fling in port, they were no longer conducted for some reason.

After a few days he emerged, sheepishly, and began to mingle with everyone. By arrival time in Melbourne, his eye had cleared and no one was the wiser. And he never offered an explanation of the cause of the black eye.

Winter trips in the North Atlantic found few, if any, passengers willing to fight the severe storms that were often encountered. The company was just as pleased with this because the passengers were not wise to the ways of a sailor who could tolerate the rolling and pitching of the ship. Also, there was always that potential for fingers getting jammed in a closing door which the passenger had forgotten to hook open, or slipping on a wet deck, or even having their hot soup spilled into their lap during meals while the ship rolled or pitched. Summer trips, however, were usually filled to capacity with students, vacationers, and senior citizens wanting a leisurely trip to Europe, Australia, or the Far East. The company would carry passengers to the Far East providing their final destination was not Hong Kong. Discharging passengers there required the ship to dock first at a passenger terminal for processing and then shifting to the cargo berth. This was not only costly, but time consuming as well, since the ship's primary function was to deliver its cargo with due dispatch.

Aboard the SS *Pioneer Ming*, we carried a single passenger on one voyage, a lady en route to Kobe, Japan, to join her husband who had arrived there earlier to set up an office for a major American oil company. At the end of the first week at sea after leaving the last American port, we were to hold our first weekly fire and boat drill as required by law. United States Coast Guard rules require a drill every seven days, at which time the crew shall be mustered at their stations, wearing their life jackets, fire hoses strung out from their hydrants, and water pressure from the engine room pumps circulated through them. Upon completion of the fire drill, the lifeboats are to be swung out on their davits, safe conditions permitting, the crew instructed and, upon completion, the boats stowed properly for sea.

These drills are conducted routinely and the different stages of the drill are performed upon hearing commands from the ship's whistle and the general alarm bells which are located throughout the living quarters and work areas of the ship.

The captain notified the chief steward to tell the lady passenger that it would not be necessary for her to attend the drills. She was to be told to put her life jacket on and stay in her room until the all clear signal. There was only one thing wrong with this, the captain forgot that the chief steward was a naturalized Greek whose English was not the most fluent. When the ship's whistle and the general alarm bells began their loud, ear-splitting noises at 3:30 P.M. that day, the lady started out of her cabin to see what was going on. There outside her cabin stood the steward. He wouldn't let her leave her cabin. He screamed at her in broken English to hurry and put on her life jacket but she would not be allowed out of her cabin, "Captain's orders!" he shouted and then slammed the door behind her. She rushed to her porthole to see the fire hoses being strung out and again attempted to leave the room, but the steward was holding the door closed. He kept shouting, "Fire dreel, fire dreel, no come out, captain say you must stay in room!"

The woman was now in a cold sweat imagining the worst possible scenario aboard ship—fire and she was unable to leave! Moments later, more bells and whistles calling the crew to lifeboat drill. She again went to her porthole and saw the crew outside her room apparently launching the lifeboat to which she was assigned. It was then she fainted.

After the all clear was given, the steward opened her door to tell her it would be all right for her to come out and found her slumped in her chair, incoherent, and in a cold sweat. He called the captain and with the help of the purser and mate she was revived.

She threatened to sue the company. However, after observing the routine for another few weeks, she was almost like another crew member and somewhat sorry to be leaving when we eventually arrived at Kobe. On subsequent trips to Kobe, she invited some of the officers to her home for a Japanese meal, but not the chief steward!

CHAPTER THIRTEEN

MEALTIMES

Mealtimes aboard our ships brought many laughs, occasional arguments and disagreements, but hardly a day went by without some incident during the preparation, serving, eating, or cleaning up after a meal. The menus were selected by a nutritionist hired by the company to assure a balanced diet, and agreed to by the various unions whose members were aboard.

The company was cost conscious, but at the same time watched the feeding costs closely. It was aware that the crew would report to their patrolman any time the food slipped below the established standards. Sometimes the ship's cook would take a vacation and the relief cook was not as good. That's when the union members would report problems with the food with a tendency to blame the company. The company, however, would merely produce the receipts for the food which had been put aboard for that trip and compare it with that of another ship which had just given its steward department a vote of confidence. The same purveyor furnished the food for both ships, thus the company would blame the poor food on the cook. The issue would die, particularly since both the good cook and the bad one were in the same union as the complainants.

The food was wholesome and plentiful in contrast to that which was served during the 1920s when the crew often ate from chipped enamel dishware. At that time conditions were often unsanitary in the galley and refrigerators and food handlers were not trained in sanitary habits.

The reforms in the culinary department were a direct result of the labor unions forcing the issue. At one point in U.S. Lines, the cooks were cutting the steaks a little thinner than usual, but after a hearing between the company and the unions, it was agreed that all steaks would be cut to a minimum of 3/4 inch thick. With the advent of automation on the container ships, crews were reduced, portion control introduced, frozen desserts furnished, and the butcher block became an ornament in a housewife's kitchen instead of a piece of galley equipment. Now everyone's hamburger, veal cutlet, steak, etc. is the same size whether served to the captain or ordinary seaman.

At dinner one evening aboard the SS *Pioneer Ming*, the main course was a veal cutlet served with mashed potatoes, gravy, and string beans. I had just finished eating when the captain, John Hart appeared at the pantry door, which was just outside the entrance to the officers' dining room. He looked in at the steam table and asked the pantryman what they were serving that evening and was told "veal cutlets, mashed potatoes, and string beans."

The captain said, "I'll have a nice cutlet with the vegetables." Everyone in the dining room could hear him place his order with the pantryman. He then entered the dining room and took his place at the table next to me. The pantryman could be heard talking on the intercom to the galley and he told them to prepare a nice cutlet for the captain. This irritated everyone in the room because the rest of us had to get our cutlets from the pantry steam table where they had been lying since 3:30 that afternoon.

Moments later the chief mate, John Tucker, a very capable chief mate who eventually became captain of the SS *United States*, entered and took his seat opposite the captain at our table. The messman appeared and asked him what he would like for dinner. He replied, "Veal cutlet, potatoes, and string beans." The messman left for the pantry and reappeared a few seconds later with the mate's dinner.

The cutlet was dried up and curled at the edges and had obviously been cooked much earlier. He looked at it disgustedly and looked up at the captain who was still waiting to be served. The mate asked, "What did you order, Captain?" He replied, "The same thing you have, Mr. Tucker." Tucker then lifted up his plate and placed it down in the captain's place and said, "Then this must be yours, you were in here ahead of me!" The captain picked up the plate and placed it back in front of the mate and said, "No it isn't, mine is coming soon." Again, the mate placed it before the captain and once again he returned it to the mate's place. I started to laugh at this Keystone Comedy taking place when the messman shouted from across the dining room to make room; the captain's plate was very hot and beginning to slip from the napkin in which he was holding it. The cutlet was freshly cooked, hot, and spitting. The mate looked at it and said, "That's my cutlet!" The captain replied, "No it isn't, this is mine, that's yours," pointing to the cold plate in front of the mate. The mate threw down his knife and fork and stormed out of the dining room. The captain turned to talk to me and I walked out, too.

On another occasion on the same ship but with a different chief mate, Bill Atterbury, the captain sat down one evening to start dinner and was served a sliced cucumber salad in vinegar and oil. The chief mate had just finished his salad and was about to start eating his main course which included mashed potatoes, served with gravy floating in a crater neatly placed in the center of the potatoes.

The captain picked up a cucumber slice in his fingers and began waving it up and down, criticizing the cooks for making a salad in which the cucumbers slices were soaked for so long they were limp. In his rage he threw it down into his salad; it bounced out and across the table where it landed directly in the gravy of the mate's mashed potatoes. It landed with a splash and threw gravy into the mate's lap and onto his new shirt. He looked up at the captain in disgust. Before he could say anything, the captain reached across the table and plucked it out of the mashed potatoes and put it on his own plate.

He said, "I'm sorry, Mate, I just got carried away!" Atterbury also threw down his utensils and stalked off without finishing his meal.

CHAPTER FOURTEEN

UNIFORMS

U.S. Lines had a company rule book which detailed the duties of the ship's officers, reports to be turned in at the completion of each voyage, and the uniforms to be worn on board while eating in the saloon, particularly if there were passengers aboard. These rules applied to the freighters as well as the passenger ships.

A copy of these rules was placed aboard each ship. If a new mate or engineer reported aboard, the book was handed to him to read in order for him to obtain the necessary clothes to dress as the book dictated. Some people balked at this, but generally it was accepted.

The saloon would look pretty shabby if people came in at mealtimes in tee shirts, dungarees, etc., but when everyone wore clean khakis, it made for a pleasant atmosphere.

The uniform of the day was to be determined by the master. Most of the time khakis were worn, however in cold weather the deck officers might wear blues. But the engineers always got away with khakis. Whenever khakis were worn, the officers wore their shoulder boards on their khaki jackets, or if not on the jackets, the shoulder boards were worn on their shirts.

While I was aboard the SS *Pioneer Star* as first assistant engineer, our ship had just left the Panama Canal bound for Australia. I found it necessary to dash to the engine room for emergencies during dinner on three consecutive days. The following day, a Sunday, I appeared at lunchtime wearing civilian clothes.

The chief mate, Stanley Kirby, asked, "Mr. Murphy, don't you have any khakis to wear during the lunch hour. They are the uniform of the day, you know."

I bristled when I heard this, and replied, "Yeah, I got khakis; you've seen me wearing them at other mealtimes. It just so happens that they were soiled from running to the engine room during meal-times for an emergency, and they are in the washing machine at this very moment!"

Captain Smith gave Kirby a disgusted look for making an issue of this, and the chief engineer told him to mind his own business. That evening at dinner, all the engineers entered the dining room wearing their civilian clothes to spite Kirby.

Captain Smith smiled when he saw this and knew very well what their intention was and said to me, "Mr. Murphy, the engineers look very nice this evening," while Kirby did a slow burn.

We thought this was the end of the matter because for the next meal my khakis were clean and I wore them at each meal thereafter. But the following Sunday at the evening meal, all the passengers appeared in their best clothes, while we were just in our usual khakis.

Talking to them after dinner, they told us they thought it was the ship's routine for everyone to dress nicely every Sunday evening because it happened last week. We told them it was merely a feud between the chief mate and the engine department.

During one voyage to the Far East aboard the SS *Pioneer Minx*, Captain Heather set the example by wearing a khaki jacket with shoulder boards upon leaving the West Coast. One evening he entered the saloon without his coat, so I said, "Did you forget your jacket?" I said this to him because he was constantly reminding me when one of the engineers forgot his.

He didn't want to give the impression that he had forgotten it, so he said, "We're in tropical waters now, so tell your men jackets won't be required any longer." A few days later he forgot his necktie, and when he saw me looking at mine, he said, "Oh, by the way, Chief, no neckties from now on. The weather is getting too warm for them."

Several days later after leaving the Philippines for Inchon, Korea, he entered the saloon wearing his jacket and necktie. He told me this would be the uniform until further notice due to the cold weather in Korea. After several days we left Korea for the Philippines again. It began, first, no jackets, then no ties, but after leaving Manila, back to ties and then jackets. A few days out of Manila, he went back to only shirts, no ties.

By then I had had it, and so had the engineers. At the next meal I entered the saloon wearing a necktie. He said, "Chief, no ties now, we're in the tropics, remember?"

I reached to my neck an gave the tie a slight tug and it came loose from my shirt, but all that came loose was the knot and tie, without anything from around my neck! He stared at me and asked, "How in hell did you do that?"

I replied, "Like this," and I placed the knot up to my neck and it remained there. I had implanted a small magnet in the knot, cut the loop of the tie off flush with the sides of the knot, and placed a paper clip over the top button of my shirt. Thus by merely touching the knot to the paper clip, the tie remained in place.

I told him he had changed the uniform so frequently, this saved wear and tear on the tie, and just in case he changed the uniform in the middle of the meal, I'd be ready. This ended the uniform craze and he became more realistic.

At breakfast one morning aboard the *Pioneer Ming*, Captain John Hart looked across the dining room to where the second assistant engineer, Walter Wood, was seated. The captain leaned over to me and quietly said, "After breakfast, tell that second assistant to wear socks when he comes into the dining room to eat." I looked over in his direction and turned to the captain and said, "He is wearing socks." Hart insisted he wasn't, so I said I would check later.

After breakfast Walter left the dining room and returned to his room. I left shortly after and stopped in to see him. He was seated at his desk with his feet up reading a book, so I reached over and pulled up his pant leg. He said, "What in the world are you doing?"

I told him about our conversation in the dining room and he laughed. He proved to be wearing socks just as I had thought.

I left to go directly to the captain's office where he was seated at his desk, his feet also up. I said, "The second assistant is wearing socks, KHAKI socks. He is more in uniform than you are. You're wearing white cotton slop chest socks that are falling down into your loafers because the elastic is gone in them. I think you owe him an apology." He just laughed it off, however.

Captain Hart was in the habit of removing his jacket after each meal and hanging it over the back of his office chair. Someone slipped into his office just after the incident with the second assistant's socks and reversed his shoulder boards so the pointed ends headed outward instead of inward as they were designed. He didn't notice it for over a week and no one would tell him. I asked the second assistant engineer if he knew anything about it. He claimed he had nothing to do with it, but I have my suspicions.

A new licensed junior engineer reported aboard the SS *Pioneer Ming* one afternoon in New York, just prior to sailing on our outward journey to the Far East. When he entered the dining room for his first meal aboard, he was dressed in old khakis, which looked like they had been used for tank cleaning, and old work shoes with white socks, which seemed to disappear into the backs of his shoes. This was quite a contrast to the rest of the officers in the saloon.

After the meal I took him aside and told him about company rules for proper dress in the dining room, and handed the company rule book to him to read. I added that since we would be boarding passengers in one of the coastwise ports, uniforms would be worn by all the engineers, as well.

He was understanding and said it was his intention to purchase some clothing in one of the coastwise ports while there to load cargo. In Baltimore he bought a couple of sets of khaki shirts and trousers, and looked much more presentable after that. That is for a few days anyway!

This man's problem was that of so many who go to sea, he was a natural "dirt magnet." He seemed to get filthy just by opening the door to the engine room. Whenever he went below on watch wearing clean clothes, he was filthy within an hour. But he was a very conscientious worker, a nice lad, and valued aid to the second assistant engineer with whom he stood a watch.

One of his attributes was that he wasn't afraid to dig into a problem, whether it be a machinery malfunction or a routine weekly changeover of vital machinery. He gave no thought to the clothes he was wearing. Thus his new clothes were soon soiled beyond the capabilities of our washing machine.

Our schedule brought us to Honolulu where we worked commercial cargo, and then a shift of ship to Pearl Harbor where we were to load military for the Far East. After tying up to the pier at Pearl, he came to my room to ask if I needed anything from the Navy commissary. I asked who was going and he said he was. I told him I didn't think he would be admitted without a proper ID card authorizing him to enter and purchase goods there, but he told me he intended to dress as a naval officer and just walk in.

I had to hide my laughter when he, of all people, was going there impersonating a naval officer. I told him I couldn't think of anything I needed, but to please come to my office just before he left in case I thought of anything. Actually, I wanted to see what he would look like as a naval officer.

He reappeared in a half hour, dressed in wrinkled khaki trousers spotted with fuel oil. His shirt needed pressing and one elbow had a tear; the collar held a propeller on one side and an anchor on the other, which he had borrowed from our two cadets; and his black necktie had a lunch stain on it. I loaned him a large tie clasp which covered it and I suggested he roll up his sleeves to conceal the torn elbow. He planned to carry the cadet's hat in his hand, upside down, so the emblem wouldn't show. His trousers had shrunk from repeated washings and ended a few inches above his shoes, exposing his white slop chest socks. I told him I couldn't think of anything I needed, so he left for the commissary. He returned about a half hour later and came to my office to ask if I cared to have a cold beer with him. I told him I didn't want one at the time, but asked how he made out at the commissary.

He replied, "Great, the commissary is only about a ten minute walk from our gangway. I was admitted without any problem and no one asked for an ID, so I bought some clothes, a pen and pencil set for the second assistant, and two cases of beer."

"When I left the commissary, I began walking to the ship, struggling to carry the beer, when a car carrying a four-striper in the back seat stopped next to me and asked if he could give me a lift. I got in the back seat with him. His driver, a sailor, put my beer in the trunk and they drove me right up to our gangway. When we stopped, the driver helped me carry the beer aboard!"

I just had to shake my head in disbelief.

CHAPTER FIFTEEN

CONTRABAND

I believe smuggling and black-market activities have been going on as long as ships have plied the oceans, and I suspect that cigarettes have been the common denominator involved in many of the transactions.

Cigarettes were always sold at nearly cost aboard ship and with no tax because they were consumed outside the United States. Therefore they were a cheap commodity to buy and their demand was unbelievable in some countries. I once asked a man in Belgium what he planned to do with some I had sold to him and he said he would trade them for either clothing or groceries, but not smoke them.

I then asked who would eventually smoke them, in other words, where did the chain end? He replied, "The farmer, the man who has what everyone requires, food!"

Onboard ship, tobacco products are kept locked in a small locker called the "slop chest." It is fitted with a type of padlock arrangement which usually has a steel box covering the lock which can accept a seal, usually put there by the customs officials upon entering a port.

A ration of tobacco products, i.e., one carton of cigarettes, one pound of tobacco or fifty cigars, were permitted every five days while in port. After five days, a customs man would board the vessel, examine the seal, and then break it to allow the slop chest to be opened. In U.S. Lines, the chief steward usually operated the slop chest and kept an account of each crew member's orders. The account was given to the purser at the end of the trip for deduction from the men's wages. The customs man would stand by and witness the handing out of the tobacco and reseal the door upon completion.

I recall one time aboard the SS *Pioneer Star* while docked in Australia, the ship had been in port for five days so a tobacco ration was due. The captain informed our agent of this and requested that he call customs for unsealing. He placed the call in the morning, but by late afternoon no customs officials had appeared. The captain then instructed the chief mate to lower the Australian flag from our foremast, tie an overhand knot in it, and hoist it aloft again.

The mate did this and within an hour the customs officials were aboard. The customs officials apologized for being late and then politely told the captain he could untie the knot in their flag. Later I questioned the captain about the flag and the possibility of the Australians being insulted, but he assured me it was a practice used in the British Isles to call customs.

He must have been correct because the customs inspector recognized the signal and casually told him to remove the knot after it had served its purpose.

Just after World War II, I made a relief trip on a ship carrying a full load of potatoes to Hamburg, Germany. The ship had been in port for three days, so many of us were able to go ashore each night to have a nice meal and a beer in the seamen's club located in the pier area.

One evening a German man approached me at the club bar and asked if I would be interested in purchasing a prewar German camera. Having been a camera buff for many years, I told him perhaps I would be if I could examine it. He told me he had it with him and I could see it if we went over to a booth where we would not be observed.

It turned out to be a Zeiss-Ikon folding camera and in excellent condition. He told me it was mine for three cartons of Lucky Strike cigarettes. I backed off then, telling him there was no way in the world I would risk taking three cartons of cigarettes through the newly organized German customs or the GI sentries at the terminal gates.

"Oh, don't worry about that. I'll come alongside your ship in my boat about 10:00 tonight and we'll make the exchange then."

This sounded pretty foolproof to me so I agreed and left the club to return to my ship. At 10:00 P.M. I was standing out on the boat deck in the darkness, looking up and down the river for a small boat. A large three-hatch coastal steamer was tying up to us on our offshore side, at the time, and our mate on watch had sailors fore and aft to receive his mooring lines. I assumed this ship was alongside for receiving our cargo first thing in the morning, because we had been discharging into barges offshore for three days, as well as onto the pier. My thought now was, "How in hell is the small boat going to come alongside our ship with this monster blocking the way."

Our boat deck was on a level with the bridge of the steamer, so I thought if necessary, my man could tie up to the offshore side of the coaster and I could cross that ship to make the exchange.

The captain of the steamer came out on his bridge in uniform, and I thought crossing over him is out of the question, now. He looked over at me and asked, "Do you have the cigarettes, I have the camera here!"

I took another look and sure enough it was the man in the seamen's club!

"Yes, I have them right here with me."

We made the exchange from ship to ship, and then he asked me if I would be kind enough to have our mate on watch let his lines go so he could leave. I told the third mate on watch, and he said, "What the hell is going on here? I just tied him up to us!"

"Don't ask any questions, we just completed a business transaction." He laughed and told his watch mates to let the lines go.

As the coaster proceeded up the river, I watched it and after running slowly for a quarter of a mile, he tied up to another American ship. I don't know how many cameras he sold that night in this manner, but apparently the cigarettes were valuable enough to keep a ship that size in operation, and at the same time risk being caught by the river police patrols.

As for the camera, it was in extremely good condition and served me well for many years.

While at sea on this ship, we were holding a routine inspection of the living quarters, and noticed an old bicycle tied up to the handrails on the main deck inside the house. The handlebars had been turned ninety degrees so as not to protrude out into the passageway and strike someone passing.

Out of curiosity, the captain asked one of the crew who the bike belonged to. He was told it belonged to a crew member who was on vacation at that time, but would be returning to the ship upon our arrival in New York. He went on to tell us about the bike.

The owner had learned several trips prior to this one that there was a shortage of cigarette lighter flints in Europe. It seems no one had matches because the ingredients, such as sulfur, needed to manufacture them were unavailable because of the war. The sulfur and other chemicals were reserved for munitions, etc., so anyone who had a need for matches was using lighters. Lighter fluid seemed to be plentiful, but the flints were difficult to obtain.

This crew member scouted around New York and found he could purchase them by the pound in lower Manhattan. He bought several pounds there, but then was confronted with the problem of how to get them through the customs gate in each foreign port. So he dreamed up the idea of an old bicycle.

He would remove the bicycle seat from the frame and pour hundreds of flints into the tubing of the frame, leaving enough slack to insert the seat post. He would then ride out through the gate, being searched occasionally by the customs, but his bike was never suspected.

He would pedal to a local bar, ride the bike into a back room where his contact was waiting, remove the seat, and pour out the flints. I never found out if he sold them by the pound or individually. He claimed his only worry was that he might be suspected if he made too many trips through the gate each day, and that he could be stuck with thousands of flints if he were to return to Europe and find someone had flooded the market with them.

CHAPTER SIXTEEN

CARGOES

U.S. Lines, like most shipping companies, would accept any cargo which paid revenue, and do its utmost to deliver it to its destination in good order. But strangely it was sometimes called upon to carry the cargo only half way, and then dump it overboard.

Such was the case one time when a major U.S. automobile manufacturer had shipped some spare parts to Antwerp on one of our ships. These parts were to be picked up from our pier by its European representative and distributed to their various dealers in Belgium and Holland. For some reason they were never removed from the pier.

U.S. Lines allowed incoming cargo to remain on its pier for a minimum period of time without a penalty. After that the consignee would be billed on a per diem basis as long as it remained there. This was to discourage people from using our allotted pier space as a warehouse. Our facilities there were quite limited, being city owned piers, so we needed all the space we had to accommodate incoming and outgoing cargo on a weekly basis.

After the automobile spares had been there for a long time, the dealers realized that the rental would soon exceed the value of the goods so they weighed several factors, continuing to rent space, shipping it back to the United States, or junking it. They learned if they chose to junk it there, customs duty would have to be paid (it remained duty free as long as it was on the pier). They also learned that shipping it back home would cost more than it was worth, so they made an agreement with U.S. Lines to load it aboard its next vessel, carry it to mid-Atlantic, and jettison it. They agreed to pay all expenses involved, including longshoremen costs to load, securing it for sea on deck, paying our crew longshoreman wages to discharge it overboard, delay of the vessel, etc.

The ship left Antwerp for Amsterdam and Rotterdam and finally headed for the States; the discharging and loading of the Dutch cargo taking place over the deck cargo of automobile parts.

Of course, as soon as the ship got outside the port on its way to New York, the crew began investigating the contents of the wooden boxes. It was no secret that the boxes were to be thrown overboard, so why not look in them?

The first box opened contained engine blocks, not much use on a ship. The second contained steering wheels. I brought a number of them to the engine room and replaced many of the valve wheels with steering wheels and they really dressed up the place. Another contained seat covers. All hands took some of those and soon everyone's settee was covered with a classy looking cover. If a fellow was cutting one to fit and he made a mistake and cut it too short, he just took another and started over.

Still another box contained dashboard clocks, hundreds of them. Everyone had at least one in his room and soon all three departments ran out of flashlight batteries to power them.

The last box contained automobile spotlights. These were distributed so all hands got at least one, some even had many more. Everyone planned to take them home and mount them on their car or at least that's what we thought.

When we reached mid-Atlantic, it was time to stop the ship and get on with the longshore work. This turned out not to be an easy task because no one had thought to pick up a quick-release hook from Antwerp. It's easy enough to hook onto a sling wrapped around a heavy box and winch it out over the side, but once it's out there, how do you release it? We ended up bringing it back aboard, removing the contents, and throwing everything overboard—everything that is, except what was held by the crew.

When we arrived in Boston, our first American port, the "forty thieves" came aboard to search for contraband. (Forty thieves is the name given to U.S. customs searchers.) Naturally they found hundreds of spotlights, clocks, steering wheels, seat covers, etc. Our argument when questioned about it, "It's all made in America, so we don't have to pay any duty on it!"

Their argument, "Yes, it was manufactured here, but no taxes were ever paid on it because it was destined for export! Also, it should have been manifested if it was going to be re-landed in the United States." They had us.

But because there was so much involved, they made a deal. If we promised to throw it all overboard between Boston and New York, our next port, there would be nothing done about it, providing the New York customs informed Boston they couldn't find any of it remaining on board.

That night after leaving Boston, the crew spent a couple of hours throwing stuff over the side, just outside the Cape Cod Canal. We held a ship search to be sure there wasn't anything remaining on board and made a log entry to that effect. If something was found, the company might be spared a fine if we could convince the customs we had made a diligent effort to find it, and the log entry would prove that, we hoped!

The next day we arrived in New York and no customs officials ever boarded the ship. The Boston customs had bluffed us. Some spotlights did make it off the ship, however, but they were the two dozen the Boston customs took ashore for evidence, they said at the time.

I assume every customs inspector and searcher in Boston had one mounted on his car shortly after we left!

After a cargo was booked by the freight sales department, many factors (whether it was hazardous or flammable which would require deck stowage, or pilferable which would require extra security during loading, carriage and discharge, or its weight which could affect stability) affected the loading operation. The company had no control, however, over the cargo once it left the ship.

There was an instance in Australia when the *Pioneer Gem* carried four of the largest tractors manufactured in the United States on the fore deck. The first tractor was discharged using the ship's heavy lift boom and lowered onto a waiting low-boy trailer on the pier alongside the ship. The truck pulling the trailer began to slowly move it down the pier, away from shipside along the stringpiece, and had traveled about one hundred feet away from the ship when the trailer broke into two pieces, sagging in its middle! With its center resting on the roadway, the rig could not be moved. Unfortunately, they were out of reach of our jumbo boom so we couldn't assist them by taking the weight of the tractor from the trailer to enable them to move the trailer out from under it. Also, the tractors were packed for shipment by sea, which meant they were completely boxed in to prevent exposure to the elements during the long sea passage. This meant they could not simply be started up and driven off. Many components necessary for their operation were packed in other crates within the ship, so a call went out for the largest "over-the-road crane" in the area.

The largest available did not have sufficient capacity to lift the tractor from the trailer, so the tractor had to be dismantled by mechanics to lighten it up so the crane could lift it clear and place it on another trailer. This delayed discharge of the other three tractors and delayed the ship. Our freight department learned from this experience to be certain that facilities at the port of discharge for future cargoes were in readiness and capable of handling the cargo.

Australia had always had good Liberty ports because the break bulk ships usually spent at least five days in each port. The longshoremen there had a poor reputation for working cargo efficiently, such as not wanting to work if it threatened rain.

If the forecast predicted a rainy day, many would not show up for work. If it started to rain or even looked threatening while they were working, they would walk off the ship, leaving the hatches open and exposed to the shower. In a break bulk cargo ship much of the cargo is in cardboard boxes which could be damaged if exposed to the weather. Many times, the captain and mate called the engine room to send men on deck to help the deck crew close the hatches when longshoremen walked off in a shower.

Many stories were told about them, such as the time they were discharging prize cattle from the holds using a belly sling around each animal. When the noon whistle sounded while a cow was in the air between the ship and pier, the winch driver turned off the winch to leave the animal suspended in the air. Only the magnetic brake held the winch in the stopped position. The mate saw this and reportedly lowered the cow into the cargo hold until the longshoremen returned from lunch.

If the cargo contained pilferable goods, the longshoremen were paid "temptation money," extra compensation not to break into it. One ship was discharging toilet bowls which were crated in a partial box which allowed the bowls to be seen, so the longshoremen requested "embarrassment money!"

During one trip to Australia Pete Strachota was the chief mate. He and I called a taxi to pick us up at the ship to go uptown to eat dinner. We were each wearing half Wellington boots, a type of boot which reached halfway up the calf of the leg and which contained a pocket on the side of each boot to hold a pack of cigarettes.

After boarding the cab, we headed for the gate where the customs guard stopped the cab and inquired if we had anything to declare. The taxi driver, who had a special permit which allowed him entry to the pier area, replied that he had picked us up at the ship's gangway and we had nothing with us.

This would have normally allowed him to pass through without further questioning. The customs official knew the value of a pier pass and knew a cab driver wouldn't jeopardize it by lying to him. Just then, however, Pete and I said, "We have cigarettes in the boot!" To an Australian the boot is the trunk of an automobile! At this, the driver spoke up, saying, "No they haven't, I never opened the boot for them, they're crazy!"

The customs inspector made us get out of the cab and made the driver open the trunk which proved to hold only his spare tire. The customs inspector and driver stared at us with a puzzled look. With a flourish, we lifted the legs of our trousers and exposed our boots, each containing a pack of cigarettes. We thought we were really clever to pull off something like this, but neither of them thought it a bit funny. We had to listen to a tirade of curse words from the driver all the way to town.

Another incident occurred aboard one of the ships which showed the importance of getting orders in writing. This particular ship arrived in New York carrying a load of imported wine bound for Baltimore in one of its refrigerated cargo boxes.

Often refrigerated boxes are used for "special cargo" i.e. pilferable cargo, but not necessarily cargo under refrigeration. The reason for this is because they can be secured against any entry, either by shore personnel or ship's people.

While discharging the New York cargo, the captain and mate received word from the office that a load of refrigerated cargo was scheduled to be loaded in Baltimore. They were supposed to tell the chief engineer to bring down one reefer box to zero degrees, and that is just how they told him.

He understood them to mean to bring down "Number One" box to zero degrees, not knowing this was the box where the wine was stowed! While still in New York, he started up the machinery to freeze the box, but because the lights were out in the cargo compartment, he never saw any cargo stowed in the area.

When they arrived in Baltimore and opened the hatch to discharge the wine, they discovered all the bottles frozen and every one cracked! The stevedores had to move quickly to discharge as much wine as possible before it thawed, but only managed to discharge a small amount before it became fluid and had to be pumped out.

The arguments then started between the deck and engine departments as to whose fault it was. The captain and mate insisted they said any box, and the chief claimed they clearly said "Number One!"

The company then issued a circular letter to all ships which stated that in the future, the chief engineer would be on the distribution list for all refrigeration cargo notices.

Charlie Higgins was the port engineer handling the ship that trip and he said, "We found ourselves with a batch of Dubonnet Popsicles on our hands!"

On another occasion, the company booked two lions for shipment to a zoo in Belgium. They were delivered to the company piers in cages and placed in a remote area until the SS *American Jurist* was due to sail for Antwerp. The company had told the shipper to deliver them on a certain day, at which time they would be the last cargo loaded and the ship would be on its way. The keeper who accompanied them to the pier fed them some horse meat on their arrival and then left, leaving them in the company's care for eventual loading on the deck of the ship.

For some reason, the *Jurist* was delayed in its sailing so the animals were left on the pier for two days without being fed. As a matter of fact everyone had forgotten about them until just before we were due to leave. When the chief mate was looking through his cargo papers, he saw them on the manifest and reminded the shore officials. They delayed the sailing while the lions were loaded at the last minute.

It was decided to load them onto #4 hatch, just behind the midship house where they would be protected from the weather and seas. The cages were housed in on all sides for their protection from the elements except for a small sliding door at the floor level of each cage used for feeding them. The lions could not be seen.

The ship's carpenter was appointed by the mate to do the feeding each day. He would be compensated at the overtime rate. A large quantity of horse meat was placed aboard in the ship's refrigerators and was to be cut up each day and placed on their trays and then the door slid open. At least that was the way the carpenter had been instructed!

At sea the next day it was time for the first feeding and, of course, they hadn't eaten in three days at this point. A number of crew members gathered on the boat deck, just above the cages, to witness the feeding. The carpenter cut off a large chunk of meat and carried it to the main deck. He was holding it in his left hand while he reached over to slide open the door. He had expected to merely lay the meat on the shelf and the lion would reach out with its paw and draw it into its cage and eat it at his leisure.

What he expected and what happened were two entirely different scenarios! As he opened the door, a huge paw which looked about ten inches wide, reached out like a flash, hooked onto the meat with one claw, and nearly pulled the carpenter in with it as he let out a ferocious roar!

The carpenter jumped back about five feet and broke into a cold sweat! From then on he fed them at the end of a long boat hook while standing on the boat deck about ten feet above.

After our arrival in Antwerp, a young lady about twenty-two years old, dressed like a circus animal trainer, came aboard to accept delivery of the lions for the zoo. She asked to meet the man who had cared for them during the voyage, so the mate introduced her to Chips.

Together they walked to the after deck and, as she approached their cages, she began talking to them in soothing tones. As she slid open the feeding port, a huge limp paw came out through the opening and rested on the shelf where she stroked it like it was a house cat! The carpenter couldn't believe his eyes. Of course, half the crew was there to witness this, so he became the laughing stock and subject of a lot of razzing. He had the last laugh, though, when he showed them his overtime sheet at the end of the trip.

CHAPTER SEVENTEEN

SEAMANSHIP

One time while docking the SS *Pioneer Ming* after an unusual number of telegraph bells, the ship was finally secured to the pier. After securing the plant, I went above to eat dinner which had been delayed a half hour due to the late docking. I took my place next to Captain Hart and was just seated when he said, "Your men did a good job down there helping us dock the ship. We had a docking pilot who got carried away with the telegraph and really overdid it." I agreed, saying, "That's true, for some of the bells we didn't even have time to put our hands on the throttle before we had a countermanding order. Anyway, Captain, thanks for the compliment, I'll tell the oiler who was on watch, he was at the throttle."

He screamed, "What, you had an oiler operating the throttle instead of an engineer?" I replied, "Who did you have on the helm, an AB or a mate ?" He replied, "An AB, of course."

I said, "Well, what's the difference? Shouldn't you have a mate on the helm if we're required to have an engineer on the throttle? A wrong turn on the wheel can have just as serious consequences as the wrong direction or speed of the propeller!"

He paused for a moment and said, "You know, I never gave that any thought, but you have a point there." I put his mind at ease and assured him that either the first assistant engineer or I were usually at the throttle; if not, the engineer on watch would be.

We then began to speculate on how an admiralty court would rule under such conditions in the event of a casualty.

Being confined to the engineering spaces, often times the engine room crew would miss out on interesting happenings and sights while maneuvering the vessel in and out of various ports. For instance they might miss out on transiting the Panama Canal, entering a port during a festival when fireboats are spraying their hoses, or during the welcoming ceremonies of the arrival of a new ship to a port.

Down below the scenery is always the same. Some masters and mates took the engine room into consideration during long maneuvering sessions, calling us on the phone to describe something happening in the bay. When this happened, we would relieve each other to go topside to view the scene.

Still to other masters and mates, we were just a bunch of guys whose job it was to answer the telegraph orders and bring the ship into and out of port. We occasionally would remind the men on the bridge of this, especially in view of the fact they had a pilot up there who was calling the shots in navigating from outside the harbor all the way through tying up the ship at the pier. We would simply say they only had to get the ship somewhere close to the port and then turn it over to the pilot. This would always start an argument as to who was still in command of the ship in spite of the pilot being aboard.

In the port of Kobe, Japan, we were maneuvering the SS *Pioneer Ming* in the inner harbor, approaching the pier, when we began receiving telegraph signals rapidly, terminating in a "full astern." I opened the astern throttle to produce 45-50 propeller RPM, the normal full-astern maneuvering speed. Just moments later, another full astern was rung, so I increased the RPM to 60-65. Almost at once it rang full astern a third time followed by a frantic jingling of the telegraph bell. Normally this is done in desperation, so I told all the men around me to pick an escape route out of the engine room because we could be in a collision situation If we were struck in the engine room, we would have to evacuate quickly.

Usually in an extreme case such as this, the bridge would call to tell us what was going on up there either to put our minds at ease, or to alert us to be ready to vacate the engine spaces quickly! Seconds later, the phone rang and I thought that was it. Everyone was watching me for my signal and after a few words, they witnessed a chief engineer really lose his cool!

The call was from the young third mate who said, "Chief, you're pouring dense, black smoke out of the smokestack up here!" I couldn't believe what I was hearing, so I said, "We are also going all out down here to give you guys a triple full astern. Smoking is the least of our worries at this point!" and hung up. Furious, I sent the oiler topside to see what was going on up there. He returned to say we were merely in the turning basin, had three tugs secured to us, and were turning 180 degrees prior to being breasted into the pier.

Still fuming, I waited a few minutes. After we had received a stop bell and a few other necessary telegraph commands for docking, I telephoned the bridge. The third mate answered, and I said, "Will you please check the smokestack and see if we have stopped smoking?" He replied, "I can't be bothered with something like that, we are trying to dock this big ship!"

Later after the ship was tied up to the pier, the captain approached me and said, "You shouldn't call the bridge at a time like that, Chief. We are very busy up there." I told him I did it on purpose because the bridge called us during what to us was an emergency full astern, to tell us we were smoking. I told him smoking was the least of our worries at a time like that, especially when we get no phone call to keep us informed as to what the reason is for the furious jingling of the telegraph bell.

He then realized what we were up against, so he informed his mates of this and peace was maintained between the departments.

U.S. Lines had one master who would send a new mate into the engine room during maneuvers to let him witness just what goes on down there before he would let him assist in docking or undocking the ship. This was a good practice because it gave the mate some idea of what happens down below when the telegraph is rung.

On another ship while preparing to get underway from an anchorage, the captain told the third mate to telephone the engine room crew to put water on deck in order to wash the mud from the anchor chain prior to being stowed in the chain locker. He rang the engine room and talked to the third assistant engineer, who was a personal friend of the third mate, and asked, "Will you give us water on deck, please?" The captain, standing near the third mate, over-heard this and said, "You don't have to ask those engineers to put water on deck, just give them a direct order to do so. That's why they're down there!"

Later on the third mate told the third engineer about the captain's remark. He said, "In the future, if the old man is within earshot, I'll have to make it sound like a direct order." The engineer replied, "Okay., but I can't be responsible for my reply," and they both laughed.

Not long after, the same situation presented itself and the captain stood nearby when the mate ordered, "Water on Deck immediately," in his best authoritative voice. The engineer replied, "Go shit in your hat, Jim, Ho Ho Ho."

The captain had a satisfying smirk on his face and asked, "That's better, what was his reply?" The mate replied, "He said, 'Yes sir!'"

During the reactivation period of the SS *Gopher Mariner*, later renamed SS *Pioneer Minx*, I asked Captain Heather, the first master of the ship for U.S. Lines, how it would feel to be traveling at a speed of twenty plus knots instead of the usual fifteen to which he had been accustomed on the C-2 Class ships. He just shrugged his shoulders and said, "It won't make any difference to me on the bridge, I'll adjust to it without any problems."

Shortly after that we left the fitting out yard at Newport News and headed for New York to begin loading for our maiden voyage. As we approached the pilot boat at Ambrose Light, the captain rang the engine room telegraph to reduce speed. After a flurry of tele-graph signals, including a few full asterns, we received a half ahead signal which lasted about fifteen minutes, then a stop, an astern, another stop, and after being stopped for about ten minutes, a full ahead, and we were finally on our way into New York harbor.

After tying up at Pier 62, I went up topside and saw the chief mate. I asked him why we received so many telegraph signals at the pilot station. He said we overshot the pilot boat by at least a mile doing ten knots and it was necessary to go out and come around again for another approach.

Captain Heather then realized the Mariner Class vessel was a much greater mass in the water, which, when traveling at twenty knots, would require more time than a C-2 to bring to a stop. Soon after a letter was issued to each of the Mariner Class ships that, due to the high 850 degrees superheat in the turbines, the ship would require a reduction in speed at least one hour prior to making arrival at a pilot station in order to gradually reduce the intense heat in the turbine.

Many masters thought this requirement unreasonable probably because it was issued from the superintendent engineer's office, but also because one hour translated into twenty miles distance from the pilot station. They soon realized, however, it served a dual purpose. It not only gave time to cool the turbine, but gave them a realistic speed to approach the pilot boat, not like the *Pioneer Minx's* approach in New York harbor!

During World War II the British government set up a signal station at Land's End, the outermost tip of England on the Atlantic and a landfall for traffic heading into the English Channel. The signalman on duty would send a blinker light message to each approaching vessel requesting the vessel's code name and other identification. It was a practice which was started in order to attempt to screen all ships entering the coastal waters of Britain.

After the war the government shut the station down, but soon an enterprising group of Brits set up their own signal station in the same area. It was manned around the clock and its function was to request the name, company, and destination of each cargo ship entering the channel. Upon acknowledgment by the ship, the signalman would blink back to the ship, "Thank-you, I will notify your agents of your arrival in the English Channel." For this unsolicited service, an invoice would be forwarded to the company agency.

Our U.S. Lines management found out about this scheme soon after we resumed our peacetime cargo operations to Britain and northern Europe. A circular letter was sent to all masters to ignore the signalman because each ship was already under orders to keep management informed of its ETA at intervals of ninety-six, forty-eight, and twenty-four hours prior to arrival in the channel.

One morning aboard the SS *American Jurist*, we made the land fall at 0500 hours while the second mate was on watch. He received the blinker message, "WHAT SHIP?"

He replied, "WHAT ISLAND?"

The Brit promptly secured his light and U.S. Lines ships, with their distinctive red, white and blue smokestacks, were never bothered again!

The *Pioneer Ming* was en route through the busy Inland Sea between Kobe and Yokohama one sunny Sunday afternoon amidst a large fleet of Japanese fishing vessels, pleasure boats, and other small craft. The third mate, a man about fifty-five years old, was an experienced sailor. He had served many years as master on several types of ships in his career, but never in U.S. Lines. His company, like so many after the war, went into bankruptcy forcing him to begin his career over by shipping out of the union hall. He had made up his mind that he would not pursue a master's job again. He had forgotten how good things were sailing as third mate without the responsibilities of a skipper.

I strolled up to the bridge to observe the fishermen and to chat with him. He was an interesting type who enjoyed talking of his experiences in his early shipping days and I enjoyed listening to his tales.

We couldn't do much talking, however, because of his concentration on the heavy traffic around us, so I just observed. But he did point out an interesting situation developing and one which only an old hand with a knowledge of Far East customs could anticipate.

We were steaming along smoothly about sixteen knots when he pointed out a small one-man fishing boat hundreds of yards off approaching on our starboard bow. He checked the radar scope to determine his distance off and, after some fast mental arithmetic, determined his speed. He reasoned that we could soon be on a collision course if both vessels maintained their course and speed. He alerted me to this possibility and told me to watch the boat closely and see what the fisherman's plan might be. This puzzled me, but I watched anyway.

As the vessels closed, he alerted our quartermaster on the wheel to stand by. In a few more minutes, the fisherman stopped his small diesel engine and heaved up a sail. The third mate gave the order to the helmsman to go hard right. Our ship turned to starboard and we passed closely behind the small craft. After clearing him, the third mate told the helmsman to come about and resume our original course.

My first thought was that the fisherman must have been crazy, he could have been cut in half! The mate explained to me that we originally had the right of way, or as they say, we were "privileged" and he was "burdened" by virtue of both of us being power vessels. But when he killed his engine and became a sailboat the roles changed; he became privileged and we became burdened.

Of course, it would have been a lot easier for the little guy to change course rather than us, but he had other ideas. After he passed under our bow, he hauled down his sail and started up his small engine and went merrily on his way, never changing course one degree. The mate explained that most fisherman in those waters are quite superstitious and believe their boat is followed by evil spirits. If they can cause something to pass between them and the spirits, the near miss will sever the imaginary tow line connecting them. The closer the near miss, the longer the spirit will stay away, and the better the catch! All I could think was he should come in with one hell of a catch that afternoon.

One cold winter evening after completing cargo operations in Antwerp, the *American Jurist* was preparing to depart for Amsterdam. One of the routine functions of the first assistant engineer, which was the position I held, was to check on the presence of the engine room crew one hour before sailing time and report to the captain any who might be missing. I held off reporting to him this particular evening because the only engine department man missing was the chief engineer!

Usually when a ship is transiting between ports such as these, the vessel may leave port short of certain crew members if they are ratings which are not required by the vessel's safety certificate which is issued by the U.S. Coast Guard. If, however, a required rating is missing, the vessel may still leave providing there is someone aboard who has the necessary documents to fill the missing man's position. Upon leaving the pier, the company agent is supposed to notify the authorities in that port that a crew member has failed to join because he now could be in the country as an illegal alien.

I knew the chief engineer had gone ashore after dinner to have a few drinks, even though he knew the ship was sailing in a few hours. I also knew the bar where he usually spent time, so after waiting a few more minutes, I decided to catch a cab and go there to bring him back. I found him there drunk, paid his bill, poured him into the cab, and rushed back to the pier. We arrived at the ship's gangway about fifteen minutes before sailing, but as we drove up I saw the captain watching us from the bridge. I told the chief to try to act sober because we were being watched from the bridge. As he climbed out of the cab, he fell down! I helped him up and managed to get him aboard where I put him into his bunk. I went directly to the engine room and called the captain on the phone and told him all engine room personnel were aboard. I could tell by the tone of his voice that he was quite peeved.

He rang up "standby engines" on the telegraph and in a few minutes we were on our way. The ship had been tied up in a section of Antwerp whose water level in the harbor was higher than that of the sea, so it would require us to enter a lock to be lowered to sea level. The weather was worsening and a gale was blowing as we approached the lock. The front gate was closed as we entered, and after becoming secure in the lock, the rear gate was closed. In a few minutes, the water level in the lock was lowered and the front gate opened.

The pilot gave a pull on the whistle lever to signal the lock attendants that we were leaving, but the lever came loose in his hand and hung downward broken. He informed the captain who tried the whistle and found it not working so the captain called me out of the engine room to hurry to the bridge to locate and correct the problem. At the same time, he said, "And send that chief engineer up here, too!" I told him I'd be up right away.

On my way to the bridge, I stopped off at the chief's room and woke him to tell him he was wanted on the bridge by the old man. I told him about the whistle problem, but I don't think it penetrated his drunken stupor. After examining the whistle pull mechanism, I determined the problem to be in a section of chain located up in the stack next to the whistle. I had to climb a vertical ladder located between the outer and inner stacks in order to reach the area. I returned to the bridge to tell them I was going back to the machine shop to get a new section of chain and the necessary tools. On my way back to the shop, I looked in on the chief and he was now sitting on the edge of his bed.

After getting all the materials I needed, I left for the whistle, climbing up that long ladder again. I made temporary repairs, climbed back down, and entered the wheelhouse to tell them the whistle was repaired but that I would like to test it before leaving. We tried it and it proved OK.

The captain told the pilot we were now ready to leave, so the pilot shouted to our tugboats through a megaphone, speaking Flemish, to haul the ship out of the lock. In the howling gale, however, the chief mate, who was standing by the anchor windlass, thought he heard the captain instructing him to drop the starboard anchor. He released the windlass brake, dropping not only the five-ton anchor, but several tons of anchor chain with it onto the concrete floor of the lock.

The captain screamed frantically to him to stop the windlass and secure it, but the mate could not hear him due to the roar of the tumbling anchor and chain paying out.

The captain's immediate thought was automatic, "When dropping the anchor, you must put the ship astern to tighten up the anchor's bite on the bottom." He rang "slow astern" on the engine room telegraph, but the quick-thinking third mate immediately returned the telegraph to stop, reminding the captain the rear gate of the lock was closed. If the engines had gone astern, we would have broken through the gate, the water level in the harbor would have equalized with sea level, and the many ships in the harbor would have ended up sitting in the mud or capsized!

After heaving up the anchor, the captain and pilot had a heated argument over who was to give the orders from this point on. The pilot informed the captain he was filing a full report with the port authorities, and if any damage was found to the lock, U.S. Lines would be held responsible.

I was still on the bridge during this debacle when the captain turned around and saw me still standing there. He said, "Get down below where you belong!" Just at that point, a voice spoke up and said, "Did you want me, Captain?"

It was the chief engineer standing in the doorway to the wheelhouse. The captain asked, "How long have you been standing there?" The chief replied, "I saw the whole thing!"

I believe it had been the captain's intention to file a report to the company on the chief's drunken conduct leaving the port. After the fiasco in the lock, I think he was afraid the chief would retaliate with his own report on the lock incident, so nothing was said by either one.

The author in kilts in Glasgow, 1944.

Liberty ship, SS *Charles Morgan* at Utah Beach, after taking a
bomb in #5 cargo hold. Photo courtesy of Captain Frank Hayden.

V-1 and V-2 rockets fired on Antwerp, but not exloded, 1945.

SS *Pioneer Ming*,
Pusan, Korea.

SS *Pioneer Ming* alongside a pier in Keelung, Taiwan.

Taxi lines, Kowloon, Hong Kong.

Rickshaws carry cargo and people in Hong Kong.

Korean man waiting for someone to hire him to deliver goods.

SS *American Traveler* in heavy weather, North Atlantic, 1946.

Laundry day,
Hong Kong.

SS *American Reliance* at the home office in New York after weathering a severe snow and ice storm while crossing the North Atlantic. The captain brought the ship in iced up to impress the office of the hazardous conditions at sea.

Mobile "bar and night club", Bugo, Philippines, which arrived alongside SS *Pioneer Ming* after docking. It was equipped with a bar with four stools, and behind a plywood partition, a bed and wash basin. It was manned by a driver and two "ladies of the evening" for the entertainment of anyone who wished to partake of their services.

CHAPTER EIGHTEEN

PIONEER MING

After completing a trip to the Far East in 1960, the *Pioneer Ming* made its usual coastwise voyage discharging inbound cargo in Philadelphia, Baltimore, Norfolk, and Boston, but did not backload any outbound cargo for Far East ports. This led to all sorts of speculation about our future—were we going back to the Far East, were we destined for a different run, were we to be laid up? Questions were put to everyone in our offices along the coast, but no one seemed to have any idea about our coming voyage if there was to be one. Not even the cooks or the company chauffeur knew, and when one of these didn't know, it was truly a mystery.

Upon our return to New York empty of any cargo, we waited at the company piers. The following day the U.S. shipping commissioner appeared aboard, signed on the crew, and still we lay there for another two days.

None of us really cared at this point, except those few lovers who had purchased nylons and ladies' intimate underwear to pave the way for their amorous ventures in Japan. They were afraid they would be traveling to some port where these goods were not appreciated and they would be stuck with them! The rest of us didn't care because we were now on shipping articles, so we knew it wasn't to lay up and we were on the payroll.

The news broke after a few more days. In Cuba, Batista had been overthrown by Castro and we were headed there to load a full cargo of raw sugar for Vietnam. The company had signed a contract with our government to carry it on behalf of the United Nations. We were told the sugar crop in Vietnam had suffered because of heavy rains, so the United Nations was shipping an emergency supply to them.

The following day, the purser and a company official had to go to the Cuban Consulate in New York to present him with a certified crew list for his perusal. When they entered his office, his secretary greeted them and announced their arrival over an intercom. His voice came back over her intercom telling her to have the crew list slid under his office door, along with the fifty-dollar fee, in cash, in U.S. dollars!

They unfolded the newspaper-size crew list and flattened it enough to be able to fit it under the door along with the money. An unseen hand pulled it from them on the other side, and they were instructed to wait in the outer office. A half hour passed when a voice told them everything appeared to be in order, and the crew list was slid out to them from under the door. It now contained a large red seal in the corner.

It was apparent to our people that no one was taking any chances in any dealings with the new regime in Cuba. After all, how could the individual in that office be certain that our men were legitimate, and not Batista's men, or for that matter, Castro's?

We sailed the following day for Bahia Honda, Cuba, after fueling ship the previous night. We arrived in Cuba in three days and commenced loading. One fast observation, and quite obvious, was that all the men in the country were sporting beards. Men in the cities, countryside, longshoremen, all with beards. The reason, we were told by our agent, also bearded, was that when it became apparent that the whiskered Castro and his hirsute followers were about to take over the country from his mountain headquarters, anyone found without a beard was suspected of being a Batista supporter. This resulted in many men staying under cover until their beards grew out.

Our cargo of raw sugar came aboard in burlap bags stacked on wooden pallets. Cargo checkers on the pier had several boxes of cardboard tags with the United Nations logo and a red, white and blue crest printed on them with the wording, "Gift of UNRRA" (United Nations Relief and Rehabilitation Administration), in smaller letters. These men were to staple at least one tag on each bag before it entered the ship. Some bags had two or three tags because men would tag them at each end. The bags themselves were stenciled in large, black prominent letters, "PRODUCT OF CUBA." Some checkers were stationed in each cargo hold to ensure that no bags missed being tagged.

I was in my office on the ship the day before sailing from Cuba when a man passed by in the passageway. He saw me at my desk and asked if I smoked. I said I did, but only cigars. He reached into his bag and produced a Cuban cigar. He said, "Take this with my compliments and let me know if you enjoy it."

I lit it and it was, without a doubt, the best cigar I had ever smoked. He said, "It's 100 percent pure Havana tobacco; could I sell you a box?" I said, "Sure, these are excellent, make that two boxes!"

Just at that point, John Tucker, chief mate, walked by and I called to him, "Hey, John, you smoke cigars. Try one of these, they're great!" The salesman said, "Don't open one of your boxes, I'll be glad to give him one of my samples." He lit the sample cigar and admitted how good they were, so he ordered a box. I said, "Hey John, we're leaving here tomorrow for a long trip. You'll never be able to get these again, better get two boxes." So he did.

After leaving Cuba the following day, I opened one of the boxes and lit a cigar after lunch. After only a couple of puffs I had a horrible taste in my mouth, and the aroma was like something I had never smelled before. The cigar was terrible! I put it out and lit a second thinking maybe the first one was made with some bad tobacco. But the second was just as bad! Then it dawned on me why the salesman didn't want me to give one to the mate.

Just then, John Tucker came into my room. "Did you light up one of those cigars yet?"

I said, "Yeah, they're terrible. I think we got taken!" He agreed, so we threw them overboard, went to the chief steward and asked him to get some Dutch Masters out of the slop chest for us. We had a good laugh over it. Even today, in retirement, when we see each other, his first words are, "Hey, John, these are great, you better buy two boxes!"

After picking up our pilot outside Vietnam, we started our perilous trip up the Saigon River, a serpentine-shaped seaway cut through extremely high reeds which were home and hideout for the Vietcong. (The high reeds gave ample coverage to the Vietcong so when the Vietnam War started, they were some of the areas burned out by Agent Orange.) Snipers were not uncommon so everyone stayed under cover during the transit. If one were to go out on deck, the city could be seen on the port side of the ship in the distance. Moments later it appeared behind us, then off our starboard side, and then dead ahead. The trip up that river was a fright, and the only thing on my mind at the time was "What if?—What if we had a power failure at that time, or a steering gear failure, or many of the countless other things that seem to go wrong onboard ship at the most inopportune times?"

One of our sister ships had taken a mortar shell in the boatswain's room only a few weeks earlier. It did considerable damage to the midship house, but no one was injured.

When we reached the pier in downtown Saigon, stevedore gangs came aboard in droves and began slinging the bags onto pallets which were then landed on the pier. From there, other stevedores removed them and threw them up onto waiting trucks.

At the end of the first day, we noticed many of the United Nations tags were laying loose all over the cargo holds. We thought they were pulled off accidentally by the stevedores as they grabbed bags by opposite ends to sling them onto the pallet. When the trucks drove away from the pier headed for the interior of Vietnam, we discovered hundreds more of the tags on the pier. The following day, we observed the discharging operation more closely and found the stevedores were deliberately tearing the tags loose from the bags. Whenever a pallet load left the hold, it was nearly stripped of its tags. The tags that weren't torn loose there were taken off by the men on the pier, before the sugar was loaded onto the truck.

The people in the interior of the country who were to receive the sugar received bags which had only one identifying mark on them, "PRODUCT OF CUBA!" Nothing remained to inform them of the generosity of the United Nations.

We protested to our agent in Saigon and he said he would relay our complaint to the U.S. Government officials in Vietnam, but we never heard any results from it.

One of my more distressing experiences occurred aboard the SS *Pioneer Ming* in the Pacific Ocean while homeward bound from the Far East. I received a call from the bridge that our speed had dropped off from twenty knots to eighteen and was asked if we were experiencing any propulsion problems in the engine room. I went below and checked over the machinery and found nothing wrong; all pressures and temperatures were normal and there was no loss of propeller revolutions.

I went up to the bridge to report this. While we were checking things up there we noticed a wide, white, foamy wake alongside each side of the ship. Also, the normally narrow, white wake behind our stern was now wider than the ship's hull.

These wakes were indicative of something clinging to our hull so we rushed forward to look overboard and discovered a huge whale "wrapped" around our bow! It was dead and its back obviously broken judging from the way it was hung up on the bow. It was a sad sight to behold, and we felt a lump in our stomachs as we waited for it to dislodge itself. After waiting a few minutes, it still appeared to be firmly attached, probably hung up on the hook at the bottom of our bow used for attaching a paravane during wartime. We stopped the ship and had to run astern for a few minutes to shake it loose.

Our "lookout" felt badly about the whale, blaming himself for not sighting it ahead of the ship, but he was told he wasn't expected to see anything as remote as a whale which was swimming under water at the time.

On one voyage of the SS *Pioneer Ming* the relief captain was a man named Robert McNamara, an upperclassman over me at Massachusetts Maritime Academy. We had seen each other in the company at various times, but this was to be our first time sailing together. He had mellowed since his cadet days and was known to be a competent shipmaster so I looked forward to making a trip with him.

The first assistant engineer was John Suarez, a man much older than the captain and I. We were about thirty-six, while Suarez was at least sixty-five.

We had gone ashore in Kobe, Japan, to a Japanese restaurant to eat some of that weird stuff they served over there—stuff you didn't ask about until you were through eating it! We returned to the ship and were sitting in my office having a nightcap when Suarez decided to take a turn through the engine room to see if the plant was quiet.

When he returned, he was huffing and puffing and remarked how much farther the lower engine room seems to get with each passing day. The captain said, "You're just out of condition, John, that's all. Why, I could make it down to the lower engine room and back before you even got out the door!"

"That'll be the day. When I'm in a hurry I slide down the handrails and I defy anyone to beat me!"

The captain replied, "I'll bet you five bucks I can get to the lower engine room and back here to the chief's office before you can, and I'm not even accustomed to going down there."

Suarez reached into his wallet and took out five dollars and handed it to me and said, "I'm calling his bluff, Chief. Here's my five, you be the referee."

McNamara handed five to me and said, "You're on!"

They both poised outside my door and I said, "GO!" Suarez ran to the engine room fiddley door on our deck while McNamara ran outside on the boat deck. At that point I quickly phoned the engine room, talked to the engineer on watch who was a pretty savvy guy, and told him about the bet. I told him to quickly go to the lower engine room to await the first assistant. When he showed up he was to ask Suarez why the captain had just come down to that level, said hello, turned around and ran back up the ladder.

In the meantime, McNamara merely circled the boat deck and returned to my office and sat down to await the arrival of the first assistant. When he arrived, he was sweating, panting, and completely out of breath!

Suarez exhaustedly said, "You bastard, I don't know how you did it, but there's something fishy here!"

I told Suarez how sorry I was for him but the captain was the winner by far and he hadn't even raised a sweat! I then presented the ten dollars to the captain.

Later McNamara said, "I think we should tell Suarez the truth and return his five." But I said, "No way, if he's that gullible he deserves to lose!"

CHAPTER NINETEEN

KOREA

Shore leave in Pusan, later called Busan, Korea, could be hazardous to your health. Whenever one of our ships entered this port, it was routine to remove all life preservers from their stowage racks on deck, the sound-powered telephone handsets, all fire hoses and nozzles from the fire stations, and all brass sounding tube plugs from the decks. These were all stowed inside the midship house until the ship left port. All of these items were pilferable by the hundreds of people who boarded the ship as stevedores, hold cleaners, painters, cleanup crews, laundry women, etc.

Brass was a highly prized commodity in the black market. Entrepreneurs could fashion almost anything from it, as well as from beer cans, coffee cans, etc. I recall buying what appeared to be a Ronson lighter from a man for a pack of cigarettes. After I had used it for awhile, the soldered seam on the side split open and revealed the printing on a beer can label inside.

Brass couplings could be cut from the canvas jacketed fire hoses with a pocket knife, the nozzle removed from its rack, and stowed vertically inside a man's pant leg while he strolled ashore under the eyes of a watchman. The flushmounted sounding tube plug could be unscrewed from its socket in the deck by using a square wrench, or by merely standing on the plug with the heel of a shoe or boot and constantly turning the foot. Eventually it would loosen from its threads and be easily removed.

The black market was located in the center of Pusan, an area of several acres made up of various sized booths, much like a flea market. Everything was available here for a price: GI uniforms and vehicles of every description, either pilfered, salvaged from U.S. Government scrap piles, or bought on the black market in wholesale quantities for distribution at the counters. The name given to this area best explains its function—"Thieves' Market!"

Korea was a devastated country after its wartime period from 1950 to 1955. The main road leading into the city was in poor condition, blocks of concrete were missing from sidewalks, and there were no streetlights. One man from my ship went ashore one evening. He forgot to bring a flashlight with him and stepped into one of the open sidewalk areas in pitch darkness.

The problem was that the sidewalk was also a covering for the sewer system! The drop into a sewer on one leg was enough not only to cause one to suffer from a bad fall, but also could result in a broken leg. It at least meant the saturation of one's sock, shoe, and trouser leg with raw sewage, which is what happened to the man in this case.

Along this road a wooden fence about six feet high ran for several hundred yards. It appeared to be nothing unusual, until a board moved suddenly upward from the walk and a person stepped out. Many families used this fence as the front of their meager house built against it with the loose board acting as a door! Whenever a crew member went through the security gate leaving the pier area, he would be rushed by gangs of children, varying in age from six to eighteen. These youngsters would swarm all around a man jostling and bumping him, their hands all over him, including in his pockets. For this reason no one ever wore jewelry or watches, or carried a wallet.

It was impossible to shoo them away. They kept up a constant chatter in Korean among themselves. The only English they spoke was learned from GIs and it was mostly for begging. The name given to these boys by the GIs was "Slickey Boys!"

The only way to get rid of the children was to select one to be your escort for the day. He would then signal the others that he had been chosen and they would leave. He expected to remain with you until you returned to the ship. If you stopped in a bar or restaurant, he would accompany you and probably receive a commission for having steered you there, though he had nothing to do with your choice of restaurant or bar.

Robert Bach, third assistant engineer aboard the SS *Pioneer Ming*, and I were heading to the Thieves' Market one afternoon and picked a young slickey boy from the group. He asked us if we wanted a taxi, a rare commodity in Pusan, so we said we would if one came along. Moments later, he hailed a jeep driven by a Korean, which claimed to be a taxi. However it had no meter, sign, or any other indication of being a taxi. We climbed aboard, Bob sitting on the outside, the boy in the middle, and I was on the other side of the back seat.

While riding through the noisy street teeming with pedestrians in the center of the city, a Korean youth, about eighteen, ran alongside our jeep and suddenly, with one sweep of his hand, hooked Bob's wristwatch off his wrist and took off through the crowd. We attempted to jump from the jeep to pursue him, but our driver told us to stay aboard and he would chase him. The thief was wearing blue jeans, a white T-shirt, and a red bandanna around his neck, so he was easy to follow.

The driver speeded up and managed to keep the lad in sight, weaving in and out of the pedestrians, horn blowing steadily, people leaping out of the way! The boy turned into an alley too narrow for the jeep, so Bach and I leaped out and followed him down the alley.

About fifty feet into the alley, he made an abrupt turn to the left into another alley, just as Bach was catching up to him. As the kid made the turn, he leaped over a large mud puddle, unseen by Bach, and Bach skidded and landed flat on his rear end as he tried to dodge it at the last second.

I was directly behind him and saw him fall so I was able to skirt the puddle and keep up the pursuit. The lad had run into a blind alley and now had no place to go. He turned to face me and we both realized it was now one on one. A thought went quickly through my mind, "What in the world am I doing in this predicament? Is a lousy watch worth this?"

As I walked slowly toward him, wristwatch still clutched in his fist, he looked desperately for a way out, realizing the only way was to get by me. He suddenly got a terrified look on his face and I thought he's really afraid of me now, when out of nowhere, a man from behind me grabbed me by the shoulder, pushed me out of the way, and headed for the boy!

My immediate thought was that he was a gang member, or even worse, a rival gang member. The man shouted, "I am police, stand back!" He drew his gun and walked up to the boy, took the watch from his hand and handcuffed him. Directly behind him were two ROK Army MPs who, like the cop, had seen the chase and came to assist.

As the four of us were walking out of the alley, I spotted Bach poised just around the corner with a large rock held over his head ready to crown the boy. I shouted to him that everything was under control, Bach put the rock down, and we left the alley. The cop took the boy to the police station in an unmarked car asking us to follow in our jeep.

At the station, they took the captive upstairs to interrogate him. We could hear loud screams from there a minute later, so he was being more than just questioned. They wrote up statements for us to sign, returned the watch to Bob, and thanked us. Apparently they had been looking for this kid for a long time.

As we were leaving, they brought him downstairs (he was bleeding), put him into a police car, and drove away. We asked what would happen to him, and were told he would be tried, found guilty, and sentenced to an indefinite term in a special division of the ROK Army. The cop said that division was far worse than any jail!

On a subsequent voyage to Pusan, our agent was reviewing our cargo plan, one afternoon just after we docked, and discussing it with the mate and captain. It was decided at that time the ship could leave the port the following noon.

The radio operator stopped by the captain's room to ask if the sailing time had been determined yet and was told it would be noon the following day, so he told them he was going ashore.

A few hours after the radio operator left the ship, the agent found he could obtain more labor to work than anticipated, so it would be possible to sail from the port at 0800 instead of noon the following day. I was going ashore in an hour, so the captain asked me to keep an eye out for Sparks. I was to inform him of the change in sailing time in the event he stayed ashore that night, planning to return just before noon.

At the gate I selected a slickey boy and we walked to town together. In the first bar I entered I asked the Korean barmaid if she had seen an American radio operator from a U.S. Lines ship, a man who wore glasses. She replied that no Yanks had been there that day, so we moved to the next bar. There I asked the young lady behind the bar and she said several Americans had been in and some were upstairs with "her" girls. The slickey boy and I went upstairs to the second floor. We faced a long corridor with rooms along each side separated by thin walls made of a rice paper material.

I knocked on the first door and a girl answered in Korean. The slickey boy explained in Korean who I was looking for, but the girl didn't seem to understand. I spoke up and said, "American radio operator, thick glasses, from U.S. Lines ship." She replied in broken English, "Not here, Yank."

We moved to the next room and knocked, but before we could ask, a voice came through the closed door and said, "Not here, either." After knocking at the next door, came an American voice, "States Marine Lines!" Almost immediately, another American voice, "Moore McCormack Lines," and then, "American President Lines!"

I started to laugh, and then all the Americans in the different rooms began laughing. I thanked all of them through closed doors and went on to the next bar.

I eventually found him in a store and told him of the change in sailing time. He thanked me and said he had only gone ashore to do some shopping and would be returning in a couple of hours anyway.

It was important to find him because the ship is not permitted to leave one foreign port for another foreign port without a radio operator, and no one aboard who can fill in for him.

The following morning an hour before sailing, the third mate was going through the routine of "testing gear," which meant he was to sound the whistle, both mechanically and electrically; run the engine room telegraph through all its segments with the third assistant engineer returning the signals; test the steering gear, both gyro steering and mechanical telemotor; and finally test the telephone system. Everything tested normal except the telephone system.

It was discovered the handsets were missing from the three telephones exposed on deck; the bow phone, stern phone, and flying bridge phone! We had forgotten to remove them after tying up the ship at the pier and someone had cut them off at the wire connection. Since we had only one spare aboard, we inquired from our agent if there were any electronic stores where we could purchase two.

He laughed and said we had two choices. We could wait about two hours to give the thief a chance to put them on sale at the Thieves' Market and then buy them back, or go directly there and buy two others! So as not to delay the sailing, we chose to go shopping.

The electrician and I rushed uptown to the "market" in the agent's car. We found two of them for sale which were compatible with our system and bought them for $3.00 each.

The electrician was installing them when he discovered a small stencil on each, "PROPERTY OF AMERICAN PRESIDENT LINES!"

CHAPTER TWENTY

BLOOMINGTON VICTORY

During the Korean War, I was assigned to the SS *Bloomington Victory* as chief engineer. The ship had been taken out of the lay-up fleet at Suisan Bay a few months before for the exclusive purpose of carrying ammunition from various ammunition depots in the United States to Korea. It had already completed two voyages when I joined it, but the only U.S. Lines people aboard were the master, Wilbur Lange, and the chief mate, Owen Clancy. They had made the last trip and had lots to say about the condition of the ship when I boarded.

Apparently there had been a complete change of crew in the engine department each voyage since the ship had been broken out, but the engine room logbooks and voyage records could give no reason for it. I joined the ship in Houston, Texas, at the ammunition depot in San Jacinto. Upon reaching the gate of the facility, the taxi in which I was riding had to stop on the orders of a guard and remove the cigarette lighter from the dashboard. The driver and I had to surrender any matches on our person. I soon realized why they were so serious about taking such precautions when I saw the railroad cars and warehouses loaded with bombs, artillery shells, etc.

One of the first things Clancy and Lange told me to buy was a pellet pistol from ashore with lots of pellets or BBs. After having just viewed the bombs and artillery shells, I had to laugh at their suggestion! They explained it would be necessary to keep it visible as a sidearm to repel boarders once we anchored in Korean ports. I asked, facetiously, "North Koreans or Pirates?"

Lange said, "Neither, whores!"

They explained it became necessary occasionally to fire a BB at them to keep them away from the side of the ship. They said it wouldn't hurt them through the heavy quilted clothing they wore due to the cold December weather.

We stayed in San Jacinto for several days loading, so Mrs. Clancy and Mrs. Lange joined their husbands there. I was now on my own when evenings came around. One night I walked outside the gate to have a beer in a nearby bar with one of the new assistant engineers who had reported aboard the day before.

It was a small neighborhood place, with about ten men seated at the bar. My friend and I were seated at a table, when the door was suddenly thrust open and a man was standing in the doorway holding a gun.

He announced, "OK everybody, this is a stickup!"

I nearly fainted at the table, but then the men at the bar shouted, "Come on in, Tex, have a beer!"

He put his gun away and laughed, and joined his friends at the bar. This was my first experience with Texas humor and I hoped my last. We finished our beer and returned to the comparative safety (and sanity) of the ship.

A few evenings later upon returning to the pier area from a shopping expedition, I stopped in another waterfront bar for a beer. Just as I entered the place, a man went hurrying by me to get out the door. As he was leaving, he shouted to the bartender, "You better be ready, mister. I'll be back!" I asked the bartender what the problem was and he said they had an argument over the payment for his drinks. I ordered a beer and after serving it, the bartender disappeared into the back room. Moments later I heard a shot!

Startled, I looked behind me to see if the guy had returned, but the bartender appeared from the back room with a revolver in his hand. He placed it on the counter behind the bar saying, "Well, it works OK, now let the son of a bitch come back!"

Needless to say, I quickly finished my beer and left. I began to wonder about these Texans.

After loading at San Jacinto, we left for the Panama Canal and on to Concord, California, another ammunition loading berth where we were to top-off our cargo. The security was just as tight as in Texas; cigarette lighters checked at the gate, no matches allowed on anyone's person, and smoking only permitted in special concrete bunkers jutting out over the water.

These special smoking houses were constructed of concrete and were windowless. Large cans of sand were spaced at regular intervals inside as ash trays. The U.S. Coast Guard was aboard each ship patrolling the decks and peering into portholes watching for smokers. Smoking was strictly prohibited aboard and rigidly enforced!

Bordering Concord had been the town of Port Chicago which was literally blown off the face off the earth when two ammunition ships blew up at the pier during World War II. Having witnessed the earlier tragedy, Concord was doubly cautious of fire.

After loading we left the West Coast for Inchon, Korea, and after only a few days at sea, encountered our first heavy weather, high winds and rough seas. The ship began to roll heavily and after one severe roll, the generator tripped off the main switchboard and we were without power.

The ship got caught up in the trough of the sea and we began to roll heavily, which was worsened because we had no steering gear or propulsion power to keep the ship headed into the seas. I rushed to the engine room and found the generator turbine had tripped out, causing the circuit breaker to trip off the switchboard.

The emergency generator had started automatically, but had only sufficient power to provide lights. I reset the main generator trip and restarted the turbine. Once it was up to speed, I engaged the main circuit breaker and after restarting some of the machinery, the plant was restored and main engine once again in operation.

After rechecking all the machinery to be sure everything was operating properly, I checked the generator to determine the cause of the failure, but could not find anything abnormal. I had served aboard other vessels when they suffered power failures, but we were always able to determine the cause. In this instance I was baffled.

On the other vessels we were carrying general cargo, not a full load of ammunition. I had visions of 500-pound bombs tumbling down in the cargo holds while the ship was wallowing in high seas out of control! As long as I hadn't determined the cause, I would have to anticipate it happening again.

I returned to my office and broke out the generator manual to study the construction of the unit for a clue to the cause of the power failure, when we had another heavy roll, and another power failure! Once again it was the generator turbine which had tripped out. After restoring it and restarting the plant, I changed over to the other generator and secured the troublesome unit. The weather subsided for a few days and we had no more problems, so I thought it must be in that one generator. After a few more days, we again encountered heavy weather and again more power failures, but with the generator which I thought was operating so well. I reasoned the problem had to be something common to the plant or at least tied to the heavy weather.

When the weather let up, I drained the lubricating oil from the idle generator sump, something like draining the oil from the crankcase of an automobile. I removed the inspection doors on the side of the sump to check the oil pump and strainer, realizing that a clogged strainer could cause the trip to operate.

What I discovered was something I had never expected. The interior of the sump was supposed to be constructed like a honeycomb with small bulkheads to retain the oil in several small compartments. This was to prevent the oil from swashing from side to side during the roll of the vessel and causing the oil pump to lose suction which would trip the turbine.

I discovered, much to my surprise, that the swash plates were never installed, which accounted for the generator turbine tripping out only during heavy weather. The generator oil pump would lose suction and the turbine tripped out through its built-in low-oil pressure protection feature.

I felt much relieved once I had found the cause. I immediately disconnected that safety feature from the turbine, connected a large oil pressure gauge to the lubricating oil tubing, and had the gauge facing the maneuvering platform where the engineer stood his watch. I issued instructions to observe the pressure periodically, especially during heavy rolling, and if the pressure failed to restore itself, to trip the turbine out manually so it would not destroy itself.

I examined the other generator and found the same condition. It too was then rigged with a gauge and we had no more trouble. Subsequently, other crew members in the deck department told me this had happened several times on the two previous trips, and this was the reason no engine department crew members would make more than one trip on board. They were worried about the type of cargo being carried aboard a ship which had repeated power failures, and rightfully so!

Upon our return to the West Coast, I submitted a repair request to have swash plates installed in each sump and they had no more problems.

A similar situation occurred aboard the M.V. *John Erickson*, a passenger ship converted for carrying troops during World War II, and later, war brides from Europe. The ship was returning to New York in 1945, immediately following the war, and was loaded with several thousand troops. As it proceeded up the lower bay escorted by an armada of small craft and larger vessels, whistles were sounding and fire boats were shooting streams of water into the air. It was a warm greeting for the homesick troops, and as they got closer to the Statue of Liberty, all the soldiers rushed to the port side to get a glimpse of it. The ship heeled over and developed a list to port and stayed that way as long as the men stayed there.

Once clear of the statue, a large boat carrying USO girls and show girls appeared off the starboard side, resulting in the troops rushing across the ship to that side and causing a list to starboard!

In the meantime, Louis De Raey, first assistant engineer who was manning the throttles, called the bridge to inform the ship's captain, John Andersen, that the generators were in danger of shutting themselves down if the list remained, due to loss of oil suction in the generator sumps. Captain Andersen, a very capable man, readily solved the problem by sounding the general alarms calling all the troops to General Quarters. The regulation oriented troops dutifully reported to their boat stations on each side of the ship, and the ship regained its even keel. It remained that way until the ship was secure at its pier one hour later.

Upon our arrival in Inchon, we proceeded to an ammunition anchorage to discharge our cargo. That night about 11:00 P.M. the captain and mate called me to bring my pellet gun and give them a hand; the boarders were alongside! We were surrounded by cargo barges into which the cargo was to be discharged, but sandwiched between them were small row boats, each manned by at least two young Korean women. They tied up to the barges, or threw grappling hooks up over our bulwarks to fetch up on anything their hooks would cling to. In an instant the girls were climbing up the ropes, hand over hand, onto the deck and disappearing into the midship house!

There, almost by a silent signal or maybe instinct, the crew seemed ready to receive them. Our first orders to the crew were to lock all staterooms, storerooms, and public spaces and we began our search.

After a couple of hours we thought we had located all of them, much to the disappointment of many crew members. Some of the young ladies insisted they were not prostitutes, but on board to do the crew's laundry. We told them if that were true, they could produce a pass issued by the U.S. Army, which of course they didn't have.

We escorted them to the ship's gangway and made sure they left the vessel safely. We then made one final round on the decks, and as we approached the stern, we heard laughter coming from the after gun tub. There was no gun fitted in the tub, but it had been built into the ship at the time of construction during World War II. Climbing the short vertical ladder to the tub, we found the chief cook and a young lady in a compromising position on a cot. We shone our flashlights on them and told the chief he would have to get her off the ship.

He pleaded for a few more minutes, but the captain said, "No, she's the last one aboard, she has to go." Frightened, she made a dash for the ladder from the gun tub, descended to the deck, and jumped overboard, hoping to land in the water near her boat and then swim for it!

She misjudged her jump in the darkness, and landed partly in her boat and in the water. She struck her arm on the side of her boat and let out a scream. We rushed to the side to see her attempting to climb into her boat, screaming in pain.

We lowered a ladder to assist her, while the captain called the Army medics on our ship-to-shore phone. They soon arrived and brought her by launch to the Army hospital where she was treated for a broken arm.

Word must have spread quickly ashore among the girls, because we were not bothered any more in Inchon.

A few days later, Clancy and I were standing at #3 hatch watching the ship's electrician repair a resistor bank on one of the winches. It wasn't snowing, but was windy and stinging cold. The Korean stevedores were taking turns standing next to the air cooling outlet from the winch resitor bank to keep warm.

The winches were known as "unit winches," which meant their resistor bank was mounted on the side of the winch controller instead of inside the mast house several feet away. As the winch driver speeded up or slowed down the winch during cargo discharge, the resistor bank would become normally very hot. A fan under the bank drove atmospheric air upward through the resistors to cool them. As a result, the air leaving them through an opening at the top was quite hot, so some stevedores would leave a container of tea or their lunch boxes across the outlet to keep them warm.

While this was a practical use of the wasted heat, it would also block the passage of cooling air, causing the resistors to overheat and burn out. This in turn caused the winch to trip out and create another headache for the engineering department.

While standing there, Clancy and I saw smoke rising from #2 hatch. Both of us feared the worst—fire! A fire aboard any ship is cause for alarm, but, needless to say, aboard an ammunition ship it is an extremely dangerous situation. We rushed to the hatch to see what was burning before sounding the general alarm, and found the stevedores huddled around a bonfire they had started on a steel plate in the lower hold.

Bombs, artillery shells, and all sorts of other explosives were stacked around them as they took turns standing near the open flame. The fire was confined to the area around the steel plate, so we put it out with hand fire extinguishers.

My thoughts went back to San Jacinto, Port Chicago, and Concord, where cars and drivers entering the base had to check their lighters at the gate, and smokers puffing away in the cinder block house suspended over the water. If those enforcement officers had ever witnessed this bonfire...

CHAPTER TWENTY-ONE

SHIPYARDS

For many years U.S. Lines enjoyed good relations with several shipyards throughout the United States as well as overseas. For a long time Newport News Shipbuilding and Dry-dock Company claimed U.S. Lines as their best customer. The yard had built the SS *America* and the SS *United States* for our passenger ship service as well as several Challenger I-type general cargo ships. Whenever it became necessary for a routine dry-docking of a freighter, or even an emergency, Newport News always managed to find a dry dock or lay berth to accommodate us. However our earlier management also realized the importance of doing business with other yards in the United States, such as Bethlehem Steel Corporation yards and Todd Shipyards.

U.S. Lines needed them and they needed us. When a union contract would be nearing its termination date and a long strike seemed imminent, U.S. Lines would begin seeking lay berths in the shipyards for the stranded vessels. Strikes often occurred in the winter when it would be necessary to locate a lay berth in a yard which could furnish steam to prevent the ships from freezing as well as electricity to operate bilge pumps to remove minor leakage.

After many ownership changes over the years, U.S. Lines began to look overseas to dry-dock its vessels for economical reasons and scheduling purposes, but the port engineers always attempted to convince management that this was poor policy, especially if a strike was called.

American shipyards then had every right to tell us (and often did) that no berths were available. Also, if one of our vessels were to become involved in a collision or grounding in an American port, we would have no place to go for repairs without being held for ransom, but our arguments fell on deaf ears.

On one occasion, the general manager of Bethlehem Shipyard in Hoboken, New Jersey, told me, "You people have some colossal nerve calling yourselves 'United States Lines' and then sending all your repair work to foreign shipyards!" I could only agree.

With the facilities available in a modern shipyard: the massive dry docks, wet berths, machine shops, and power plants where power was available to suit any vessel from any country in the world, perhaps the most popular place in the yard was a room variously called "the pump room," "blue room," "anchor room" and many other names. This was a refuge of sorts for customers, port engineers, surveyors, inspectors, shipyard management personnel and other occasional guests. Yes, sometimes even captains went to this room, but they were usually frowned on because this room was considered a haven for engineering types.

The main attraction of this room was, of course, the bar, but at noon management would have sandwiches or sometimes hot dishes brought in from a local deli. After 5:00 P.M., however, the room really came to life. Some problems of the day were discussed, however, most of the men present were chomping at the bit to tell the latest joke, or the most recent sea story.

The Newport News Shipyard room was called the blue room for reasons I never found out, and was under the capable guidance and supervision of a fine man named Gene Jaeger, a former U.S. Lines port engineer. Gene had several other duties in the yard management, but at 5:00 P.M. he assumed command of the blue room.

I recall one evening just after he had opened the blue room for business, I wanted to make a martini, but found the gin bottle empty, so I asked Gene if he could arrange to get another. "No problem," he said, "I'll be right back," and left the room through a rear door which he first had to unlock.

I followed him down a flight of stairs which led to the office of the vice president of ship repair. There he unlocked the vice president's desk and removed another key which opened a locker just outside the office. Inside the locker was a large safe which he opened and produced a new bottle of gin. He handed it to me and we returned to the blue room.

I remarked about the tight security in the yard, and he said it was the result of pressure from Admiral Hyman Rickover to insure security of the shipyard during construction, repair, and refueling of nuclear submarines in the yard.

I laughed at this and said, "I'm referring to the security of the shipyard liquor. The security of the submarines doesn't seem to be nearly as stringent as that of the company booze!"

When he thought about it, he said, "You have a good point."

Todd Shipyards Corporation had a room in each of its many yards throughout the country. The one in Brooklyn, New York, was called "Pump Room East" and the one in Alameda, California, "Pump Room West." I don't recall the name of the one in the Hoboken, New Jersey, yard, but I do remember their management had it completely redecorated with a new bar, new pine paneling throughout, and new floor tile. Then they closed the yard a month later!

One favorite story to come out of the Brooklyn pump room was about a wooden shipping crate which was kept prominently placed in a corner of the room with an address to someone in Liverpool, England, on a label on its cover. The box was securely nailed together and had small air holes drilled frequently around its sides. Whenever a new port engineer, marine surveyor, or other gullible individual would appear in the room for the first time, someone would ask the yardman present when they intended to ship the mongoose to England.

He would reply, "The Express Company is due here this afternoon to pick it up." They then turned to the new surveyor to explain that a British ship had to make an emergency stop for repairs in the yard a couple of weeks ago, en route from India to South America. A sailor on the ship had purchased the mongoose in India and had intended to take it home when his ship returned to England.

While the ship was in the yard, he was stricken with appendicitis and had to be hospitalized and the ship left without him.

When he was well enough to leave the hospital he was to return home, but he stopped in the yard and gave them some money to ship it for him. They then asked the surveyor if he had ever seen a mongoose, and the chances were that he hadn't, so they told him it would be possible for him to view it if he wished.

They told him to stand in a certain spot in the room and he could view it through the feeding port located on the top of the box, but to be very careful because the mongoose was a natural enemy of the dreaded hooded cobra and it had a natural instinct to attack.

They further explained that the cobra usually raised itself off the ground about two feet high just before spreading its hood, which was an indication it was about to strike. At this point the mongoose would attack and go instinctively for the cobra's neck, therefore just in case the mongoose escaped from the box, he should protect himself in the crotch area to escape its sharp teeth!

With the stage set, they handed the surveyor a flashlight and told him to stand in the designated area and shine the light through the feeding port while they opened it.

An accomplice opened the feeding port with a quick flourish and a large furry object leaped from the box headed directly for the surveyor! Frightened, he grabbed his crotch in both hands and began leaping around the room in a frenzy, to the laughter of all present!

When he realized he had been had, he began to laugh and walked across the room where he retrieved the ball of fur and handed it back to the yardman who then opened the cover of the box, recocked the spring, and placed the fur ball in position for the next victim!

The usual routine for having any work done in the shipyard is to have the repair item first submitted to the chief engineer by the captain, chief mate, or chief steward. The chief engineer would then determine if it could be accomplished by the engine department and thus save the expense of having the yard perform it. However, if the repair was beyond the capabilities of the engineers or they didn't have the time, it would be submitted by the chief engineer to the port engineer who would then turn the item over to the yard for completion.

It was very important that the request for repairs be thoroughly and completely written up with nothing left to guesswork or assumption. Also, all dimensions, sizes, material required, etc., were to be listed because all of this had a bearing on the cost of the job, and often was all that was available to a yard estimator who would be submitting a bid.

I illustrated this point one time when one ship submitted a standard request for overhauling the magnetic compass. The compass was mounted in gimbals, a device to hold it level whenever the ship rolled or pitched. The usual procedure was to remove it from the gimbals and send it ashore to an instrument repair facility where it would be opened up, glycerine drained, glass lens cleaned, refilled with glycerine, returned to the ship, and installed in place.

A common fault with a magnetic compass was its tendency to develop an air bubble in the surface of the glycerine. This was usually caused by a minor air leak in a gasket, as the gasket deteriorated from the weather, etc.

The repair item was written as follows: "Furnish necessary labor and material to remove vessel's magnetic compass from its gimbals, transport to shop, remove air bubble, repaint numerals on rim as necessary, clean, return to vessel, and install."

While it was a standard item, I always kidded the yard about not reading each item thoroughly before putting an item in hand, so I added an extra line to the request, "Upon completion, return bubble to chief mate."

The ship completed its yard stay and left to resume its scheduled operation. About two weeks later I had a call from the yard that the paperwork was completed and they were ready to negotiate the bill.

The marine industry was the only one I had ever known where "You perform all the work as indicated in these specifications, plus whatever other work may develop during the vessel's stay at your facility and upon completion, we will sit down and negotiate the price." If you ever treated a garage mechanic in this manner, your car would never be delivered. Nor would any home repair contractor work this way!

I went to the yard, sat down at the negotiating table, and settled on a fair price for all the work done, but I did make an issue of the compass item. I told the yard they didn't read the compass item carefully because no one questioned me about the intent of returning the bubble to the chief mate.

They reread the item and agreed it should have been questioned. I told them of my purpose in including that line and they laughed. The item had passed through the ship's supervisor and his superior, through the yard estimator's office, on through the production department, on to the individual who was assigned the task of the compass removal, and finally to the instrument shop who performed the actual work without anyone ever questioning the return of the bubble!

Of course, the shipyard had the last laugh here because the estimator said, "Well, you know we charge by the length of the written repair request and every item contained in it has a price. If we had discovered it, we might have charged you for the transportation of the bubble to the mate's office!"

When the first of our new Lancer Class ships was ready to leave Sun Shipyard on its maiden voyage, the vessel received some basic stores in the shipyard, but the bulk of them were delivered from our regular ship chandlers in New York when the ship arrived there the following day.

The superintendent engineer, Dick Bower, boarded on the morning of sailing day for a final check of things and was talking to the chief engineer, Ed Wickham. On an important day like this for the company, the first trip for a new vessel, Dick was understandably nervous and very serious. Wickham was just the opposite!

Bower asked him if there was anything he could think of that he might need for the voyage that wasn't already aboard. Wickham replied, "Yes, Mr. Bower, I am the only person on this ship who doesn't have a bulletin board in his room! Everyone else has one except me."

Bower explained that the vendor who supplied them had been one short in his delivery to the ship, but he would see to it that he received his upon the vessel's return to New York. Bower also said it was he who made the decision to have the chief engineer be short because he knew he'd understand.

The chief replied, "Yeah, but Mr. Bower, this is June and Fathers' Day is coming in the middle of the month. I expect to receive Fathers' Day cards from all over the world and I won't have any place to hang them up!"

At that, Bower knew Wickham was zinging him, but Wickham added, "Seriously, though, I checked with the chief steward and found he had no cranberry juice on board. Being a Cape Codder, I like my cranberry cooler each evening before dinner; that's vodka and cranberry juice. I already have two cases of vodka in my bedroom, but no juice."

Again he knew he was getting ribbed because Wickham didn't drink. However Bower went ashore and brought back two large bottles of cranberry juice for him!

A month later when the next vessel in the series, the SS *American Legion*, was ready to leave on its maiden voyage, the chief engineer, Tony Wong, our first Chinese chief engineer, was asked by Bower if there was anything he could think of he might need for the trip and he replied, "Yeah, you gave Wickham two bottles of cranberry juice for his first trip, how about a case of soy sauce for me!" This time Bower didn't fall for it.

CHAPTER TWENTY-TWO

PRACTICAL JOKES

A ship can be a dull place to live and work or it can be an enjoyable environment depending on the individual personalities and dispositions of its officers and crew. Some people pass their free time reading, playing cards, chess, or checkers, while others enjoy photography, building ship models, and one other pastime, playing practical jokes on others. Many of the practical jokes can be humorous when the victim is good-natured, but the jokester must expect retaliation.

Several years ago the SS *American Banker,* making its first trip after delivery to the company, left for a long trip to India carrying relief supplies. This was an unusual venture for a brand new ship because they are most often scheduled for a short voyage as a sort of shakedown.

The ship arrived in India without incident, and was tied up there for several days discharging cargo. Early on sailing day, the first assistant engineer went ashore to do some final sightseeing and shopping. He passed a street vendor who was selling live snakes!

Realizing the potential for a good practical joke, he purchased one, a hooded cobra and carried it back to the ship in a burlap sack. He then dumped it into a large cardboard box and left the box in the middle of the chief engineer's office on the deck.

When the chief returned from ashore, he opened his office door and saw the box. Wisely, he kicked the box causing it to move, but then it moved again without a kick. He became suspicious and peered down through the folded top with a flashlight and quickly stepped back when he saw the cobra peering up at him.

The chief suspected the first because of his weird sense of humor, which the chief had learned early in the voyage not to appreciate. The first then appeared laughing, "What's the matter, Chief?"

"Have you gone mad, get this thing off the ship, NOW!" the chief said.

"I bought it from a street vendor, it's been defanged," replied the first.

"I don't give a shit, get rid of it and get your ass down below and get the plant ready. We're sailing in a few hours!"

The first removed the snake, the chief closed his office door, and the chief went to the engine room to check out the plant prior to sailing.

Several hours later, at 2:00 A.M. after dropping the pilot, the ship was brought up to full speed on its way for the long voyage back to New York. After checking out all the machinery, the chief engineer and first left the engine room telling the watch engineer everything had settled down and he was now in charge of the watch.

When the first returned to his room to turn in, suddenly he became worried and called the chief, "Chief, I know you told me to get rid of the snake ashore, but instead I put the box in my room, and now the box has been tipped over and the snake is missing. He's somewhere loose in the ship!"

Now livid the chief called the captain and mate and they broke out all hands, forty-four men, and started a search of the ship. Many crew members refused to participate for fear of finding it in the darkness, so they locked themselves in their rooms! About an hour after the search had begun, they found the snake in the steering gear room, huddled up against a radiator for warmth.

The first managed to get a rope around its neck, and in the presence of the entire search squad dropped it overboard. The chief retaliated to this joke by firing the first when the ship arrived in New York!

Crew members who were permanently assigned to a vessel would take their annual vacation and return upon completion. These men, officers and crew alike, were often called "Homesteaders." Homesteaders made for a cohesive, friendly, cooperative ship's complement who knew what was expected of them, reported for their watches on time, and generally made for a smooth running ship. The company encouraged homesteading.

When a vacation relief man reported aboard, he soon realized he was working in the midst of a group of men (and women) who had a great deal of pride in their ship and its upkeep. Most relief people fit right in, but occasionally an agitator would show up. However he was usually straightened out very soon by his fellow workers.

Today, sadly, homesteaders are a thing of the past due to rotary shipping rules imposed by the unions.

One such homesteader was the radio operator aboard the *Pioneer Ming,* Eugene Kauder. He came aboard about the time U.S. Lines obtained the vessel from the Maritime Administration and served aboard for several years during the period I was chief engineer. He was a fine guy and good shipmate, however he was also the butt of many practical jokes.

One evening while en route to the Far East from Honolulu, the first assistant engineer, Dick Lenox, and I were playing cribbage in my office when I received a phone call from the bridge. It was the second mate calling to tell me the bow lookout refused to go onto the forecastle head to stand his watch because there was a huge sea bird standing on the deck that growled each time the lookout approached. I asked why he was telling this to me and he said he needed help to chase the bird away and thought Dick and I could help him. The second mate was due to go off watch in fifteen minutes so I told him to call us when he was ready.

He soon showed up in my room and we proceeded to the bow armed with three flashlights, heavy weather oilskins, and a huge cardboard box. As we approached the bow, dressed in the oilskins, each of us took a different route around the anchor windlass. We heard the roar which the lookout had mentioned. It sounded like a huge bear, so we stepped back to be sure what we were about to encounter was something we could safely handle. It was a huge albatross which could have weighed thirty-five pounds. It spread its wings momentarily and its wingspan seemed yards long, but it was confused by the bright flashlights shining in its eyes. Dick and I kept our lights on it while the second mate crawled behind it and pulled the big cardboard box down over it. The three of us landed on the box to hold it down then we lifted it slightly to tuck in the flaps on the bottom to close it.

Our original intention was to carry it aft and release it from there, but after talking it over we thought it might be a good trick to release it in the radio operator's toilet and shower. Sparks was due to go off watch in the radio room in about twenty minutes, so we carried it to his room, opened his bathroom door, placed the box on the deck, opened the flaps, released the bird, removed the box, and slammed the door closed!

Through the door we could hear the bird flapping its wings in a frenzy as well as the loud growling sound. We then took up positions outside Sparks' room peering through his porthole to wait for him to return. At 9:00 P.M. he turned on his "auto alarm," which we could hear because it gives a momentary audible alarm, and returned to his room. He opened the toilet door and was greeted with the ferocious growling noise of an "enraged animal," as he later described it. We left the scene immediately for my room and had just seated ourselves when he came storming through the door.

We asked if there was anything wrong and he could barely talk. He sputtered and gasped and finally was able to ask us to come to his room and see the animal in his shower. We told him there was no way any kind of an animal could board the ship out in the middle of the Pacific Ocean at 9:00 P.M. We followed him and when we arrived at his room, he said, "Stand clear and watch." When he opened the door, we heard the sounds of the wings and the roar once again. He slammed the door closed and turned to us with a bewildered look. I said, "Get some heavy weather gear and a large box, we'll have to capture it!"

The second mate and Dick left to get the gear and returned almost at once with it. It was then that Sparks realized we were the culprits. He said, "How come you were able to get this gear so quickly, you bastards, you did this!" We owned up to it, but then our immediate job was to get the monster out of his shower and off the ship. We managed to get the box over it and carried it out onto the open deck where we opened the flaps and dropped it overboard. We kept our flashlights shining on it and the albatross crawled out and flew off into the night.

When we returned to Sparks' room, the mess in his shower was beyond belief. There were bird droppings on the walls, deck, medicine cabinet, lights, toilet, shower curtain, and loose feathers stuck to everything, but worst of all was the stench. It was an overpowering smell of fish and bird droppings! It was a week before it was finally cleaned, repainted, and ready for use. Sparks swore revenge!

Eugene Kauder (Sparks) called Dick Lenox and me to his room after leaving New York for the Far East to see the new ham radio set he had just purchased in New York. He filled us in on its specifications, power, capabilities, etc., all of which meant nothing to us because it was far too technical. He was like a little boy with a new toy and could hardly wait for the ship to get off shore far enough to give it a good test.

He enjoyed listening and talking to various people around the world, especially ham operators on other vessels called Maritime Mobile Stations. He mounted the set on a bookshelf over the desk in his room where he could secure it against the rolling and pitching of the ship. The back of the radio rested against a steel bulkhead on the other side of which was a small closet containing cleaning gear used by the room steward.

One afternoon while he was on watch in the radio shack, which was about twenty feet from his room, Dick and I slipped into the cleaning locker and drilled a small quarter-inch hole through the bulkhead directly behind the radio. Later that evening when he finished his watch, Sparks went to his room and tuned the radio to begin his nightly chatting with the other hams. Dick came to his room to watch and listen to him while I quietly ducked into the cleaning gear locker and closed the door.

I lit up a big cigar and, holding my lips to the hole, began blowing smoke through it. The smoke had begun to rise slowly behind his new radio when Dick said. "Sparks, where the hell is that smoke coming from?" Sparks nearly panicked and yelled, "My new $700 radio is going up in smoke!" He quickly pulled its plug and lifted it from the shelf. After it was removed, he spotted the stream of smoke coming through the hole and quickly rushed out of the room, opened the cleaning gear locker door, and caught me red-handed with my mouth to the wall. I had no way of knowing he had removed the radio because Dick was laughing too hard to clue me in. Once again he called us a couple of bastards and vowed to get even some day.

One fine man with whom I sailed on two different ships was a fellow named Cornelius Frost. Any man named Cornelius had better grow up to be on the defensive and ready for some heckling about his name. Frost was not anyone to be ridiculed, however, because he was about six-feet-eight-inches tall and had a build to go with it. But for a monster of a man, he was a pussy cat, easy to get along with and did his job as second assistant engineer very well. Of course, no one called him Cornelius, his nickname was "Slim."

He was returning to the ship which was tied up at Pier 74 at the foot of Thirty-fourth Street in New York one evening after having gone to the movies, when he passed a department store with a "Going out of business" sign in its window. Beneath the sign was another one which read, "Everything must go, even the store fixtures."

He stepped into the store to look around and saw a pile of mannequin arms, legs, torsos, heads, and wigs stacked in a corner. He was told they were for sale so he purchased enough components to make a woman. The store packed them into two large paper bags for him and he carried them back to the ship and slipped aboard unobserved.

The ship had just completed its coastwise voyage and was about to leave for ports in the Gulf of Mexico, on to the Panama Canal and from there to Brisbane, Australia. The passage from Panama to Brisbane was to be twenty-two days.

We left the next day and after calling at the Gulf Ports and transiting the canal we were on our way. Normally, we would have picked up a number of passengers along the coast, but this trip there were none.

At midpoint in the Pacific between Panama and Brisbane, Slim put his plan into action. Standing the 0400-0800 watch in the morning and the 1600-2000 in the afternoon, he would always be called by the 12-4 oiler at 3:30 A.M. or P.M. to get ready for his watch.

On this particular day, he set his alarm clock to awaken at 3:00 A.M. He quickly removed the mannequin from his locker and assembled the "woman." He then laid it out in his bunk with a sheet casually draped over it, turned off his light, and retired to his toilet waiting for the oiler to call him.

At 0330 the oiler opened his door, snapped on the light switch to his room and announced, "3:30 Mr. Frost." Slim opened the door to his toilet and said, "OK, thanks, I woke up ahead of time."

The oiler stared at the "woman" for a brief moment and then turned off the light! Slim left the toilet and quickly disassembled the mannequin and put it back into his locker. When he entered the engine room twenty minutes later to assume the watch, the 12-4 oiler approached him with a grin and quietly said, "Hey, Mr. Frost, I don't know how you got her aboard, or where she came from, but your secret is safe with me!" Slim replied, "What are you talking about?"

"The girl I saw in your sack when I called you to go on watch!" the oiler said. But Slim said, "You must be seeing things, there are no women aboard this trip."

The oiler walked away, scratching his head. The next day the oiler was seen standing on the main deck looking upward toward the boat deck where Slim lived, hoping to catch a glimpse of her. He was then observed hanging around the officers' pantry, maybe to catch Slim bringing a tray of food to her, but of course there was nothing to see. Several times in the next eight or nine days he was seen out on deck, always looking up in the direction of Slim's room.

At the completion of the voyage four months later, the oiler, who was a relief man, signed off the ship. At payoff I asked Slim if he was going to clue the oiler in on the truth. He said, "I was going to, but I think it's more fun to let him think he was seeing things!"

As far as I know, the oiler never found out the truth!

When Slim was off watch he passed the time by building ship models. He wasn't satisfied making them from a kit; he would construct them from the keel up using raw materials. He asked the chief mate, Bill Hurley, to keep his eye open for a 4 x 4 from the ship's dunnage so he could begin carving a hull for a model sailboat.

Hurley asked him how long a piece he needed and Slim said, "Length isn't important, I'll cut it to size." Hurley told him he might have a piece in the carpenter's shop and would look then next morning, but jokingly added, "Be sure to return what you have left over."

Hurley knew he had an extra long piece in the shop, so he asked me to help him carry it to Slim's room, but not until he had taken a couple of measurements. We waited for Slim to go on watch and then slipped into his room with a tape measure and measured the distance from one upper corner of his room to the opposite lower corner and made a note of this.

We sawed the timber to that length and carried it to his room. By opening his porthole, entry door, and door to his toilet, we were able to jockey the timber through the porthole, out his door, into the toilet, and back into his room and by sawing off small pieces. We made it fit in his room at an angle between the corners! When he came off watch at 8:00 P.M. he stopped off at the saloon for a cup of coffee where Hurley and I were sitting.

The mate told him he put the wood in his room and not to forget to return any that was left over. We accompanied Slim to his room after he finished his coffee and when he opened his door, he let out a big laugh that could be heard throughout the ship! He thanked Hurley for the wood and at once his evil mind began thinking "Payback!"

A couple of weeks later after completing the hull, he returned what wood he had left over in the form of a bucket of sawdust distributed evenly between the sheets of Hurley's bunk!

At another time aboard the same ship, someone smeared white Pepsodent tooth paste all over the white toilet seat of one of the mate's while he was on watch, and then removed the holding down bolts of the seat from the toilet bowl. When the mate came off watch and sat down to use the toilet (the ship was in heavy weather), he slid off the bowl with the next roll of the ship! The seat stuck to his rear end because of paste. After he pulled it loose, his rear end began to burn and smart because of the toothpaste on such a sensitive area of his posterior!

On another occasion, Bill Hurley and I took the steward's steam radiator apart telling him we were vacuuming the dirt from all the radiators prior to cold weather setting in so he would be assured of plenty of heat. This we did. But before closing it up, we placed a huge fish on top of the heating coil.

Later that day when the weather turned cold, he turned the steam on the radiator and the fish began to ripen. He went crazy searching his room trying to find the cause of the smell, never suspecting the radiator. He even asked me to check his sink and shower drains, which I did, and told him the smell didn't seem to be coming from them.

We clued the skipper in on our trick and whenever he walked by the steward's room on the way to the saloon, he would ask the steward about the smell. The odor eventually disappeared as the fish dried up, so in a few days Hurley and I were back in his room taking the radiator apart again, telling him we misplaced a screwdriver the day we vacuumed and were checking all the rooms to find it. This time he hung over us to watch and when he saw us pick up the dead fish, he swore revenge.

The next morning when I awoke, I slipped off the edge of my bunk into my slippers and found my feet were ankle deep in grape jam. He had stayed up late that night to sneak into my bedroom to fill them. I took a shower and went into the saloon to eat breakfast. Hurley was already eating, so I started to tell him about my slippers. He already knew, he had found the same thing in his. The steward walked into the saloon with a big grin on his face, but Hurley and I didn't say a word.

There is one thing which every port in the world seems to have in common—seagulls, thousands of them! They hover over a ship in port, like vultures awaiting some unfortunate victim, but the gull's target is the ship's garbage. When a ship is in port, the garbage is usually stowed in steel barrels secured to the stern rail. It is later dumped overboard when at sea.

Gulls have followed my ship across the entire width of the Atlantic just to eat. They dive for the garbage when it is thrown overboard, hoping to beat the fish to it. When they rest, they perch on the mate's rigging, slopping up his paint work.

One afternoon, the galley utility man carried the noon garbage to the stern to throw it overboard and amused himself by observing the gulls diving for pieces he would throw into the air. After the next meal, he brought a reel of fish line with him when he carried the garbage aft. He tied a piece of meat to the line and threw it overboard, stupidly holding onto the other end! A gull seized it in midair and swallowed it, diving crazily while the utility man attempted to reel in the gull. But he quickly released the line when the gull became enraged and dove at him. The utility man dove for cover!

He then tied a piece of meat to each end of another line and threw that into the air. Both pieces were immediately grabbed by two gulls who then attempted to fly off in two different directions. They had apparently swallowed the pieces because they began to fly wildly, first one pulling the other, and then the other pulling the first one! They began diving and trying to outmaneuver each other until one of them finally disgorged his piece! The other gull flew off with the line trailing behind him.

I thought this was sadistic but I guess the guy enjoyed himself. As mentioned earlier, the sea gulls compete with the fish for garbage thrown into the sea, which accounts for an occasional gull with one leg missing.

Ships' crews are not the only humorists in this marine industry; shipyard workers have also been known to pull their share of pranks on unsuspecting victims. One I have seen occasionally is when a welder using an electric welding outfit removes his helmet to go to lunch and leaves it where a prankster can get to it. The helmet contains a window with dark glass to protect his eyesight from the brilliant arc of the welding process.

The glass is subject to weld "spatter" as the welding rod arcs with the metal being welded, so a clear glass lens is used over the colored glass to absorb the spatter. This clear glass is changed frequently as it becomes scarred and etched. The prankster will remove the outer clear glass and insert a piece of carbon paper between the two pieces of glass.

When the welder returns to the job, he sets up to commence welding, places a new rod in the handle, and strikes an arc to be sure his equipment is functioning normally. He will then pull the hood over his eyes and attempt to resume welding. He can see the arc from around the sides of the helmet but cannot see it through the glass. He might adjust the helmet again, try once more and then realize someone has been playing games with his equipment!

Shipyard employees have a subtle way of telling someone what they think of him without ever saying a word; for instance, when a floating dry dock is lifting a ship out of the water, many fish, crabs, eels, and other marine life will be stranded on the floor of the dry dock. One time the welding department foreman was up on a scaffold with several others examining a crack in the rudder of one of our ships. After giving it a lot of thought, he discussed his recommendations for making the repairs and carefully explained the proper procedure to be used. He was a highly skilled man in his field and everyone respected his opinion.

A young Coast Guard inspector on the scene had absorbed this bit of information and later was heard explaining it to another inspector as if it was his own recommendation!

A yard welder who was present during the original inspection overheard the conversation between the Coast Guard inspectors. So he reached down to the floor of the dry dock, caught a wiggling fish with his hands, and dropped it into the rear pocket of the inspector's coveralls! The young inspector blushed and gave him a weak smile as he removed the fish! Message delivered!

Newport News Shipyard was a safety conscious yard as were most. For those who didn't take safety seriously, OSHA (Office of Safety and Health Administration) soon saw that they did. To promote safe working habits in the yard at Newport News, a large showcase was placed in the center of one of the main thoroughfares within the yard showing all the safety equipment available to the workers.

When the head of the safety department retired, the yard held a party for him at a local restaurant. One of his workers dressed up in one of every piece of safety equipment available and dragged himself into the room. He was wearing safety shoes with steel caps, instep protectors, knee guards, a welder's leather coat and pants, hard hat, welder's helmet, welder's goggles, leather gauntlets, etc. The man could hardly make it into the room, having to nearly crawl, because of the tremendous weight he was carrying!

Speaking about OSHA, the yard was given a work order to open the high-pressure turbine on one of our ships for a survey, but first had to remove the asbestos insulation covering. The OSHA inspector roped off the area surrounding the turbine, and forbade anyone from entering the area until the insulation was removed. After its removal, the area was wetted down and again roped off, but anyone could enter the area if necessary by donning a set of paper coveralls, paper hat, a mask, and paper covering for his shoes.

The rope barrier had been tied from a handrail next to the turbine, along a walkway to a pipeline, and to the other side of the ship. Included in the prohibited area was a spare-parts box for a pump which was being worked on by the first assistant engineer. He found it necessary to get to the box to obtain a part from it. Because it was just inside the barrier, he had to dress in the paper costume, as he called it.

After obtaining the part, he climbed out from under the rope, shed his paper outfit, stowed the suit in a plastic bag, and sealed the bag, under the direction of the OSHA inspector.

He went back to the pump on which he was working and discovered he had removed the wrong part from the box. So he asked the OSHA man if he could slip through the barrier for one second to exchange the part.

"Sure, just get dressed again with a new outfit!" the OSHA inspector said.

This he did, retrieved the proper part, undressed, stowed the suit in another bag, and left the scene. I asked the OSHA man why he couldn't change the barrier to the other side of the box and then it would be accessible without the fuss of dressing up. But he said, "Nothing doing, I'm just doing my job!" So much for the rules!

Stories have been written about children putting messages in bottles and casting them on the waters hoping to contact other children in remote parts of the world. This practice wasn't limited to children, however, because selected ships were given bottles by the U.S. Weather Bureau with instructions to fill out a form stating the ship's position, weather and sea conditions, ship's name, company, hailing port, and date with instructions to drop them overboard in selected areas in the various oceans.

When recovered, the forms were to be forwarded to the Weather Bureau in Washington for compilation and study of the oceans' currents. This was not a case where a bottle would be tossing about forever, and the cooperating ship never learn of its recovery. The bureau would send out periodic reports of recovered bottles stating where they were found, the finder, how long at sea, etc. Thus the ships could appreciate that their efforts were not in vain.

One evening Dick Lenox, first assistant engineer, and I were playing cribbage aboard the *Pioneer Ming* while en route to Honolulu from Yokohama. Walter Wood, second assistant engineer, came off watch at 8:00 P.M. and came into my office holding an empty Chianti bottle. He had decided to clean his room this particular night and rid it of many loose things he had accumulated.

He said, "Well, this is all that remains of an expensive dinner the second mate and I had in Saigon last trip, so it's sayonara, Chianti bottle, you're going overboard."

I said, "Woody, you never throw a bottle overboard without a note in it, that's bad luck." I had never heard of this but it sounded good!

"What'll I write on the note?" he asked.

"I'll type it out for you," I said and then I typed, "If the person who recovers this bottle will forward this note to me at the address below, I will send him one dollar in American money, anywhere in the world." And we typed his name and company address at the bottom.

He folded the note, stuffed it into the bottle, sealed it with a tight cork, and threw it out my porthole, saying, "Nobody will ever find this, we're in the middle of the Pacific!"

He returned to his room to resume his cleaning, so Dick and I immediately typed a similar note, exactly like his, to set our plan into action! The *Pioneer Ming* was about 500 miles west of the Hawaiian Islands at the time and would be arriving in Honolulu in about twenty-five hours.

When we arrived there the following day, we had already placed the duplicate note in an envelope addressed to Woody with a hand written note inside which read, "While I was riding in my outrigger canoe off Waikiki yesterday, there upon the waters lay a bottle. Inside was your note, please send me the dollar." We included the name and address of a man we knew in Honolulu who would mail it for us a couple of days after we left there for New York.

We docked in New York about three weeks later and the mail was delivered to the ship. I received the engine department mail and going through it found the letter for Woody. I called Dick Lenox and the two of us waited for him to come to my office to pick it up along with his other mail.

Looking through it in my office, he said, "Here's one from Honolulu; I don't know anyone from there who would be writing to me."

"Well, open it and you'll find out who it is," Dick said. He opened it and his eyes lit up, "Some guy found my bottle off Waikiki Beach!"

"No kidding, you're going to send him the buck aren't you?" Dick said.

"Of course, I promised!" and he walked out of the office. Dick and I looked at each other in disbelief. "Woody is smarter than that," he said. "Doesn't he realize that bottle would have to drift at a rate of about 18 knots and make a half dozen course changes to find its way into Waikiki Beach in that time?"

"Yeah," I said, "I think we're the ones whose ass is being dragged now, he's too smart to fall for this!"

The next day Dick asked him if he still intended to mail the dollar and he said, "Of course!" Now, Dick was convinced he was wise to us.

About six weeks later after our arrival in Honolulu once again, our friend came aboard and told us he had received a dollar from Woody! "What'll I do with it, give it back?" Dick and I looked at each other and began laughing, "Hell, no," Dick said, "Keep it for your trouble."

We decided not to tell Woody the truth about the bottle as long as he stayed on the ship. After two more trips, he left the *Pioneer Ming* to raise his license and request a first assistant's job in the fleet, so we told him the truth.

His original bottle is still adrift somewhere out there, but if it is ever found, I'm afraid it will go unanswered because the *Pioneer Ming* is no more, and U.S. Lines is gone also!

Aboard the *Pioneer Ming* at sea one afternoon, during a routine fire and boat drill, a 2-1/2-inch fire hose burst at its coupling while being tested. The hose was replaced with a spare taken from the deck storeroom and the damaged one brought to the ship's machine shop where the brass couplings were cut off to be added to the scrap brass bin.

This scrap was saved, along with lathe turnings and drill press scrap, and traded off in Japan for chrome plating of the throttle wheels of the main engine, valve wheels, and gauges and thermometers in the engine room. Most of the ships on the Far East run sported engine rooms which were showplaces; clean and well kept, the crews were justly proud of the machinery spaces.

This was due partly to the gleaming chrome and the well-maintained and freshly painted machinery. It was routine in Far East ports to hire shore labor for painting and cleaning in the engine room, as well as on deck, with payment usually made in cigarettes or cash paid by the chief engineer or captain.

A wiper was dragging the remains of the discarded fire hose up to the main deck to throw it overboard and it reminded him of a huge snake. That's when the idea struck him. He stretched it out to its full length on the after deck, pounded a tapered wooden plug into one end, and whipped it with marline to keep it in place.

Into the opposite end he pounded another plug which contained a pipe fitting and he secured this one in the same manner. Using compressed air, he inflated the hose through the fitting and then plugged the fitting. He painted a pair of eyes at one end, and a series of circles and stripes along its length, using several different colors. When finished, it resembled a fifty-foot sea serpent!

He threw it overboard and it floated off behind us while everyone on deck had a good laugh over it, imagining a lookout on some ship spotting it in a few days and reporting a sighting of a large sea serpent!

One thing he overlooked, however, was that the ship's name was stenciled on the hose as required by law. Common sense dictated that he should have cut the hose at that point so as not to be identifiable, but nothing was ever heard about it so I assume it eventually sank.

CHAPTER TWENTY-THREE

MEDICAL

Many steamship companies operated large fleets during the war but the vessels were under a bareboat charter agreement with the government. This meant the ships would be operated by the company who would hire the crew and pay all expenses of the ship's operations, but would not own the vessel and would be reimbursed by the government for performing services. Due to the numerous crew members needed, many companies set up their own medical offices, usually within the vicinity of the operations office, to take physical exams for each new crew member prior to his assignment aboard ship.

One of the main things the doctor would examine for was a hernia to preclude a seaman from alleging he suffered one aboard a company vessel, thus prompting a lawsuit. A young man reported to the U.S. Lines medical office for a physical one morning and astounded the doctor when he dropped his trousers and underwear for the hernia check.

The doctor said, "Young man, in all my years of medical practice I have never seen anyone as well endowed as you; do you mind if I call in two other doctors to see that?" He replied, "No sir, as long as they are doctors." The doctor assured him they were and called in two senior port engineers, Bob Lurye and Leo Vam Damme, telling them on the phone to wear their suit coats and talk like doctors. They left the engineering office and reported to the medical department next door and carried it off well. Both men managed to keep a straight face while they admired the young man's endowment. One of them asked if that was all his and he replied, "Yes sir, owned and operated by me!" The engineer/doctors thanked the young man and returned to their office, not only envious, but still not sure of what they had just witnessed!

After the war United States Lines established its peacetime trade routes, one of which was the Far East run. Any crew member signing aboard one of these vessels was required to have a series of inoculations to prevent typhus, typhoid, yellow fever, smallpox, etc. A routine was set up in New York. The company doctor would board the vessel, after completion of its coastwise run, either upon its arrival from or just prior to its sailing for the Far East. On one occasion, the doctor came aboard when the vessel arrived and set up temporary facilities in the officers' lounge to give the inoculations to those crew members making the next voyage.

One engineer, who shall remain nameless, was taking off the coastwise trip to go home to Boston for a few days vacation. He thought it would be smart to have his shots prior to going home because sometimes an individual would have a sore arm or feel miserable for a half day after the shots. If this were to happen, at least he would be at home. The doctor administered his shots and signed the man's yellow World Health Organization card, entering the date, shots received, and manufacturer and expiration date of the serums used.

The engineer went home to Boston. A day or so later he thought it might be smart to have a blood test taken because he had frequented a couple of houses of ill repute while in the Far East. The day after the blood test at the Boston Marine Hospital, he told his mother, with whom he lived, that he was going to the neighborhood bar to have a few beers and see his buddies.

A few hours later, the hospital called his mother to inquire of his whereabouts. She told them where he could be found, and soon a Boston policeman entered the bar and asked for this individual. He identified himself to the cop, and was asked to please get into the police car and accompany him to the marine hospital. The engineer became a nervous wreck on the way to the hospital, envisioning himself as having contracted a rare Far East strain of either gonorrhea or syphilis, both of which strains were reputed to be incurable at that time.

When he arrived at the hospital, the doctors immediately put him into quarantine and now he was sure of it. He asked which of the two venereal diseases he had contracted and they said, "Neither, you are a walking epidemic. You have typhus, typhoid, etc." He said, "Is that all! I can explain that." He produced his World Health Organization card, and after studying the card, the doctors gave him a clean bill of health. He asked about any venereal infections and they reassured him he was clean.

He asked the cop to give him a lift back to the bar where he could explain this to his buddies. The cop said he wasn't operating a taxi service and told him to take a cab back, but to stop off at home and put his mother's mind at ease before going off to the bar.

This is just what he did, and when he returned to the bar all his buddies were gone. He didn't see them again before he had to return to New York to rejoin his ship. He often wondered if they ever thought why he was "arrested" that day.

Many years ago while serving as first assistant engineer, my chief engineer had been frequenting some houses of ill repute in Europe. Eventually he decided to go to the outpatient department of the U.S. Public Health hospital in lower Manhattan for a checkup after feeling somewhat under the weather. A blood test proved he had syphilis.

He didn't want to sign off the ship to be treated for fear the office might find out about his condition so he asked the doctors to furnish enough medication for treatment aboard ship. They provided him with a sufficient amount of a new sulfa drug which had just been approved and enough peanut oil to be administered with it. The intent was to have the ship's purser, a maritime service pharmacist mate, mix a specific quantity of the drug with a measured amount of peanut oil and administer it by injection into his buttocks. The theory was that the sulfa would remain in his body longer if it were in suspension in the peanut oil rather than just by itself.

After the first day of treatment, I stepped into the chief engineer's office to speak to him and found him sitting sideways at his desk making routine entries in the engine room logbook. I asked why he was sitting in such a weird fashion. He said he had received his first "shot" and the lump on his rear end felt like a golf ball and it hurt to sit on it!

The following day at the same time, I again called on him and this time he was seated in another strange position. He told me he had just received his second injection on the other side, the "golf ball" was now reduced to a large marble, and now both sides hurt.

On the third day, I found him writing log entries in a standing position with the logbook perched on the top of his file cabinet! After several more shots, he completed the course of treatment and a subsequent blood test proved he had been cured.

I asked if the shots had begun to hurt and he said, "Not really, but my ass began to feel like hobnailed glass!"

Probably one of the most unusual medical treatments aboard ship occurred on one of our Far East ships which was moored in Yokohama for several days awaiting cargo. The first assistant engineer had read an ad in an English language newspaper for a doctor who specialized in vasectomies. This particular engineer thought it would be a good chance for him to have the operation performed because the ship would be in port long enough, and more than likely the operation would be much cheaper than in the United States.

He phoned the doctor and was told he would need a letter from his wife authorizing the procedure, so he immediately composed a letter, signed his wife's name, and reported to the doctor's office the next morning.

The operation was performed in the office, a few stitches put in to close the incision, the area bandaged, and he was sent back to the ship. Everything seemed normal the next day and the following day the ship left port for Honolulu.

One day after leaving Yokohama, he noticed traces of blood on his underwear. He removed his clothing, stepped into the shower, and examined the area with a hand mirror. He discovered the stitches had pulled out completely on one side and the incision open! Not wishing to inform any of his shipmates of his condition, he "repaired" it by wrapping Scotch tape around the entire area until the bleeding stopped!

Upon his arrival in Honolulu, he reported to a clinic where he told the attending doctor about the operation and subsequent bleeding, but not his temporary repair! When the doctor examined him he wanted to know who the "butcher" was who performed the operation and used Scotch tape instead of stitches to close it.

The engineer then told him about the appearance of blood and that he had made the temporary repair himself. Everyone in the clinic had a good laugh over it. They stitched it closed and he thanked them for their understanding and assistance.

Ironically, when he returned home and told his wife about his operation, to which she had not agreed, she filed for divorce!

CHAPTER TWENTY-FOUR

BURIAL AT SEA

For many years U.S. Lines would accept the ashes of a deceased person aboard company ships for scattering at sea. This request was usually made by a member of the family of a person who was a friend of the company, such as a shipper, a relative of a company official, a government official, or a crew member from one of our ships. This occurred frequently enough so that eventually a routine was set forth by the company. The ceremony was always one of dignity, whereby the master would select the site in the ocean, usually determined by weather and sea conditions, and the crew and officers assembled on deck in uniform. The captain would read an appropriate passage from the Bible, ask anyone if he would care to say a few words, and conclude with "I commit thee to the deep, may your soul rest in peace," or other solemn words, and cast the ashes upon the water.

Upon arrival at the next port, the master would send a letter to the next of kin in which he described the ceremony, gave the ship's position and the weather conditions, and listed those in attendance. This letter was a source of final consolation to those left behind.

Today if a crew member dies at sea, his body is placed in one of the empty refrigerated boxes on board until arrival at the next port where it is removed and handled according to the wishes of the next of kin and under direction of port authorities.

Many years ago before laws governing the disposal of bodies were enacted, it was routine for a deceased crew member to be sewn in a canvas bag, the bag weighted, and the body buried at sea. Tradition had it that the boatswain would do the sewing, and the last stitch was to be put through the nose of the deceased to prevent him or his spirit from attempting to free himself. Payment for this was to be a bottle of whiskey from the captain, and the boatswain relieved of his duties for the rest of that day to enjoy the whiskey!

I was told about one occasion which allegedly occurred years ago, where the family of a prominent shipper had requested their father's body be buried at sea in the middle of the Atlantic. This was somewhat unusual because up to that point only ashes had been scattered at sea, but the company said it would make an exception this time because of the individual's close business association with U.S. Lines.

When this individual was waked, his family had him laid out in his favorite tuxedo. After the shoreside services, the casket was placed in a wooden box and transported to the company piers to await its final voyage to a resting place in the Atlantic. The next ship bound for Europe was to have the box loaded aboard and stowed in a deck locker with instructions to the master concerning its disposal.

His orders were to conduct the burial at a point in mid-ocean, weather conditions permitting. However soon after leaving New York, the weather took a turn for the worse and stayed at gale force for nearly the entire crossing. In the meantime as the days wore on, the boatswain had been observing the box in the locker and, after giving it much thought, came to the conclusion that it might possibly float when put overboard.

Without consulting anyone, he pried open a top board from the box and filled the area between the casket and box with old hardware and junk from his storerooms and renailed the board. Eventually the weather let up when the ship was not too far from the English coast, so the captain notified the mate to quickly prepare for the burial while the weather was favorable.

All hands were assembled on deck at the rail, the vessel slowed, the box was placed upon a hatch board, lifted to the caprail and held in position while balanced by the boatswain. After the reading when the captain said the words, "I commit thee to the deep," the boatswain upended the hatch board. Instead of the box sliding overboard, the weights in the box shifted to the low end and punched out the end of the box!

The weights and casket slid out while the box remained on the hatch cover. The casket remained afloat, bobbing up and down on the water, while the crew tried to decide what to do next! Someone suggested launching a lifeboat to retrieve it, but the captain decided against it because the sea was still too rough.

Someone else suggested getting the ship's revolvers out of the safe and shooting it full of holes to release the air and maybe it would sink. This seemed to be the best suggestion, so the guns were broken out, loaded, and the captain and mate shot the casket full of holes!

The casket slowly settled and eventually sank after the air was released. The ship resumed its voyage, and when it arrived in Europe, the captain sent the letter to the next of kin giving only the proper details of the ceremony, nothing about the fiasco that occurred!

Meanwhile unknown to the ship, as the casket was plummeting to the ocean bottom, the lid popped open and the body floated to the surface and eventually washed ashore somewhere in England. When found by the authorities, they were confronted with a body dressed in a tuxedo, fully embalmed, and shot full of bullet holes!

The identity of the deceased was traced through the labels in the tuxedo jacket and the next of kin notified, much to the embarrassment of U.S. Lines! Needless to say, this ended any further burials at sea.

CHAPTER TWENTY-FIVE

STOWAWAYS

Stowaways have been troublesome aboard ship I suppose from Columbus' time or maybe even before. In U.S. Lines we had our share. Most I have encountered have been pathetic souls seeking a better life, some escaping poverty, oppression, and even the law.

Upon leaving the pier, each department's personnel would commence a stowaway search of their compartments. The steward would search the mess rooms, pantries, storerooms, and walk-in refrigerators which, even though locked, could have been invaded earlier when the cooks were removing food.

The chief mate would search the cargo holds, storerooms, mast houses, and deck lockers. The chief engineer or first assistant engineer would check the engine department spaces, machine shop, storerooms, steering gear room, and shaft alley.

The search had to be carried out hurriedly so as to enable the ship to disembark any undesirables at the pilot boat if the crew of the boat would accept them. If they refused, we would inform our agency in the port we just left to have officials waiting on the pier, or to dispatch a boat out to us in the bay to remove the stowaways when we returned to the harbor.

If by chance a stowaway was not found during the search but surfaced later, a decision had to be made whether to return him (or her) to the port, or if too far out to sea, proceed with him aboard. In any event, whether he remained aboard or was returned to port, he was immediately handcuffed and locked in the ship's hospital, interrogated, and searched for contraband and identification papers.

Meals would be brought to him at the same time the crew was eating and he ate the same fare as the rest of the ship. Although they were fugitives in the eyes of the immigration laws, stowaways were treated humanely. On some ships, problems arose when some crew members, feeling sympathetic, would attempt to bring a stowaway extra food or clothing or give him money.

We tried to discourage this attitude, lest the crew member be persuaded to assist him in an escape attempt at a subsequent port. When the ship reached the next port, efforts were made to land him there, particularly if we were still in the same country. If authorities would not permit him to land we were "stuck" with him. In these ports a watchman was usually hired by our local office to guard the individual.

In the event we turned back to land a stowaway in any port, our office was immediately notified so that our insurers would add a "rider" to the ship's insurance policies. It has been argued in court that if a vessel had not turned back to land a stowaway, it might not have been in a certain place later when it was involved in a collision!

I recall one evening after leaving Pusan, Korea, I was searching the refrigerated diffuser rooms for stowaways when I heard a noise in the cargo compartment of the hold. (A diffuser room holds the machinery used to cool the cargo space, but is separated from the cargo by heavy metal screening. This is to allow access to the machinery without having access to the cargo.) I turned off my flashlight momentarily and listened. I could hear the noise again, so I turned my light on and shone it in the direction of the noise but saw nothing. A minute later I saw another flashlight.

I became frightened in the darkness alone. Another noise and another flash from the light! Whoever was down there with me in the bowels of the ship was stalking me. Knowing the desperation of stowaways, it was frightening.

I turned and aimed my light at the next sound and suddenly was caught in the beam of the other light! We were each blinded by the brightness when I heard a voice, "Chief, is that you?"

It was the voice of the chief mate coming from the cargo hold. I shouted, "Yeah, you scared the shit out of me!" He laughed and admitted to the same thing. Then we climbed out of the compartment and reported to the bridge that no stowaways had been found.

We quickly learned the best way to prevent stowaways was to tell a lie on the sailing board. The sailing board is a sign placed at the head of the gangway twenty-four hours prior to sailing from a port. It gives the particulars of the vessel's planned departure from that port, stating the date and time of leaving and the name of the next port. The date and time of leaving would usually be correct, but the destination would be a lie to discourage anyone from hiding aboard until after leaving.

If the ship was in Hong Kong and the sailing board read, "SS *PIONEER MING* sails on March 3, 1960, at 2300 hours for New York," we could plan on at least a half dozen stowaways. New York and San Francisco with their large Chinatown populations were popular destinations for stowaways. Thus the sailing board would read "SS *Pioneer Ming* sails on March 3, 1960, at 2300 hours for Pusan, Korea." No Chinese stowaways wanted to go there. Of course we had to be certain our crew was well informed of our true destination in case one of them missed the ship.

The *American Jurist* was docked in Boston and one of our oilers was making the rounds of some of the bars on Washington Street. Washington Street in those days took on the air of what used to be Scollay Square in another part of the city.

The oiler had lined up what was to be an exciting evening with a young "lady" he met at one of the bars, but there was only one possible drawback to his plans. Would the ship be leaving that night or the next morning? No sailing board had been posted at the time he left the ship. If it were leaving in the morning, he was home free; but if leaving that night, he would have to give up his plans.

He put the girl on "hold" while he dashed back to the ship by cab to check the board. Feeling no pain, he rushed up the gangway to find the board posted, "SS *American Jurist* sails for New York at 0100 hours on that date." He was done in but then he had a brilliant idea. If the board had no writing on it, he had every right to stay ashore because union rules required it to be posted at least eight hours before sailing on a weekend and this was Saturday night!

Now, to put his plan into action. He stood at the head of the gangway, unzipped his fly and urinated all over the board, washing off the chalk printing and leaving the board bare. Unfortunately, the chief mate happened to be walking by the gangway and witnessed the act!

The chief mate sent the oiler to his room, hosed off the sailing board, and rewrote it. When the oiler reached his room, his temper flared and he woke his roommate. The roommate, seeing his condition, left the room to get away from him. The oiler became violent, tore the table lamp from its screwed-down base, yanked all the linen from the two bunks and tore it into shreds, and then threw a bottle of hair tonic at the sink and cracked the porcelain sink.

His roommate had gone to get the mate and when the mate arrived, he had to have help subduing the oiler. He was placed in irons in the ship's hospital until he sobered up. The following morning he was brought before the captain who logged him one day's pay plus the cost of replacing the damaged goods in the room. When the ship docked in New York, he was fired.

His name was then sent to the Marine Index Bureau where he would go on record as a trouble maker. In the future whenever he would be dispatched from the union hall for a job, his future employer could scan his record and he could be denied employment. Insurance companies have often declared a known "fighter" on board can make for an unseaworthy ship, so many companies are reluctant to hire them.

CHAPTER TWENTY-SIX

PORT ENGINEERING

After having served aboard the SS *PIONEER MING* as chief engineer for several years, I was about to leave for another trip to the Far East when I was approached by Mr. Joseph Cragin, superintendent engineer. He asked me if I would be interested in leaving the sea and accepting a job in the superintendent engineer's office as a port engineer. If so it would be necessary for me to complete the coming voyage and sign off the ship on its return to New York, about May 30, 1961. I quickly called my wife and told her of this news and she was thrilled. Up to now I had been living in Massachusetts and only getting home on weekends and having an occasional coastwise trip off. Her first reaction was, "Good, now you can help me raise the kids!"

Needless to say, the trip dragged. At times I had second thoughts and questions about the new job, the reduction in pay, and the responsibility. I wondered if I would fit in with the other port engineers, whether the job change would mean selling my house in Massachusetts and moving to the New York area, or whether I would be assigned to the Bethlehem Steel Shipyard in Quincy, Massachusetts, as part of our new construction group. All of these things went through my mind. On our return to New York on a Friday, I called Mr. Cragin and he said I was to start the following Monday. I would be assigned permanently to his staff in New York. I had to rush home, return with my station wagon, load up five-years worth of accumulated gear, rush back to Massachusetts, unload, and return to New York for an eight o'clock start on Monday.

In my haste I had overlooked one important factor; I had no place to live in the New York area! I quickly called my brother, Howard, who lived in Hillsdale, New Jersey. He and his wife, Bar-

bara, graciously took me in until I could sell my house in Massachusetts and move to New Jersey.

On my first assignment in my new job I was assigned to Tom Wilhelmsen, a very capable port engineer who was to teach me the duties of a port engineer. His first lesson was to inform me that a port engineer always brought two things to a job: a flashlight and a good appetite! His first project that day was to contact the contractor who was working his ship to tell him there would be an extra man for lunch. That taken care of, we proceeded to the Brooklyn Army Base where our ship was just tying up. As we approached the army base gate, he informed me that smoking was prohibited in the army base so he taught me the second important thing I should know: how to carry a lit cigar through the gate without getting caught! He accomplished this feat by holding it in his hand concealed up his coat sleeve. He thought this quite important because he knew I smoked cigars, and a cigar never tasted the same once it had been extinguished and relit. Tom was a good teacher.

In 1963, U.S. Lines sent five port engineers to the Bailey Meter Plant in Cleveland, Ohio, to learn about the automation which was being installed in our new ships. Our boss, Bob Lurye, assistant superintendent engineer, also came along, not as a chaperone as some wags suggested, but to learn about the ships. At least that's what he told the superintendent engineer, Joe Cragin, but Lurye really was there as an excuse to get out of the office where he had been desk ridden for years.

Lurye had graduated from New York State Nautical School, at Fort Schuyler in the early 1930s and shipped out as a company cadet with U.S. Lines when he couldn't find a job as a third assistant. By accepting a cadet's berth he at least had his foot in the U.S. Lines' door when an opening came about.

He told me about his first trip to sea which was aboard an old freighter making eight knots while bound for Australia. He said the trip dragged on for what seemed like months after only a few weeks.

Somewhere in the mid-Pacific one evening, he came off the 4-8 watch and walked out on the after deck where a group of men had gathered. He sat down with them and heard music playing. The men were listening to phonograph records played on a crank-type phonograph, a state of the art machine for the times. He was enjoying the music when he saw the crusty old boatswain stand up, walk over to the carpenter and invite him to dance!

The carpenter accepted and the two began a two step on the after deck to the music. Moments later, two ABs stood up and began to dance together also. Lurye had never seen anything like this in his young life. His first thought, "Let one of them ask me and I'll punch him in the nose!"

Disillusioned, he returned to his room and sat in bewilderment. He thought, "Is this what going to sea gets to be? If so, I don't want any part of it." It was later explained to him that these rough sailors often did this to kill the monotony of long days at sea and he had nothing to worry about.

After they arrived in Sydney, he saw many of the dancers propositioning some of the girls in the bars in Kings Cross so his faith in humanity was restored. But he was determined that this would be his first and last trip on a freighter!

When he returned to New York, he asked for a transfer to a passenger ship. As he said, "Even though I wouldn't be allowed to mingle or associate with the passengers, at least I could look out on deck once in a while and see women and girls and know that they still existed!"

Bob Lurye was a an excellent man to work for. We could call him at 3:00 A.M. from a ship to explain our problem and he'd listen patiently and give us his recommendation. He instilled in the port engineers a certain faith that if we were to make a wrong decision on a job, we were to tell him at once so he could be prepared to defend us when management learned about it.

I often wondered what his wife thought when their phone would ring at 3:00 A.M., but she was a lovely, understanding lady who knew he was just doing his job.

He was extremely outspoken, but was still the one who was consulted by the marine department when they needed answers or advice concerning a vessel's operations. He and his wife, Heidi, were attending a dinner dance in one of the large hotel ballrooms in New York with a group of five U.S. Lines port captains and their wives one Saturday evening many years ago, when a couple came to their table to say hello to one of the captains. As the introductions were being made, "this is Captain Green, this is Captain Kolbe, this is Captain Howard, this is Mr. Lurye, this is Captain Devlin, etc.," the man knew he wouldn't be able to remember all the names, so he just decided to call everyone captain and take his chances.

His only mistake? He addressed Lurye as "Captain!" Lurye piped out in a loud, booming voice, "Don't call me a 'captain,' I know how to read and write!" Outspoken, oh yes. Sometimes I think some of Bob Lurye rubbed off on his port engineers!

If a port engineer were to call him at home and tell him he was reluctant to send a ship to sea because of a certain condition on board, his reply would be, "Would you take that ship to sea if you were the chief engineer?"

This was a sensible question and one which all of us used as a guideline in our careers as port engineers. Because of this attitude, our responsibility was easier to understand and our decisions justified.

When the group of us landed at the Airport in Cleveland that Sunday afternoon, we took cabs to the hotel where we had reservations made by the Bailey Meter Co., our hosts for the week. In the hotel lobby after checking in, Lurye said to the group, "Now I'm gonna show you guys just how a New Yorker handles this out-of-town stuff, especially on an expense account!"

We collected our bags and headed for the elevator where the elevator operator greeted us. After telling him our floor, Lurye asked, "What's your name, young man?"

"My name is Bob, sir."

"Well, Bob, that's my name too," Lurye said. "Now, every afternoon about 4:00 P.M. the group of us will be arriving here in the hotel lobby. When you see us come in, you automatically are to bring a large bucket of ice to my room, room 323, and here's ten dollars for your trouble. After you drop us off now, you can start today with the ice."

"Yes sir, thank-you very much!"

Later while having a drink in Lurye's room, Charlie Higgins said, "Boy, Bob, you're a generous guy when you're out of town. Ten bucks is a big tip." And it was for those days. Lurye said, "Yeah I know, but we're on an expense account, remember. I told you guys I'd show you how a New Yorker behaves out of town."

The following day returning from school, we entered the lobby, Lurye in the lead, and headed for the elevator. A different elevator operator entered and asked for our floor. Lurye said, "Room 323, young man. By the way, where's Bob?"

"Oh, he only works on Sundays; I'm the regular elevator operator. I'll be on for the rest of the week, my name's Jack."

All of us let out a big laugh, "So you're gonna show us how a New Yorker behaves out of town? Better give Jack a ten spot, too, if you want ice for the rest of the week!"

Bob Lurye knew he'd been had, so he forked over another ten and we had ice every day! For months after whenever he gave us a hard time, we would remind him of the Cleveland ice incident.

Many times when a port engineer left home to go to the office and do some of the endless paperwork connected with the job, he had no idea whether he would return home that evening, put his feet up and get comfortable, or would have to call home to tell his wife, I'm leaving on the next available flight to Hong Kong, Japan, Korea, or some European port to survey a ship. Many times, of course, he would have lead time before going out of town; it wasn't always an emergency.

Scheduled inspections, dry-dockings, or lay-ups could always be anticipated, but it was those emergencies, such as a collision, grounding, or machinery failure which would necessitate getting a port engineer to the ship quickly. Upon arrival at the vessel, it would be our function to conduct a survey with underwriter representatives and regulatory body surveyors and inspectors to determine the seaworthiness of the vessel as well as keep the down time to a minimum.

We often found ourselves cutting corners to get a ship back on schedule. This often entailed convincing the U.S. Coast Guard inspector on the scene that the ship was safe to proceed to the next port where better repair facilities were available, or to give us enough lead time to prepare for the repairs there.

If possible, repairs were carried out concurrently with cargo operations, thus keeping the vessel on schedule. In doing this we sometimes encountered inexperienced USCG inspectors and had to advise them to call their boss late at night to get his approval to leave the port. They were always reluctant to do this, of course, saying they had the authority to make any decisions regarding sailing. When we would point out that this particular problem was experienced before and it was on record that the vessel proceeded without problems, they realized we were probably right. If they still refused to call, we would tell them we would make the call ourselves, talk to his principals, and cite some of the instances where decisions had been made to allow our ships to proceed under similar circumstances.

I was sent to San Francisco one time on an emergency, had no time to pack some clothes, and had to hurry to Newark Airport to catch the next plane. When I arrived on the West Coast, I expected to be there only a few days, so I picked up clothing locally to see me through. But once there, the office kept giving me new duties on arriving ships, so I was there for a few weeks. The theory was, Murphy's already out there, let him do it instead of sending another man out.

It was approaching Christmas season while I was there, and the San Francisco office of the Coast Guard was holding its annual Christmas party in a few days. The Officer in Charge, Marine Inspection, sent an invitation to the U.S. Lines office staff, and I soon found out this included me. I called my boss, Ray McPhail, in New York and asked him if he thought I should attend. He said, "By all means, you've got some fences to mend with those people!" I told him I didn't bring a suit with me and I would have to obtain one somewhere. He told me to find one and make that party, regardless. The next day I went to J. C. Penney's and purchased a cheap suit, shirt, and tie. I then called Ray and told him I bought the suit and he said, "I didn't tell you to buy one, and don't you expect U.S. Lines to pay for it!"

I attended the party and enjoyed it in spite of some of the ill feelings prevailing between their inspectors and me. When I returned to New York, I presented my seven-page expense account to Ray. Clipped to the first page was a little note which said, "Dear Ray, here are my expenses for my recent trip to the West Coast. Find the suit!" At least I could thank the U.S. Coast Guard for a new suit!

William J. Riley, a former U.S. Lines chief engineer, port engineer, and later manager of new ship construction, tells a story about working at Bushey's Shipyard in Brooklyn when a Yugoslavian ship was discharging a cargo of horses onto a pier next to the yard. A belly strap was secured around the middle of each animal, the animal lifted by winch from the hold of the ship, and discharged onto the pier to waiting trucks.

One morning while discharging its live cargo, a horse was suspended in midair between the ship and pier, and it apparently panicked and wiggled out of the belly strap. It fell into the bay where Riley spotted it when it began swimming to stay afloat. He signaled a shipyard worker in a small motorboat to move the boat near the horse. The boatman managed to lasso the creature with a rope he had on board, and maneuver the boat, towing the horse, a few yards toward a submerged dry dock.

The shipyard had just undocked a small tugboat from the dry dock thus the dry dock was submerged and ready to accept another load. Once in position, Riley directed the dock master to pump out the dry dock and in a few minutes the dock lifted the horse, boat, and boatman clear of the water!

The horse was then led up a ramp from the dry dock to street level where longshoremen guided the horse to a waiting truck. Bill Riley claims he is the only port engineer in the United States who ever dry-docked a horse!

For many years, the company was reluctant to allow port engineers to rent cars when out of town, citing such items as liability and collision insurance and other weak excuses. We suspected they probably thought we would use them for sightseeing and joyriding. We were always told to use taxis, subways, or buses to and from motels and shipyards, or have the yard provide a lift to us if we had to be called in the middle of the night for an inspection.

Charlie Higgins, one of our more outspoken port engineers, returned to the office after a trip to the West Coast. Charlie complained to Dick Bower, superintendent engineer, that he was forced to wait outside a pier in San Francisco for a cab in the most dangerous section of the city, and that would be the last time he would do it. He wasn't about to get mugged so "U.S. Lines could save a few bucks!"

The company caved in to our requests, particularly when we discovered hundreds of cars were rented every week by the company sales force! We were issued credit cards from one of the major car rental companies and instructed to use that company exclusively. Of course, this opened the door to us to rent cars in foreign countries as well.

Tony Wong, one of our port engineers, was the first to rent one in Europe after we received the credit card. He was sent to England to attend the SS *Pioneer Commander* which had run aground off the north coast of Scotland and was to be dry-docked in Newcastle.

Moments after leaving the car rental agency, he became confused driving in the left lane, a British custom, and as he approached a traffic circle, or roundabout as it is called there, he attempted to turn off onto one of the tangential roads from the wrong lane in a circle and sideswiped a man riding a scooter. He knocked the man down. Apparently the man wasn't injured or any damage done because Tony settled it right there on the scene, but would never tell us how much it cost him (or rather U.S. Lines)!

A few days later he drove through a one-way tunnel in the wrong direction! "There was no traffic in the tunnel," he said, "until I was halfway through and then it started coming toward me! All I could see was a bunch of headlights heading for me. I couldn't back up in the dark so I just stopped the car and waited!"

The first car came directly at him and struck the front end of his rental car. Tony couldn't understand why the Brit didn't at least stop before the collision when he saw the headlights! This is also the same story he told the police when they appeared in an attempt to put the blame on the Brit. There was a massive traffic snarl to unscramble with the traffic backed up in the tunnel so they issued a summons to Tony and took away his driving privileges in England!

I was driving a rental car in Australia several years ago and got in a similar situation, driving in the wrong lane after becoming confused leaving a rotary. But instead of stopping, I backed up on the highway when I saw traffic approaching after the light had turned green. I had four lanes coming at me. I backed and turned to get off the highway and ended up on a safety island for pedestrians who were waiting for a tram!

An Australian man came over to me and told me to turn around and head in the other direction quickly before a cop spotted me, but it was too late. I heard a loud voice shout, "Hold it right there, fella!"

I climbed out of the car and patiently listened to the cop inform me that I happened to be in refuge reserved for people who were waiting for a tram, and it was called a safety island to protect them from drivers like me!

"I'm sorry, Officer, I became confused driving in the left lane," I said.

"Oh, a Yank, huh?" he replied.

I told him I was and that I was driving a rental car. His frown turned into a smile and he asked me if I had been in the U.S. Navy in the Pacific during World War II.

"Yes, I was," I lied and he said, "We people here in Australia owe you men many thanks for keeping the enemy from our country, so to show my appreciation, I'm not going to write you up! Now, just back your vehicle around that sign while I hold the pedestrians out of the way, and drive off in that direction toward the traffic light."

I backed up and knocked over the safety island sign; he said, "Don't worry about it. I'll stand it up again as soon as you leave, but hurry up and get the hell out of here before another cop sees me not issuing you a ticket, and thanks again, Yank!"

Two places I never had any desire to drive were in Taiwan or Japan. In Taiwan, trucks, taxis, private cars, buses, and motor scooters by the hundreds line up at every traffic signal, their engines roaring, awaiting the change of lights. When the signal turns to green, it's like nothing I've ever witnessed before!

Tires screech, pedestrians still in crosswalks run for their lives, and the motor scooters dodge and weave in and out of all lanes of traffic, cutting off buses, cars, and anything else in their way, all attempting to make as many green lights as possible before they change. The timing of the lights is erratic and of unduly long duration sometimes, and short at other times, so all drivers live in a period of anticipation while in traffic. It has often been said that traffic lights in Taiwan are only a suggestion!

In Japan I saw a taxi attempt to pass a trolley car on tracks on the wrong side just as an elderly woman alighted from the trolley. The cab braked, but struck the lady just enough to knock her to the pavement. I rushed over to assist her, but she managed to get up by herself. She brushed herself off, and when the cab driver walked over to her, she and the driver exchanged some words in Japanese, but they didn't seem to be words of anger. In a few moments, they each bowed several times to each other, she stepped up onto the sidewalk, and the cab drove off.

No police, no witnesses needed, no court case, just sidewalk justice and Japanese courtesy. From what I observed it appeared that the driver accused the woman of being careless and she apologized!

In 1946 my ship, SS *Defender*, was tied up in Shanghai in the Huangpu River in the center of the city. Shanghai had few taxis due to the shortage of gasoline, but rickshaws and pedicabs were plentiful and cheap.

A pedicab is a vehicle with a bicycle front end and a rickshaw rear end which was pedaled by the driver, and which could travel much faster than a rickshaw. At the busy intersections, a traffic cop was stationed in a raised open air cubicle, about the size of a telephone booth. The cop was usually an Indian Sikh, a bearded man wearing a turban and always at least six feet tall. He made an imposing sight standing high over all others in the traffic.

The rickshaw and pedicab drivers were fearful of them and generally obeyed their stop and go signals quite respectfully. Occasionally, a driver would attempt to rush through the intersection after he has signaled a stop, so the Sikh would blow his whistle. All the drivers would stop and turn to see which one he would single out for the offense. He would point to one or two and they would return to the side of his cubicle where he would reach over the side, remove the seat from their vehicle, and stand it up alongside the cubicle.

The drivers then had to retreat to the sidewalk where they would park their rickshaw or pedicab and wait for him to return the seat. After a few minutes or, in the event of a serious violation, as long as half an hour, he would call them to the cubicle, chastise them, and then return their seat so they could continue on their way looking for a fare.

I observed one Sikh with four seats standing alongside him at one time, the four drivers sitting on the curb playing some sort of Chinese card game awaiting release of their seats.

Just as in Japan, no traffic tickets, no summons, no fines, no appeals, instant traffic court!

The second mate and I were uptown one afternoon in Shanghai and after a few beers hailed two pedicabs to take us back to the ship. I told my driver if he beat the other driver to the pier, there was an extra dollar in it for him, so he speeded up and passed the second mates' driver, shouting something in Chinese as we passed.

The other driver hearing this, also speeded up and the race was on! The other driver was an elderly man, though, and we felt sorry for him because he appeared to be getting out of breath. We stopped both drivers, told them to get in the passenger seats and the second mate and I pedaled back to the ship while the two Chinese men sat back with their feet up, laughing and shouting back and forth in Chinese.

They were probably saying, "crazy Americans" or something similar. When we arrived at the ship, we enjoyed a good laugh with them, brought them aboard and gave them coffee and cake, paid them, and called the race a draw!

CHAPTER TWENTY-SEVEN

REACTIVATING VESSELS

Several years ago, U.S. Lines had been requested by our government to break out and operate a group of ships from the Marad Layup Fleet in Suisan Bay, California. These ships had been laid up for about five years and had previously been owned and operated by States Lines, a company which went into bankruptcy as did so many others after World War II. Some of these ships had been properly laid up, their holds cleaned, deck gear lubricated, machinery drained, etc., but others had just been towed from a lay berth in San Francisco to the layup fleet and tied up to another ship without any layup preparations whatsoever.

Whenever ships are reactivated from these reserve fleets after having been idle for a long period of time, a myriad of troubles can be anticipated. Gaskets dry out, diaphragms become brittle in the automated machinery, electronic circuitry becomes damp, electrical shorts and grounds are abundant, and valve packing becomes so dry that when boilers are fired up, the engine room resembles a steam room with all the escaping vapors and heat!

Breaking out these ships was an enormous task. All their certificates were out of date so every piece of equipment had to be tested as though we were taking delivery of a new ship. The company sent Tony Wong, a U.S. Lines port engineer from New York, to set up an office in Bethlehem Steel's shipyard in San Francisco.

After the first week, he received a phone call from management in New York that several U.S. Lines officials were due in San Francisco the following Monday morning to meet with various officials in the United States Maritime Administration, the United States Coast Guard, American Bureau of Shipping, and the shipyard to expedite the breakout and to sign contracts relative to the work to be done.

When they arrived that Monday morning, they anticipated a hectic day of travel from one office to another by taxi for their appointments, so they were pleasantly surprised to learn that Tony had called everyone with whom they had appointments to meet at an exclusive Chinese restaurant in Chinatown at 11:00 A.M. His planning saved them a great deal of time because they wanted to return to New York that evening.

Up to this point, none of the U.S. Lines people really knew Tony, and some had expressed reservations about his supervising such a mammoth job. When they witnessed his organizational ability, they felt the project was in good hands. Well, almost!

About 10:30 that morning, some of the company people began to disappear and Tony became concerned. At 10:45 a stretch limousine, which he had ordered to transport the officials to the restaurant, appeared in the yard to pick them up but there were none around. They didn't know about the limo, and assumed they would have to get to the restaurant on their own, so they took taxis.

After determining that none of them remained, Tony rode the limo alone and arrived at the restaurant only to find all the company officials waiting at the curb for him! Their immediate thought, "This is the guy who is to run our breakout office at minimum cost, and he rides limousines!"

Tony blushed when he saw them and spent the next two hours trying to explain that the limo had been ordered for them, and would be waiting to take them to the airport after their meeting and a nice lunch. They managed to take care of all their business at lunch and welcomed the ride to the airport.

Subsequently, they were to learn that he was certainly the right man for heading up the office. He did a magnificent job in keeping costs to a minimum and getting the ships out on schedule.

After Tony had established the office in the shipyard, the company sent me and a few others to assist him. The company was anxious to put these ships in service as soon as possible so as to commence their charters. While all of the ships were tested and inspected to satisfy all regulatory bodies and had their certificates updated, some were pushed out before they were really ready for sea.

One such ship, which I will not identify, was assured a charter, but only when it was made available at an East Coast port. In other words, it would have to deadhead around from the West Coast to the East Coast without any cargo, and at U.S. Lines' expense. The company immediately called on our freight department to locate a one-time load for it to help defray the cost of the deadheading. They were successful in finding a cargo in San Diego, but it had to be picked up by a certain date.

This put us in a real bind because, although the ship was nearly ready as far as its inspections and surveys were concerned, it was by no means ready for sea! Instead of a sea trial, outside San Francisco Bay, where its engines and boilers could be revved up to full speed and all systems tested, it merely made a token trial at slow speed within San Francisco harbor and was declared ready. Tony and I protested, but our complaints fell on deaf ears, especially because revenue was involved. Even though we complained that there were many unknowns in the engine room, we were told to get it out!

In view of these anticipated problems, I rode the ship as an observer and as an extra hand in the event of any problems. After departing San Francisco, the captain sent an arrival message to San Diego that our arrival at the pier there would be 0800 hours the following morning.

Almost at once, our problems began in the engine room. The automation for controlling the boiler water level failed, necessitating controlling it by hand, almost a full-time job for one man. Next, the automation for the main console, the heart of any automated ship, tripped out for some unknown reason and could not be reset, thus all the remaining machinery had to be on hand control. All these problems occurred on a ship which was strange to all of us and with a reduced crew. Reduced by permission of the United States Coast Guard because it was automated!

Somehow we managed to keep the plant in operation in spite of these problems, but about 11:00 P.M. that evening our luck ran out. The chief engineer informed me we were making water in the engine room at a rapid rate and he couldn't find the cause. I rushed to the lower level with him but could not find any reason for taking on the water either, but the depth on the tanktops was about eight inches and was a mixture of fuel and water!

Whatever was leaking was below the water level on the tank tops, so our only alternative was to pump the bilges to find it. Because we were only ten miles off shore, we were not allowed to pump the oily water overboard, but would be permitted to pump it into a ship's tank, designated as a slop oil tank. Our only problem now was that the tank was already full of dirty oil! It had been filled during our yard stay and never emptied because we were told to pump it at sea when we were beyond the 100 mile limit. However we were not going out that far traveling from San Francisco to San Diego.

The ship, with no cargo and designed without bilge keels, was rolling severely even in a small sea, and with each roll loosened up more oil from the tanktops, making the mix even dirtier! Now, the water level had increased to the point where it was lapping at the boiler casings and in a short while would be entering the fireboxes. If this happened, we could anticipate a furnace explosion, a dead ship, and possible casualties.

I rushed to the bridge to explain our desperate situation to the captain, and asked him to change course from south to west to enable us to get as far off the coast as possible before we pumped the bilges overboard.

To this day I still find it hard to believe the dialogue that followed: "I can't change course, I've already sent my ETA to San Diego for 0800 hours."

"But this is an emergency, don't you realize that. If we don't find the source of the leak, we'll soon be dead in the water and we won't be anywhere at 0800!"

"Come on, I got faith in you guys down below, you'll figure something out. I'm not changing course, we're gonna be there at 0800 hours come hell or high water!"

Disgusted and angry at this morbid sense of humor, I left the bridge, telling the captain I couldn't waste any more time arguing about it and rushed below. I told the chief of our conversation and told him I was aware that he was not to pump bilges so close to shore, but there was nothing stopping me and I proceeded to line up the system.

When all the necessary valves were opened I started two pumps. In a few minutes the water began to recede. When the level was low enough we could see a huge stream of salt water spewing from between two eight-inch flanges where a gasket had blown out.

We secured the pipeline and rerouted the salt water cooling water through another system, and our leak stopped. Our emergency was over! We could renew the gasket after our arrival at the pier in San Diego. I remained down below for the remainder of the night with the chief engineer and after docking in the morning, came up above to the officers' dining room to eat breakfast, now dirty and irritable.

The captain was already seated in his uniform, and with a cheery smile, said, "Well, we made it, right on time! I knew your guys down below would figure something out, I had all the faith in the world in you. What did you end up doing?"

"I pumped about 80 tons of oily bilge water overboard, Captain, and at the rate of tide last night, it should be reaching the shore somewhere along the West Coast right about now!"

"What, you pumped bilges that close to shore, we'll get hung!"

"Well, you had your chance to help us out in an emergency, but apparently you considered your ETA more important than the safety of the ship, so we had to go to those extremes!"

Luckily, we never heard anything from it, so I assume the oily water just dissipated before it reached the beaches.

CHAPTER TWENTY-EIGHT

CLAIMS TO FAME (?)

I think every man who went to sea during World War II has his favorite sea story when it comes to claiming something unusual. Such as "I sailed on the ship with the youngest captain or chief engineer, or third mate or third assistant engineer, or I was on the first American ship to enter the port of 'Anywhere,' after the Germans or Japanese fled!"

The curriculum at Massachusetts Maritime Academy, like other maritime schools during the war, was accelerated several times to speed up the graduation of licensed officers to make them available for sea duty. Because of this, it was possible for a young man who had graduated from high school at seventeen to complete the sixteen-month course of study at the academy and graduate while still in his eighteenth year. This happened to two of my classmates.

The minimum age for a U.S. Coast Guard license was nineteen and the minimum age to be sworn as an ensign in the Naval Reserve was also nineteen at the time. One of these two men opted to enter the Merchant Marine upon graduation, so the Coast Guard issued a certificate enabling him to ship out as an "acting third assistant engineer."

The other applied for active duty with the Navy and served in a midshipman status until his nineteenth birthday, at which time he was sworn as an ensign. The third assistant engineer received his license upon return from his first trip to sea.

Now, whenever I hear anyone say they were on the ship with the youngest third assistant engineer or ensign, I ask if their name was the name of either of these two men, and of course they aren't, so I tell them the above story. In my opinion no one could be any younger in those positions than to be named to them at the minimum required age which was their birthday!

Also, many individuals lay claim to being the youngest captain or chief engineer and, after the war as the years passed, more and more seemed to be claiming that distinction.

As far as laying claim to being on the first American ship to tie up in the port of "Anywhere" after the enemy fled, I was aboard the SS *Henry W. Longfellow*, a Liberty ship which was carrying supplies to Constanza, Rumania, in the Black Sea. The Germans had just fled the country and we were told we were to be the first American ship to enter the port. The Germans had been forced out by the Russians who were now occupying the country.

After tying up to the pier, immigration officials and other port officers boarded to examine our crew list and other ship documents to determine that there were no undesirables aboard. After a lengthy delay they cleared the ship to allow us shore liberty. It was several hundred yards from the ship to the gate which was located at the top of a long, narrow stairway. At the top of the stairway stood a lone Russian sentry.

Eight of us, dressed in uniform, left the ship as a group to have a look around the city. As we climbed the long stairway in single file, the sentry stepped across the gate opening to block our exit.

This could have been very embarrassing because each of us was carrying a carton of American cigarettes concealed on our person for bartering shore! The quick thinking armed guard officer who was leading the way shouted to us, "Just do as I say, fellows!"

As we approached the sentry, he shouted, "RIGHT HAND, SALUTE!"

All of us brought our right hands to our uniform cap and held that position until the last of us cleared the sentry. In the meantime, the sentry had jumped away from the gate and came to "PRESENT ARMS" with his rifle as we passed him.

When clear of the sentry, the armed guard officer shouted, "TWO!" and all of us brought our hands to our sides and continued walking, never looking back. The sentry then came to "SHOULDER ARMS," and continued his duties pacing back and forth!

We turned the corner, out of sight of the sentry, enjoyed a good laugh, and then headed for the nearest bar only a few hundred yards up the road. Just as soon as we entered the bar we knew we were not the first American ship to enter the port because there on the tables serving as table covers were the familiar blue United States Maritime Commission bed spreads which were aboard every Liberty ship!

Some enterprising Americans had obviously been there ahead of us, and probably worn them wrapped around their bodies under their clothing to get them ashore. But I'll bet they didn't get by that sentry as cleverly as we did!

I have often thought it could have been my claim to be able to boast that I had been on the first American ship to enter a port after the enemy had fled, but it wasn't meant to be. Still it's a good one to use sometimes to counter some of those other sea stories.

While in Constanza, I purchased a 25-mm automatic hand gun from a Russian soldier in a bar. He had two of them, identical but both in poor condition, so we stripped each making one reasonably good one. I gave him $5.00 for the gun and holster and brought them back to the ship. I never checked them for fear I would be seen with them on board so they lay in my drawer until we reached our first American port of Philadelphia. We were scheduled to be in for a long weekend so I decided to go home and bring the gun with me.

I hadn't declared the gun on my customs manifest because it was illegal, so this meant I had to smuggle it ashore! I showered, dressed in my uniform, packed my suitcase, and strapped the holster and gun tightly to my upper thigh beneath my trousers.

The gate was about three hundred yards from the ship's gangway and by the time I reached there, my leg was numb due to the circulation being cut off by the tight strap!

A customs guard stepped out from the shadows and asked to inspect my suitcase which contained two cartons of undeclared cigarettes from the ship's slop chest. I told him the bag contained the cigarettes and opened it for his inspection. He didn't get angry and didn't wish to give me a hard time over them, maybe because I was in uniform and it was wartime. He told me I wasn't permitted to take them ashore if they were not on my customs manifest. He also told me to take them back to the ship and leave them in my room and nothing would be said.

I thanked him, closed my suitcase, and started back to the ship when he said, "Leave that heavy suitcase here, son, I'll watch it for you. I saw you limping as you walked toward the gate. Just take out the cigarettes and carry them back with you."

That heavy suitcase was my excuse for limping, now I had to walk that long distance without a limp and with no feeling in my leg! After a superhuman effort I reached the ship, rushed to my room, removed the holster and discovered my leg was white! I slapped it several times to restore the circulation and sat down in a cold sweat. After a few moments, it came back to life, but not wanting to subject that same leg to torture again, I strapped the holster to the other thigh, left the ship and headed for the gate.

When I arrived I picked up the suitcase, thanked the customs officer again for the break he gave me. He could have reported it and I could have been fined, perhaps searched and then be in real trouble!

I hailed a cab outside the gate and told the driver, "Penn Station." I had hoped to be able to unstrap the holster while in the backseat of the cab without the cabby seeing me and put the gun in my pocket. Just as I reached down through the waist of my trousers to unfasten the buckle, the cab came to screeching halt.

I looked up and saw another passenger boarding! The driver explained he was permitted to carry multiple fares because of the gasoline shortage, as long as the new passenger was heading in the same direction. By now, I thought my leg was ready to fall off and we still had fifteen minutes to Penn Station!

I didn't dare attempt to remove the gun with other fare sitting beside me. I had considered explaining it to them but decided against it after having visions of them hailing a cop, jail, fine, and many other unpleasant thoughts, so I said nothing.

After what seemed an eternity, we reached Penn Station. I paid the driver and headed for the men's room on one live leg and one dead one! All the toilets were pay toilets and I didn't have a nickel among all my change. Just then a man left one of the stalls and held the door for me. Maybe my luck was changing finally.

I entered, closed the door, and in one quick motion, removed my trousers and had the holster unbuckled. I sat down on the john to catch my breath, relax, and try to restore life to my immobile leg. After a while I tried standing on it and nearly fell down, so I began to shake the leg to exercise it.

Afterward I wondered what anyone in the men's room might have been thinking had they looked under the short sides of the cubicle and seen my actions from the knees down!

I boarded the train and finally arrived home several hours later. The following morning I examined the gun closely and decided it was in such poor condition, I wouldn't attempt to fire it. The interior of the barrel was badly pitted, the safety worn, and the clip was bent in several places so it wouldn't feed the shells smoothly. I eventually gave it to a friend who was an amateur gunsmith.

CHAPTER TWENTY-NINE

SEAMEN'S CLUBS

One of the most popular places for Merchant Mariners to spend idle moments in a foreign port is the seamen's club. Many are sponsored by religious denominations and are a haven for crews of ships of all nations. They are places where one can mail a letter, call home, enjoy a healthy meal at a reasonable cost, purchase souvenirs, or just lounge about in a home away from home.

The seamen's club in Rotterdam usually sent a priest to the ships to invite the crew and officers to enjoy an evening there or to assist them in any way possible. One boarded the *American Jurist* one time and was talking with a group of men gathered in the second assistant's room. The captain, James Knowlton, happened by and in his flamboyant manner exclaimed, "Aha, a sky pilot!"

"Hello, Captain, I'm Father Jones here to invite everyone to our club this evening."

"Good, Father, when you're finished here, come up to my room and I'll buy you a beer."

After the captain left, I told the priest to be prepared for a shock when he arrived in the captain's office because the bulkheads were lined with nude pastels done by him in his spare time.

Later when he was leaving the ship, the priest stopped by my office to say good-bye, so I asked how he made out in his room. He laughed and said, "Everything went OK."

In a few minutes the captain came to my office to tell me about their visit. "He's a very smart young man that priest was. He knows more about anatomy than most people except medics, I think. Why, he showed me in several drawings where the shadow of a muscle or bone would mislead you to think the arm or leg was out of proportion to the rest of the girl's torso. I even showed him the photographs which I copied the pictures from and he pointed out where I hadn't shaded the area properly or drawn certain parts in proportion which made them look wrong. He was a bright young man!"

I smiled in agreement.

Another organization which has centers throughout the world is the United Seamen's Service. During the early months of World War II German submarines were picking off American tankers seemingly at will just off the east coast of the United States.

One crew member aboard one of these torpedoed ships was the movie actor, Sterling Hayden, who spent several days in an open boat in the Caribbean before being rescued and brought to a Caribbean port. While there he attempted to obtain help from the Red Cross and a USO center, but was denied any assistance because he was a Merchant Seaman. After being repatriated to the States, he told his wife, Madeline Carrol, a movie star who had been traveling extensively about the United States to promote the sales of war bonds, about his treatment as a Merchant Seaman.

She became so upset at hearing this that she contacted Admiral Emory S. Land, chairman of the U.S. Maritime Commission, and he in turn told President Roosevelt about the lack of facilities for seamen. Roosevelt enlisted the aid of a friend, prominent financier Bernard Baruch, who immediately donated $100,000 of his personal fortune to set up some facilities for Merchant Seamen throughout the war zones.

This was the beginning of the United Seamen's Service, which today has centers in Guam, Yokohama, Okinawa, Casablanca, Naples, Diego Garcia, Pusan, Bremerhaven, and Manila. Ironically, most USO's are a thing of the past, as are the Red Cross centers, so the United Seamen's' Service centers welcome GIs to their facilities, as well as Merchant Seamen from all countries.

On the tiny atoll of Diego Garcia in the Indian Ocean, the club is the most popular watering hole on the island and a mainstay for the crews of both merchant ships and U.S. Navy ships stationed there. Merchant Seamen are welcome in the officers' club and enlisted men's club on the island as well.

There are also many other clubs for Merchant Seamen throughout the world, such as the Seamen's' Church Institute and Stella Maris, both of which do an excellent job assisting the seamen.

In 1993 the USO club closed its facility on Guam for lack of funds, but the government asked the United States Service to take over the club and operate it as a USS. This has worked out well for everyone because in a few months the USS would have been forced to vacate their quarters because of waterfront reconstruction in the port.

CHAPTER THIRTY

A SWIMMING LESSON

The *American Jurist* was ready to leave Rotterdam for Amsterdam, a short voyage of less than one day, when a crew check showed the radio operator to be the only man missing at the time. The captain wouldn't wait for him because the trip was in inland waters and longshoremen were waiting for us at the next port.

The deck crew was fore and aft and had just let the last of our mooring lines go. The vessel was free of the pier and under control of the tugs when a taxi drove up alongside the ship and came to a screeching halt. The rear door opened and out stumbled the radio operator. The ship's gangway had been raised and stowed, so he stood there trying to find another way to board.

He spotted an AB on deck and shouted to him to throw a line to him. The AB secured one end of a rope, about thirty feet long, to a deck stanchion and threw the other end toward him where it landed on the pier.

Sparks grabbed it and swung off the pier into space until he landed against the side of the hull, about five feet away! By now other members of the deck gang had seen him and began helping the AB heave in the line, while the bitter end of the line dropped off the pier into the water beneath Sparks.

He wasn't the athletic type to be able to climb up the rope hand-over-hand, so he just hung on and waited to be pulled up the fifteen feet to the deck. Soon, however, his grip on the rope began to loosen and he found the rope slowly moving through his hands!

Meanwhile the deck crew was heaving away, reeling in fathom after fathom of rope, but Sparks was staying at the same level on the hull. In a moment he ran out of dry rope and, when the wet section came to his hands, it was like trying to hang onto a slippery eel. Then he ran out of rope!

Sparks landed feet first in the water, but in the meantime the captain's attention had been called to the fiasco, and his first thought was to have the tugs hold the ship steady to keep it from slipping in toward the pier where Sparks could have been crushed.

The chief mate lowered the gangway into the water and Sparks swam toward it and climbed aboard like a wet rat. The old man called to him with a megaphone to come to the bridge right away, where he told him to pack his bags when we return to New York.

Sparks went to his room, removed his wet suit, wrung it out by twisting the jacket and trousers, and then hung it in the upper engine room to dry.

Three weeks later at payoff, he came in to see me to say good-bye, and was wearing the suit. The trouser legs and jacket arms were in a permanent twist, the result of wringing it out and drying it in the engine room heat!

I asked him if he was going to say good-bye to the captain and he said, "I hope I've seen the last of him. A guy can't even get a load on once in a while without getting fired!"

CHAPTER THIRTY-ONE

CALENDAR CRAZE

Immediately after the war, U.S. Lines began a massive publicity campaign to announce its new peacetime trade routes and passenger services and to inform the world that the "new" U.S. Lines was ready to resume its role in world shipping. To start this campaign, it had calendars printed showing our trade routes; the following year showed our cargo ships, and then our passenger ships. Soon it became a popular calendar looked forward to by many because it featured all twelve months on one large newspaper-sized page. These were printed in the United States annually and thousands were distributed all over the country.

A few months after the first of our Lancer Class container ships was delivered, the company made preparations for an aerial photo to be taken from a helicopter as one of them entered New York harbor. This was to be used for the calendar the following year so everything had to be just right.

All preparations were completed, the helicopter was aloft, the ship nicely painted, the sun was shining brightly, and the ship proceeded slowly by the Battery with Number One Broadway in the background.

A perfect picture. Until some company officials, watching the scene from the windows at One Broadway, discovered several of the containers on deck on each side were not U.S. Lines containers. But even more painful, they belonged to Sealand, our biggest competitor! The entire program was called off and a circular letter issued to all vessels stating that in the future they shall see that all exposed containers on deck are U.S. Lines. A picture was taken but not used, and after careful examination, the picture also revealed that one container on deck had the letters emblazoned on its side, U.S. LINEN! Apparently, someone in our container repair group had glued the "N" decal instead of an "S" on the side of a new aluminum panel after repairs.

After our new management took over, someone with a cost-cutting mind thought he could find a way to have the calendars produced in Taiwan much cheaper than in the United States so they contracted for several thousand to be produced there. When they were delivered they looked exactly like the ones previously produced in this country except for one glaring mistake—all the holidays were printed in red as before but they were Chinese holidays celebrated in Taiwan!

The following year the company changed the format for their calendars. They designed it to be in four panels with each one hanging from the one above by a spiral plastic binding. The top would contain a picture, the next one below would be the past month, then the current month, and the bottom panel would be the following month.

When this batch of thousands was delivered, many of them were found to have the two center panels upside down throughout the entire year! We made several attempts to find out who was responsible but no one in management would tell us. Someone up there knew!

CHAPTER THIRTY-TWO

SMOKING STACKS

Many years ago before the days of refined fuels most steamships burned coal in their boilers. A smoking stack was almost a necessity in every picture of a ship at sea, otherwise the ship would have the appearance of not being underway.

A plume of smoke emitting from the stack today signifies a problem in combustion in the boilers or in the engine in the case of diesel engine propulsion. This is a sign of inefficient operation, as well as a potential fine if the vessel is entering or leaving port or tied up to a pier.

A large hotel chain erected a new hotel on Twelfth Avenue in New York several years ago to accommodate passengers who might have arrived a day or so early to board a passenger ship. The hotel was located directly across from Pier 86 where our passenger ships tied up, so we were constantly receiving complaints in the office from the hotel about our ships' stacks smoking during the night and the smoke blowing into the open windows of the hotel, especially when the wind was blowing from the west.

We would always assure the hotel we would deal with it, but didn't dare tell them the cause of the smoke was the engineers blowing the soot from the boiler tubes at night!

I was on board one of our older ships at Pier 62 one Monday morning talking to the chief engineer about his repairs when a man entered his office and asked for the chief.

"Good morning, gentlemen, I am a smoke inspector from the City of New York Smoke Pollution Board. I was just driving my boss into work this morning, about a half hour ago on the West Side Highway, and as we drove by your ship, we found it to be smoking badly. He told me to come back here and speak to you about it after I dropped him off at the office, so here I am. I'm a marine engineer like you fellows and I have a first assistant engineer's license," he said, removing it from his pocket and showing it to us.

"I know what you're up against down below early in the morning, changing burner tips, changing the watch, cutting in boilers, so I wouldn't be here except I have to follow the boss' orders !" he continued.

He went on, "I'm in the same union as you guys, the MEBA. I even do night engineer work out of the union hall when I finish my day's work for the city!"

I spoke up at that point, "If you're the night engineer on a ship and the chief engineer instructs you to blow tubes when it gets dark, where is your loyalty? To your day job as a smoke pollution inspector, or to your responsibility as a ship's engineer to operate the boilers efficiently and obey an order from the chief?"

"That came up the other night on a Farrell Line ship. I was told to blow tubes by the chief, so about midnight I went up on the main deck and found the wind blowing over toward New Jersey, so I blew tubes!"

He had an answer for everything. He then sat at the chief's desk and wrote out a citation, still apologizing!

That ship sailed in a couple of days and another of the same class docked at the same pier the following Monday. Guess who came aboard just after eight o'clock?

"Good morning, gentlemen, I'm a smoke pollution inspector for the City of New York, and I was just driving my boss into work this morning on the West Side Highway, etc."

"That's the same story you told me last Monday aboard another of our U.S. Lines ships," I said.

Recognizing me, he blushed slightly and then realized I had heard this same story a week earlier, but still he issued the citation.

The company kept a smoke file in the office, so our procedure was to accept the citation, compose a letter using three or four of the excuses from the file, and mail it to the board. Most of the time we were able to talk our way out of any fines, but only in New York!

San Francisco was one of the first cities in the country to establish and enforce smoke pollution laws, and the city's clear atmosphere shows their efforts have paid off.

I was attending one of our ships in Todd Shipyard in Alameda, across the bay from San Francisco several years ago. While there, Captain Bill Smith, U.S. Lines port captain, purchasing agent, personnel director, and whatever other hat he had to wear to keep the operations office running smoothly, asked me to accompany him to a hearing before the Smoke Violation Board in San Francisco. One of our ships had been cited for smoking while in Concord at the ammunition pier.

We entered the hearing room, introduced ourselves, and found we were facing six men seated at a table. Bill knew two of them from previous hearings, and in his opening remarks explained to all present that I was a U.S. Lines port engineer who had just arrived from our home office in New York. He didn't want to tell a fib, but he had hoped to impress on them that I had made the trip to the coast just for the hearing. His thinking was that they would realize that U.S. Lines takes smoke pollution seriously, regardless of where it occurs.

One of the men explained to me that he was a marine engineer and held a third's license, so if I felt inclined, I could use technical terms in my testimony and he would understand. I got the impression that this guy was on my side already.

Before we started the hearing, I asked if I could say a few words. I was told I could, this hearing was informal. I began, "Gentlemen, I would like to compliment you for the work you are doing here in San Francisco. I just left Newark Airport which was literally under a thick pall of smoke hanging over the entire metropolitan area of New York and New Jersey, as well as a pungent smell of chemicals. A few minutes after take-off, the interior of the plane suddenly brightened. I thought the stewardess had turned on some additional cabin lights, but I discovered that we had broken through the cloud cover and were in bright sunlight. It remained that way all the way across the country, even after landing here in your city. What a pleasure to look up into the sky and see fluffy cumulus clouds overhead instead of a blanket of smog. So, whatever you gentlemen are doing out here to keep the atmosphere clean, it's sure working!"

I then went on to explain that our ship at Concord, like all others at the ammunition depot, must keep both boilers steaming on the line to be ready to evacuate the piers in an emergency, such as a fire, explosion, etc. This is not our company requirement, but that of the U.S. Navy, who is the charterer of the vessel.

Under these conditions with two boilers steaming and a minimum of machinery in operation, it is similar to an automobile with its engine revving up to full power with the parking brake on. It is very difficult to keep the stack clear under these conditions at such a high steaming rate and no machinery in operation to consume the steam!

I felt pretty good after that dissertation and sat back proudly. They asked a few questions which I felt I fielded quite well, including a few from my engineer "buddy," and they then asked Bill and me to kindly leave the room for a few minutes.

They called us in after a short while and said, "Captain Smith, Mr. Murphy, we appreciate your coming here today to answer our questions, and particularly you, Mr. Murphy, to come all the way from New York. We listened to your explanation about the difficulties in keeping the stack clear in order to satisfy the federal government's requirement to be in a state of readiness, but federal law does not govern our smoking regulations. These are handled on a local level, so we have decided that a violation has indeed occurred, and the minimum fine of five hundred dollars is hereby imposed!"

"And Mr. Murphy, thank-you for all the kind comments you made about our clean city, we're trying!"

All Bill could say was, "We tried, too!"

One of our chief engineers, Arthur O'Connor, nearly got into a fistfight with the stationary engineer of a nearby bakery over the bakery's smokestack. When the smoke inspector boarded Arthur's ship at Concord, California, to cite him for smoking, Arthur went out on deck to view his stack and spotted the cookie plant emitting white smoke from its stack and challenged the smoke inspector to write it up.

The inspector insisted the white smoke was only steam, so he and Arthur drove over to the bakery about two miles away and interviewed the watch engineer and determined it was indeed white smoke and he was cited.

The watch engineer threatened to punch Arthur in the nose for calling it to the inspector's attention! Arthur apologized to him, telling him he fully expected the inspector to drop any charges against his ship after discussing the smoking problem with the cookie engineer who was a local.

CHAPTER THIRTY-THREE

GOOD DUTY

In November 1971, a longshore strike along the East Coast of the United States shut down all cargo activity so U.S. Lines elected to leave one ship in Europe ready to receive westbound cargo for New York and other ports as soon as the strike broke. This seemed like a good plan because we would be there to load and deliver late Christmas cargo to our customers ahead of our competition.

The ship which fit into the schedule was the SS *American Accord*, a former Mariner-type vessel converted to a container ship. Normally, all ships in Europe would proceed homeward loaded with cargo hoping the strike would end by the time they arrived.

Many times though, they would arrive and be laid up to await the end of the strike so this was worth a try. Dick Bower, superintendent engineer, sent me to Ireland to await the ship's arrival in a shipyard in Cobh. Upon its arrival the plant was secured, shore power plugged in, and the crew paid off, bussed to Shannon Airport, and flown home.

I was to remain along with Fred Collison, the master, to husband the ship, pumping bilges as necessary and keeping the refrigeration in operation to preserve the ship's food. Fred's duties were to check on the mooring lines during the rise and fall of tides and to sound the cargo holds to check for any accumulation of water there.

It was "strenuous" duty for the two of us. The ship's slop chest remained on board, sealed by the Irish customs. At periodic intervals they would visit the ship, purportedly to examine the seals on the door to the slop chest, but they soon learned we were good for a little nip occasionally, so their visits became more and more frequent.

Occasionally they would settle for a cup of coffee, but that was only if they had other places to go that day! They told us the reason for their visits was not that they distrusted us, but that the cigarettes and tobacco in the slop chest were valuable to certain political factions in Ireland and they feared a raid on the ship to steal the tobacco products and sell them to finance their cause against the British. Fred and I thought, "If this was the case, why didn't they put a guard aboard?"

After a couple of weeks, a reporter and photographer visited the ship to interview us and then wrote a story for a Cork newspaper. It was an interesting article about two Yanks "stranded" in a foreign country due to a strike in the States. "Stranded" was not exactly the proper word to use in their story because we were enjoying every minute of it, but we didn't want New York to know this!

Each week we would enter the refrigerator boxes to check on the vegetables and fruits. We would find some of them beginning to spoil and would discard them; others such as the lettuce were starting to turn brown, so we would spend a few minutes culling them. We realized that much of the food would soon be spoiled, so we asked the owner of the only grocery store in Cobh if he would be interested in buying it. The money would be held by our agent and used to restock the ship when it was reactivated. After examining the food he agreed to purchase it, so we called New York to get their approval. They were all for it so we set it up for the following Monday. In the meantime, our custom friends came aboard for their daily libation and we told them of our plan. They told us it was a good plan, but of course, we should know we would have to pay duty on it! Another call to New York.

"We are not paying duty on old food to sell it; destroy it!" was the answer from New York. Fred and I recalled hearing about an orphanage nearby, so we asked New York about donating it to them and they said that would be all right if the customs allowed it without duty. Again we asked the customs and they said, "Sorry, but we have our rules."

This angered Fred and me, so we told them the Cork newspaper would like to hear about an American ship not being allowed to donate food to an orphanage without paying duty. We told them we already had two friends at the newspaper!

"Don't do anything yet, give us a chance to call Dublin on this," said their spokesman.

The next day they came aboard, all smiles, and told us we had a "green light" to proceed with the food to the orphanage, no duty to be paid!

At this point I had been over there for six weeks, and Dick Bower thought I must have been worn out or was becoming too Irish, so he sent Gene O'Rourke from our New York office to relieve me. Gene and Fred contacted the grocery store owner and he obligingly loaned them a van and driver and the groceries were loaded and delivered to the children the following day.

I enjoyed my six weeks in Ireland. After getting into a routine it was good duty, a shut-down ship on shore power, secure at a pier in a shipyard, what more could an engineer want? I would occasionally pump any residual water from a cargo hold bilge, check the refrigeration temperatures and compressor, and just take life easy. Fred would check the mooring lines periodically and sound the cargo holds for any water buildup so he wasn't doing too badly either.

I lived in the Commodore Hotel in beautiful downtown Cobh, a small village at the base of a mountain overlooking the harbor. Fred could have stayed here also, but he elected to stay aboard the ship, which was OK by me because then we had someone responsible on board in addition to the gangway watchman.

When I would return to the hotel each evening, I would drop into the hotel bar for a beer and soon got to know most of the patrons. I was somewhat reluctant to spend too much time there at first because I thought they would be hitting on me to buy drinks for them, but I soon learned the opposite was taking place.

Each time I attempted to order a beer, I would find one already in front of me, courtesy of a Paddy, or a Mike, or a Sean.

I then learned that when they found out I was a resident of the hotel, I became a bona fide traveler and this was an excuse for the bar to remain open beyond the usual closing time. Their closing laws were similar to England's whereby a bar may remain open after its usual closing time if a traveler was patronizing the establishment. The law dated back to earlier tavern days to accommodate stage-coach passengers and to rest the horses.

The hotel management liked this arrangement, of course, because the bar stayed open late every night as long as I stayed drinking!

One old man introduced himself as "Paddy" soon after I arrived there, but I discovered none of the patrons had much use for him. Paddy had emigrated with an uncle to Long Island, New York, when he was sixteen years old. He became a steam fitters apprentice and joined the union when he became a full-fledged fitter. He worked there for all those years, making a good union protected wage, earning Social Security benefits, and retired when he reached sixty-five.

He quickly returned to Ireland, where his steam fitters' pension and Social Security from the States allowed him to live almost like royalty. Every month after receiving the two checks, he would be in the bar waving them around while the Irishmen present did a slow burn. He would say, "I told all you fellows forty-eight years ago to come along with me to the States, that's where the money is. But NO, you would take your chances here!"

"Well, everybody have a drink on me, including you, Yank!" the old man said one night.

"No thanks, Paddy; you have one hell of a nerve carrying on like this in front of all these men. If you were any kind of a man, you would have remained in the States where you earned those pension and Social Security checks and spend it there. If you earned it there then it should stay there. If not, then don't come here every month flaunting your checks in front of these men. You're the last man on earth I would accept a drink from!"

When I finished this tirade, he walked out of the bar and I received a standing ovation from everyone in the place! And, needless to say, I never had to buy another beer!

CHAPTER THIRTY-FOUR

SAFETY

Safety is always foremost in the operation of any ship, not only for common sense, but because of the limited medical facilities available, particularly aboard a freighter. Normally when a purser/pharmacist, or marine physician's assistant is carried, he would be trained in an advanced first aid course at a marine hospital. But lately due to companies cutting operating costs, the position of purser has been eliminated, thus the only first aid available is from the ship's officers. In serious cases such as broken bones, radio contact is made for assistance and the instructions given until the victim can be treated by a doctor.

The company could not emphasize enough the importance of safety meetings held between department heads and the delegates from each department. Their purpose was to call attention to any known hazards, their correction, precautions to be taken, and general information delivered to the vessel from the company safety officer for promoting safety aboard ship.

Considerable attention was given to the safety meeting held just prior to the vessel entering a shipyard. Emphasis was placed on precautions to be taken by individuals who might be called upon to enter a boiler or a double bottom tank for examination.

One of the precautions when entering a tank was that a responsible individual be assigned to stand by the opening where a man entered the tank and to ensure that no one tried to close it while someone was inside.

One of our port engineers, Jim Gillen, a very conscientious individual, had to enter a double bottom tank one time accompanied by a wiper. He stationed the ship's third assistant engineer at the manhole opening with orders to stand by to prevent anyone from closing them in. The double bottom was eighty feet in length and four feet high with a manhole cover at each end.

It was compartmented like an egg crate with floors and frames every three feet. These small bulkheads each contained an access hole for climbing through from one compartment to the next, thus it was a chore to crawl through while examining the internals of the tank.

When they reached the midpoint of tank, they were startled to hear a rush of water entering and knew they had to evacuate the tank as soon as possible. The time had come to make a quick decision: continue on to the forward manhole opening or reverse themselves and head back the way they entered. They opted for the way they entered.

As they made their way, climbing and crawling, water was beginning to fill the tank. When they finally emerged, the water was nearly six inches deep. Jim climbed out, soaking wet, to find a shipyard worker with the manhole cover in his hands just about to place it over the opening where they had entered and bolt it down! Jim then checked the forward end of the tank and found that cover already bolted! He was lucky he chose to exit by the manhole he had entered.

Now livid, he took off looking for the third assistant whom he found in the ship's machine shop. He asked him why he had left his station by the tank access and he looked startled and said, "Oh my gosh, the first assistant gave me a job to do in the machine shop, and I completely forgot I was supposed to be standing by the manhole!"

Jim went to the first. The first said the man never told him he was standing by, so the first immediately fired him!

Many men who know they will be entering a tank carry a padlock with them and lock it through one of the manhole cover bolt holes before they enter the tank and keep the key with them. This prevents anyone from placing the cover in position to bolt down without unlocking the lock.

I recall reading many years ago a story about the ill-fated *Great Eastern*, a ship which suffered many casualties on board at various times in its career. When the vessel was finally scrapped, a body was found it one of the ship's double bottom tanks, a worker trapped there obviously during the ship's construction. Many believe this was the cause of her misfortunes.

CHAPTER THIRTY-FIVE

WOMEN ABOARD!

For many years women have been employed aboard passenger ships as nurses and nursery room attendants, as well as employees of concessionaires such as gift shop help, beauticians, gym attendants, etc. But it was only a few years ago that they came into their own as actual crew members dealing with the operation of the ship.

One of the first ships in U.S. Lines to employ women was the SS *American Aquarius*. The National Maritime Union dispatched a female member for the stewards' department while the ship was tied up at our terminal at Howland Hook, Staten Island. This was a milestone for not only the NMU, but for women as well. The union had "requested" that the chief cook give up his room with its separate bath facilities for another room which shared a head with an adjoining room occupied by a union brother.

Union officials were present as well as members of the press to record the event. One reporter asked the chief mate, who had previously served aboard our passenger ship, SS *United States,* to carry her bags up the gangway while the cameras rolled. He said, "Are you out of your mind. I never did it while I was on the *U.S.* for any crew member and I'm not about to do it now. Let her carry her own gear aboard!"

Union officials then had one of their own men assist her with the bags and the cameras recorded it for posterity.

Now that the ice had been broken more and more women began to appear on the crew lists, but mostly as members of the steward department. Soon, however, third mates and third assistant engineers began to graduate from the maritime academies and find their way onto the freighters. Most of the women officers were mates, but a few chose engineering.

This brings up an interesting point. When a young lady graduates from a maritime academy, she has passed an examination and received a license stating she is a third mate or third assistant engineer, both of which can be considered a "unisex" license. As she progresses by raising her license, her successive licenses are still unisex, i.e. first assistant engineer or chief mate. Even when she goes for the top license in the engine department it will read "chief engineer," still unisex.

On deck, however, the top license is master. This just happens to be a masculine term. Will the women's liberation movement be satisfied with that or will they go for the corresponding female term, (forgive me,) "Mistress?"

"This is to certify that Jane Doe having been duly examined and found competent by the undersigned is licensed to serve as MISTRESS of vessels of any oceans, etc."

It wasn't too long ago when they insisted on changing the title of "Master of Ceremonies" to "Mistress of Ceremonies," when a female acted as such.

Some female deck officers have gone on to gain pilotage for various bodies of water. I asked one veteran ship captain, now retired, what his reaction would be if a woman climbed aboard as his pilot to bring his ship into port.

His reply, "I'd probably pat her on the ass! Personally, I have never worked on a ship with a female officer aboard, but I have no objection to them. From reports I have heard they do a good job and are conscientious and reliable. Perhaps it's because they are pioneers in an industry which for years was dominated by men."

Crews have come to accept women as long as they perform their work, not only as the job requires, but as responsible people when it comes to the safety of the crew, ship and cargo, as could be required in fire fighting or abandon ship procedures.

CHAPTER THIRTY-SIX

ECONOMICS

One of the most frustrating things to a chief engineer was when he found it necessary to send a message to the office via the ship's radio while at sea. All messages by order of the master had to be cleared through him before the radio operator could transmit them. This was before single-side band radio communications where voice communication replaced Morse code transmissions.

The charge to the company for each word transmitted was thirty-five cents, paid to the radio and electronics company who had the contract for that ship to relay the messages from its shore station to the company. The thirty-five cents was pittance even in those days. But the masters were constantly under the gun to cut expenses and they assumed this was part of the overall expense of operating the ship, so they would want to review each message in an attempt to condense it. About the only time I found it necessary to contact the office was when I needed a spare part. This would expedite its delivery if the purchasing department was given as much lead time as possible to obtain it.

I would compose the message giving all nameplate data, sizes, quantity required, and any other information to assure the delivery of the correct part, and then submit the message to the master. He would then sit down, study it word by word, delete some, and literally chop it to pieces to the point where it made no sense! I would complain, but I would get the old story, "Yeah, but you don't have to face them when we get to New York like I do. You're spending too much on messages, Captain!"

The following day the ship would receive a reply to the message, "Chief Engr. send more information and details on parts required, Signed, Sup't. Engr."

Referring to my original write-up, I enclosed the necessary data in the next message and it went through without being "censored."

The total cost for all the messages far exceeded the original, and it was a perfect case of "I told you so," but I said nothing. After all, I had to live there.

The company with which the U.S. Lines had a contract to relay its messages from each ship put a catalogue aboard in the care of the radio operator for use when a crew member wanted to send greetings home. It contained a number of "canned" messages covering nearly every possible situation and holiday greeting. Some messages were quite lengthy and flowery while others were brief and to the point. Each message was indexed by a code number, thus when someone wanted to send greetings home from sea, he would merely have to select one from the book by number, add the address and give it to Sparks, and he would send it. The receiving station would type up the entire greeting and mail it to the recipient, all for a cost of only the address and the one index number!

I selected one for my wife, Priscilla, on our wedding anniversary one time. When I reached home a month later she told me what a beautiful message I had sent and that she never realized I was such a romantic. She also said she had never heard me express myself in such a loving way.

Not satisfied to leave well enough alone, I had to open my big mouth and tell her it was message #37 from the radio operator's *Choose Your Message* book and it only cost thirty-five cents plus the cost of the address!

CHAPTER THIRTY-SEVEN

HOLIDAYS

While everyone ashore looks forward to every holiday and spending the day celebrating with his family, members of the Merchant Marine, unless they are on vacation, spend their holidays with a different type of family—their shipboard family. Probably the one holiday missed by most is Christmas. Life must go on on Christmas Day, the watches must be maintained and the cooks have to cook, but at least there was always a Christmas spirit on board. Most ships had a Christmas tree set up in the officers' lounge and another in the crew's lounge. Some ships even had one flying from the foremast!

Prior to sailing on a voyage when we would spend Christmas at sea, the Seaman's Church Institute would deliver a number of packages aboard containing gifts to be distributed to all hands. These gifts were usually a woolen hat, gloves, or scarf knitted by some lovely ladies who were always anonymous to us. Several times we attempted to find their names and addresses so we could send a card from a foreign port to thank them, but we were never successful in locating them. The donors always remained nameless. In addition to the knitted goods were usually writing paper, candy, toothpaste and other assorted items useful to us which we might overlook buying for ourselves.

I spent seven Christmas holidays aboard the *American Jurist*, mostly because relief chiefs were not available during that time of year. Not that they didn't want to work. However there was a limited number available and the senior chiefs always got them.

I thought that as long as I had to make the Christmas trip, I would make it as enjoyable as possible. So before leaving New York, I would make several trips to the nearest five-and-dime where I bought forty-five Christmas stockings stuffed with candy and managed to bring them aboard unseen. On Christmas eve at sea, I would quietly fasten the stockings to the door of each room, one for each man in the room, including my own room.

When the men awoke on Christmas morning, they would find the stockings, but no one ever knew who the Santa Claus was! In 1954 on Christmas Eve while hanging the stockings, I got caught by a crew member who was returning to his room after playing cards in another man's room.

"So, you're the Santa Claus!" I tried to swear him to secrecy but the word got out and I was exposed.

"Yeah, and as long as I've been found out, I guess it's time to change ships," I said jokingly.

Everyone laughed, but in a couple of months the company transferred me to a C-2-type ship, a better job and higher pay, so I guess there really was a Santa Claus!

CHAPTER THIRTY-EIGHT

TOOL MONEY

The union contract for the ship's carpenter stated he should be entitled to "tool money" if he brought his own tools aboard. This was one of the biggest farces in any union contract because the only tools he would have to bring with him was a hammer and screwdriver and he qualified for the extra pay. Of course, many carpenters brought hammers, chisels, saws, and power tools with them and they were legitimately entitled to the tool money.

The point here being that there were other people on board who also brought their own tools and equipment for the purpose of doing their job but were not compensated. The ship's electrician would bring his own megohm meter, volt-ohm meter, maybe an oscilloscope, and many other expensive tools, but receive no extra pay. Others were the ship's cooks who often brought their own carving knives, cleavers, and sharpening stones and guarded them closely. It was not unusual to see the chef in the engine room borrowing a piece of emery cloth to shine his carbon steel knives.

And let us not forget the masters and mates who carried their own sextants and binoculars with them from ship to ship. The second mate was usually designated the navigation officer on most U.S. Lines ships. Although this was not cast in stone, it was usually the case, so his sextant was in use more than that of the master or mate.

Most of our masters and mates were considered "company men," that is, they stayed with one company for most of their career. This gave them a better chance for promotion within the fleet compared with someone who shipped out of the union hall.

Ordinarily, the master would surround himself with competent mates so that he could, as the sign in the rear seat of a New York taxi reads: "Sit Back, Relax, and Enjoy the Ride." Once he found a second mate he could trust, he would leave the navigation, such as laying out the course, taking morning and evening sights, etc. to the second mate. I know one captain who said, "Now that so and so is here as second mate, my sextant will get cobwebs on it." Another once kidded me about making a lamp out of his.

When it came to the chief mate, he was usually assigned to carry out the maintenance on deck as he saw fit. He seldom found use for his sextant, however in the event the second mate took ill, he was called upon to fill in for him. As for the master, he quite often confined himself to a triangular course from his room to the bridge and the dining room, thus his sextant saw little use.

Of course, this is an engineer speaking, so to be honest I must admit that the same conditions existed on many ships in the engineering department as well. Once a chief found a first assistant who was dependable, he would leave the routine operations of the department to him. This also applied to the second assistant whose duties usually consisted of blowing tubes each day, transferring fuel, and testing boiler water. This was all done while standing a watch, so he was also a key man in the operation of the machinery. I once heard a third assistant engineer say, "I have a good chief on my ship, he only comes into the engine room once a week and that's to hang up his laundry!"

CHAPTER THIRTY-NINE

SIMILAR, BUT DIFFERENT SHIPS

After the war, I was assigned to the SS *American Banker*, one of nineteen new C-2 ships delivered from a Wilmington, North Carolina, shipyard. It was painted in bright company colors, inside and out, in contrast to the drab gray of wartime. One minor problem, however, the ships could easily be confused when several were tied up at the same piers, as was the *American Banker.*

I carried my first of two suitcases to the licensed junior's room, a rather small room for two people I thought, but at least I was on a high-pressure ship. I noticed a man asleep in the lower of the bunk beds, so I kept quiet and left my suitcase there and went out to the pier to bring the other one aboard.

While carrying it along the pier I saw a watchman I knew and stopped to talk with him. He asked what ship I was headed for and I told him the *American Banker*. "Oh, that ship isn't on this pier, it's on Pier 61, the next one over," he said. I looked around the shed door and discovered I had put my suitcase aboard the wrong ship!

I asked him to keep his eye on my bag while I went aboard to remove the other one. As I entered the licensed junior's room and picked it up, the sleeping man awakened.

"Hey, who the hell are you? Are you trying to swipe my bag?" the man asked.

I didn't know him, so I quickly produced my assignment letter for the *Banker* and sheepishly explained to him I had boarded the wrong ship. He said it was OK, anyone could make a mistake like that, but I felt like a fool!

Several years later, however, a similar incident occurred in Liverpool between two U.S. Lines masters, one a rather stuffy individual and the other a happy-go-lucky guy.

One of these similar C-2's was tied up at the outer berth at our pier in Liverpool. The inner berth was reserved for another C-2 due to arrive later that day. Captain "Moon" Mullins of the earlier ship had gone ashore with one of the Englishmen from our local U.S. Lines office that day for dinner and a few drinks at a local pub.

Meanwhile, another U.S. Lines ship tied up at the inner berth just ahead of Moon's ship. This captain was not a drinking man and very sophisticated. He enjoyed going ashore to explore stately homes and estates which were open to the public by their owners in an effort to offset heavy taxes.

After assuring himself his ship was secure at the pier, he took off on one of his explorations. He stayed ashore for quite awhile and ate dinner ashore that night.

In the meantime, Moon and friend had returned to the pier feeling no pain, and decided they had better get some sleep. But they boarded the wrong ship! Moon turned in in the captain's bed and had his friend sleep on the settee in the captain's office.

A short while later the other captain came aboard, opened his office door, and found the man sleeping on his settee. He awakened him and realized it was the man from our local office, but then the man said, "Captain Mullins told me I could sleep here!"

"Captain Mullins, Moon Mullins?" the other captain asked.

"Yes, Captain."

"Where the hell is he?"

"In your bunk!"

"What! What the hell is he doing there?"

"It appears we came aboard the wrong ship, Captain." He went into his bedroom and awakened Moon and told him to get the hell off his ship and go sleep it off on his own ship! Moon suggested that this captain go on his ship to sleep instead of changing places so late at night, but he would have no part of it. Moon and friend had to get dressed and return to the proper ship.

The U.S. Lines man told about the incident in the local office the next morning. Someone there decided they had better call New York to inform the marine superintendent, Captain Topping, about it because they knew he had a sense of humor and would get a kick out of it, particularly since he knew both captains so well. They also suspected that the "injured" captain would send a report to the office in New York about it or report it when he returned.

As a matter of fact when he did return, he headed straight for the marine superintendent's office but the moment he entered he was greeted with, "Hello, Captain, that must have been one hell of a funny scene when you entered your room and found Moon in your bunk! I wish I was there to enjoy it!"

The captain, realizing he stood no chance, just grunted and shrugged it off!

CHAPTER FORTY

PETS

U.S. Lines had a policy regarding pets aboard its ships. It was a simple policy, none permitted! The reasons were understandable: each time a ship entered a port, the boarding officials would ask routinely if there were any pets aboard, and if so, it would be necessary to keep them confined, quarantine them, furnish proof of their inoculations, or have them destroyed.

In spite of the rules, occasionally one could find a cat or dog on a ship. The animal would sometimes chase a rat up the gangway and become lost on board or wander aboard looking for food. Pier-bred cats were not exactly the ideal house pet, either, growing sometimes to the size of a small fox and with a vicious temper from living an existence next to barbaric on the piers.

One good reason for not having a pet on board was the danger of it falling into an open hatch. At sea a crew member sitting on a hatch cover or standing on the deck opposite the animal might call to it to come for food and the animal would jump up onto the hatch cover to go to the crew member.

In port with the hatch open, a longshoreman could call the animal from one side of the hatch and it would jump, expecting to land on the hatch cover and fall to its death in the hold.

A cat wandered aboard the SS *Barnard Victory* in a European port and was quickly adopted as crew mascot. Upon the ship's arrival in New York, boarding officials asked the captain, George Irmler, if there were any pets on board and he told them a female cat had wandered aboard in Europe. The public health boarding officer said he would send a veterinarian aboard that afternoon to examine it, so please have it ready.

Later that day when the vet arrived on board, Captain Irmler called the chief mate, Bill McManus, to have someone find the cat and bring it to his office. Bill, not knowing where the cat might be, went onto the pier and told a longshoreman to pick up any cat from the pier and deliver it to the captain's office. "There's five dollars in it for the first cat delivered," he explained.

While they waited in the captain's office a knock came on his door. Bill opened it and accepted a snarling cat held by a longshoreman and slipped him a five dollar bill. While the vet attempted to examine the cat, he explained to the captain, "Incidentally, Captain, your cat is a male, not a female!" As he attempted to give the cat a shot, another knock came on the door. Bill opened it and there stood three more longshoremen each holding a cat with one saying, "Hey, Mate, is that offer still good—five bucks a cat?"

CHAPTER FORTY-ONE

SPECIAL PLACES

Most ships have special areas which are reserved for different ratings on the ship to assist the crew in performing their duties. For instance, the carpenter has a special area reserved to hold his sounding tape which he uses daily to sound cargo holds and ballast tanks. In the wheelhouse are wooden boxes mounted on the bulkheads to hold binoculars. One of these is usually reserved for the mate on watch and another reserved for the master's glasses.

No one ever uses another's binoculars, unless invited to view something through them because they are focused and adjusted to the owner's eyes. There is nothing more frustrating than for the master to pick up his glasses to view something and find them out of adjustment!

In the engine room the engineers also have their special areas. A locker for the second assistant might hold his sounding tape, extra boiler water testing chemicals, special tools for boiler work, etc. And the first assistant's locker might store valuable instruments, such as a tachometer, micrometers, gauge calibrating equipment, etc.

As chief engineer I didn't have a locker in the engine room, but I kept a wooden box in the log desk for my tobacco and corncob pipe. During long periods down below, such as transiting the Panama Canal or maneuvering up and down rivers, I would find it enjoyable to puff on my pipe, so I decided to leave it in the log desk instead of carrying it up and down from my room each time.

One evening I went below during maneuvering and decided to light up. I opened the box and found my corncob pipe painted silver and it weighed about a half pound. Someone had found it, "epoxied" it, wrapped it with string, painted it, and dolled it up with red and blue dots.

I noticed all the men around me snickering, when Gordon (Sam) Houston, third assistant, approached me and said, "Like the way I fixed your pipe, Chief?"

"What the hell did you do this for, you've ruined a perfectly good pipe!" I replied.

"I was reading the label on that new epoxy we just got aboard and it said 'ideal for repairing pipes of all kinds.' I noticed yours had a crack on the outside so I thought I'd do you a favor and fix it for you!" Sam said.

"Houston, you owe me a new pipe, you nitwit!" I bellowed.

On another occasion I filled my pipe from my tobacco can in the log desk and almost threw up when I lit it. I found some of my "friends" down below had been supplementing my tobacco by emptying the pencil sharpener into the can and mixing it up.

Later I gave up on the corncobs and purchased a new pipe in Antwerp. I had always heard the best way to break in a new pipe was to partially fill the bowl, smoke it down, refill it a little more the next time, smoke that, and gradually build up a cake in the bowl.

I thought this was a waste of time and a lot of work, so my engineering mind went to work. I cut a short section of rubber hose, fastened one end over the pipe mouthpiece, and attached the other end to a petcock on the main engine vacuum gauge. I filled the bowl to the top with tobacco, tamped it down, and lit it.

I slowly opened the gauge valve and let the vacuum begin to smoke the pipe for me. Apparently I opened the valve too much because the vacuum reached twenty-eight inches and sucked so much air through it so quickly that it built up a tremendous heat in the bowl and I dropped the pipe onto the floorplates. Still connected to the hose, it began to get hotter and hotter and then burst into flame!

When it burned itself out, I picked it up and found a big crack right through the bowl! I ended up throwing it away and buying another corncob in the slop chest. So much for that experiment!

CHAPTER FORTY-TWO

MILITARY AIRLIFT COMMAND

Diego Garcia is a small horseshoe-shaped atoll south of India in a group of islands known as Chagos Archipelago. It is the anchorage for several American military pre-positioned ships ready to leave on a moments notice to any area in the Middle East where trouble may flare up.

It was one of the areas that was used for the jumping-off point for ships engaged in the Operation Desert Storm in 1992. U.S. Lines has had a number of ships anchored there for many years under charter to the Military Sealift Command. The MSC charter called for a company official to visit the vessels periodically to discuss their operation and to be brought up to date by the military commanders on the island on any problem which might arise. Reed Clark who headed our MSC operations and I were selected to make the trip one year.

Since the atoll has no commercial airline service, access was only available by ship or aircraft of the Military Airlift Command. Reed and I were scheduled on a flight from the Norfolk Air Station to Madrid, Sicily, Nairobi, and finally Diego Garcia.

We left at 0930 in the morning aboard a C-130 cargo plane and had barely reached cruising altitude when the pilots reported that the "black box" was not functioning and it would be necessary to return to have it replaced. I learned the black box is an instrument which allows the plane to fly on auto-pilot. It was further explained that if our two pilots had to fly the plane manually to Madrid, they would be too exhausted to continue on another MAC flight for which they had been scheduled. I had visions that maybe these fellows up front could nap while on auto-pilot. No, I put that thought right out of my mind!

We returned to McGuire Air Force base in New Jersey, had the black box replaced, and took off once again. Three hours out over the Atlantic, an airman made his way through our compartment to check on the cargo and discovered a leaking oil drum. He reported it up front and shortly a sergeant came back to examine it. After he returned to the front a Lieutenant paid a visit to the leaker and I guessed he had enough rank to cause us to make a U-turn and return once again to McGuire!

After landing I called my boss, Tom Young, now at home eating dinner, and told him I was just reporting on our progress. He said, "Are you calling from Madrid?"

"No, Tom, I'm about twenty-five miles from your house and if I thought we'd be here long enough, I might join you for supper!"

We left once again, this time making it to Madrid without incident. After refueling, we left for Sicily and then Nairobi and finally, Diego Garcia.

After three days on Diego Garcia, consulting with the Military and the crews on our three ships, we flew aboard a C-5A Galaxy to Clark Air Force Base in the Philippines. This had to be the biggest plane I had ever seen. We climbed aboard a narrow vertical aluminum ladder into a huge empty compartment and then up another ladder to the upper level just as empty. There was no cargo aboard and a total of three passengers, Reed and I and a GI who was returning home after a death in his family.

These monstrous planes deliver all sorts of cargo to the atoll, as well as personnel, and nearly every flight out of there is a deadhead flight to either Singapore or Clark. Looking through the vastness of the compartment, I could envision a football field or a couple of basketball courts inside.

From Clark our company agent drove us to the commercial airport in Manila where we were booked on commercial flights to Tokyo, San Francisco, and finally New York. Around the world in eleven days.

Having flown on MAC flights before, I sort of knew my way around them. MAC planes do not taxi up to a loading ramp as planes do at a commercial facility. The aircraft is parked a long way from any terminal and the passengers are either bussed to it or "marched" in single file from the terminal to the side of the plane. In the case of a bus, you should always get a front-row seat, and if marching, work your way up to the front of the line by asking the airman in charge of the group some useless question as a reason to jump the line and become first! Once at the side of the aircraft, you become the first in line to board. Upon climbing that narrow aluminum ladder, the cargo compartment is in front of you and you will be directed to the seats in the after section of the compartment. The seats are secured into tracks running the length of the plane, and can be added to or removed to make room for cargo, which is also secured by lashings fastened to the tracks.

A small porthole is mounted in the body of the plane on each side just aft of the wing. These are the only "windows" in the entire plane except for those in the pilot's compartment, and they are used by the crew to periodically view the engines mounted on the wing.

Each time I boarded, I managed to sit in an outside seat next to one of these viewing ports. This was also the last row of seats in the plane, but was really the first because the seats faced aft. Aft of these portable seats the cargo was stowed. Thus there was plenty of leg room to stretch out in this row.

We were advised to dress warmly for the flight because heat in an uninsulated plane is almost non-existent. On one of the flights I made, we had to sit on canvas seats which ran longitudinally in the plane. The canvas was stretched over a pipe frame which ran along the "wall" of the compartment and seated five men. As a result whenever a man at one end changed position, the other four also changed, a situation not exactly suitable for snoozing. It was tolerable for maybe four hours, but certainly not eight which was our flight time. We learned later that this was a former carrier for paratroopers, thus the seats. As one wag said, "At least they only had to fly one way in these seats!"

To backtrack a bit, after hearing of my pending trip to Diego Garcia, I thought it would be nice if my wife made a trip to the West Coast to visit our kids there, so I booked her on an excursion round trip flight to San Francisco. It was scheduled to leave Newark the same day I left and she would return with me on the same flight from San Francisco. This was a long shot because we weren't sure of MAC flight reservations, how much priority we carried over others of the military, nor if our commercial legs of the trip would fit in our plans. But it was worth a try.

When I told her of the plans she jumped at the opportunity to head west. The travel agent used by U.S. Lines was very helpful in coordinating her ticket, but of course could not guarantee our coming home together. There was one problem with these plans—U.S. Lines had always provided first-class air travel to port engineers, per union contract, but I had booked Priscilla on a round trip excursion fare in coach! Without telling her, I inquired about the cost to have her come home first class, but immediately dismissed it when I learned it would cost about $200 more.

To break down my ticket to coach from San Francisco to Newark, so I could ride with her, would have also been extremely expensive and complicated. My ticket from Manila to Newark was non-negotiable anyway.

Our plans worked out well. Reed and I arrived in San Francisco two days before her scheduled departure so I had a chance to visit with the kids also. When we reached the airport and were waiting for the boarding announcement, I told her I wouldn't be riding with her because of the ticket arrangement and waited for her reply!

"WHAT?"

"Yeah, honey, it would have cost me $200 more to have you in first class," I said.

"Don't you think I'm worth $200?" she replied.

"Yeah, but I also know how frugal you are when it comes to wasting money," I said.

"So you can't spring once in your life?" she suggested.

I knew, or at least I thought I knew her well enough to know she was just kidding me, so I then told her, "They always board the first-class passengers first, so when they announce the boarding time, I'll have to leave you until they announce your row number for boarding back aft. Also, I'll be seated in first class with some rather dignified people, so I would appreciate it if, when you passed through our area, you didn't acknowledge me because of the possibility of being embarrassed. And one other thing, honey, don't buy any drinks back there because they charge a lot on the plane, and I will get all I want up here, and I'll sneak a couple back to you!"

As she stood there doing a slow burn, staring at me and struggling to think of a comeback, I slipped a new gold watch on her wrist! She was still standing there staring at the watch when I left her to board. I had purchased the watch in the duty-free store at the Tokyo Airport two days earlier.

She boarded about fifteen minutes later and by now I was comfortably settled in my seat sipping a Bloody Mary. When she saw me she stopped, leaned across the man seated next to me and gave me a kiss, then walked aft to her seat, never saying a word.

The man next to me asked, "Do you know her?"

"Never saw her before in my life!"

Being a port engineer involved much traveling to various world ports to survey groundings, collisions, power failures, fuel spills, as well as routine inspections and dry-dockings. For several years, the company used the Hyundai Shipyard in Korea for its dry-dockings, inspections and special survey work, and we were directed to use Korean Air Lines for all our flights. I had been a passenger on Korean Flight 007 many times leaving New York, stopping in Anchorage for fuel, and proceeding on to Seoul.

After that flight was shot down by the Soviets a few years ago, I have to thank the good Lord the company didn't have me or one of my co-workers booked on that trip.

CHAPTER FORTY-THREE

SS *AMERICAN LYNX*

A humorous incident occurred aboard the *American Lynx* one time which involved the captain, Peter Fay, the chief mate, Bill Schumacher, and the chief engineer, Frank Butler. The vessel left New York for Europe with two passengers aboard, two young ladies. One was the daughter of a company executive and the other her girl friend. They were going to Europe on a short sight-seeing trip and were riding at no cost because of the girl's father's position in the company.

There was little for them to do on board, the *American Lynx* was a container ship and carried no other passengers, so they entertained themselves by playing darts every afternoon in the officers' lounge.

The dartboard was mounted on a large square of plywood which was mounted to the bulkhead in the forward end of the lounge. Behind this bulkhead was a narrow passage way and beyond that the bulkhead against which the captain's bunk was mounted. Whenever the girls would throw a dart which missed the dartboard, it would strike the plywood with a loud resounding thud! This noise was amplified by the stiff fireproof bulkhead and sounded like a bass drum in the captain's room.

Captain Fay's usual routine was to take an afternoon nap after lunch each day; at least it had been until the two young ladies boarded! Now his nap was constantly interrupted by the repeated thuds, but he was reluctant to speak to the girls because of the father being a company executive.

The girls weren't very good at darts and missed the dartboard more than they hit it. Every time a dart struck the plywood, the point of the dart became a little more bent and the next time it struck the dartboard, the barb on the point would pull some of the paper loose from the board until the dartboard was in a shambles.

The girls left the ship in the first European port and had a short tour of Europe while the *Lynx* made its cargo ports and headed for home. As soon as they got off in Europe, Captain Fay directed the chief engineer and chief mate to get rid of "that damn dartboard and remove the plywood. There will be no more dartboards aboard the *Lynx* to interfere with my afternoon nap!"

When the girls finished their touring, they flew home and arrived in the States a few days ahead of the *Lynx*. When the ship arrived, waiting on the pier were the two young ladies, carrying a package. They boarded the ship and headed for the mate's room. They found the chief engineer sitting there and told the two of them they felt guilty about wrecking the officers' dartboard so they had purchased a new one for the ship.

Butler and Schumacker began laughing and almost at once said, "Well, that's nice, let's all go up above and you can present it to the captain. He'll be happy to receive it from you!"

When they made the presentation he was flustered and blushing, while Frank and Bill were behind him laughing hysterically! But he never let them install it!

CHAPTER FORTY-FOUR

UNITED STATES COAST GUARD INSPECTION POLICY

"As stated in the Merchant Marine Act of 1936, it is our national policy to foster the development and encourage the maintenance of a Merchant Marine composed of the best equipped, safest and most suitable types of vessels. In consonance with this policy, it is the aim of the Coast Guard to administer the vessel inspection laws and regulations in such a manner as to obtain safe, well equipped vessels that are suitable for their intended service. Since it is also the national policy to foster the development and operation of suitable vessels, the economic and other operational needs of the industry cannot be ignored in the application of safety standards. Thus in determining inspection requirements and procedures, inspection personnel shall keep in mind that the vessel inspection laws are intended to protect life and property and that many of them originated with a marine catastrophe; but inspection personnel shall also recognize and give due consideration to the following:

(a) that delays to vessels and failures to meet operational commitments due to inspection requirements are costly;

(b) that certain types of construction, equipment or repairs are more advantageous to the operator than others;

(c) that repairs can usually be accomplished more economically at a place and time chosen by the operator;

(d) that operating conditions, such as route, hours of operations, type of operation, and the overall safety of a vessel, may be considered in determining inspection requirements;

(e) that all efforts, competence and reputation of the operating personnel may be considered in determining the extent of required inspections, but should not substantially affect material requirements as to the condition of a vessel or its equipment;

(f) that vessels are subject to operational safety requirements of agencies other than the Coast Guard.

"A careful balance must be maintained between the needs of safety and practical operational needs. Arbitrary decisions or actions, which do not materially contribute to the aim of safety and which tend to discourage the construction or operation of vessels, are considered to be unreasonable. In the inspection of vessels, it is the intent of the commandant that inspection personnel use good judgment to provide sound and reasonable application of law and regulations, this judgment to be obtained by the adequate training and instruction of all personnel."

From U.S. Coast Guard Merchant Marine Safety Manual—CG 203, (Pages 143-144).

Port engineers and port captains have always maintained, with tongue in cheek, that if the Marine Safety Office of the United States Coast Guard was in existence during the year 1776, the course of history might have taken a different direction!

It was on December 25, 1776, when General George Washington made his historic crossing of the Delaware River. In doing so, his troops were able to surprise British-led German troops who were celebrating the holiday near Trenton.

But while doing this historic deed, he broke nearly every rule set by the Coast Guard for safe boat handling! He allowed men to stand up in the boat without life jackets, the boat had no lights during its nighttime run, the boat was overcrowded, there were insufficient oars aboard, and the boat had no name or registration number!

One of the complaints port engineers and port captains have had against the marine inspection officers was their lack of experience. Just after World War II, most of the inspectors were former marine engineers or mates and masters from the Merchant Marine and were understanding of some of the difficulties faced in maintaining a safe ship. They would interpret the rules and regulations in a practical manner, not only to keep the ship safe, but to keep it operating in an efficient manner by not delaying the sailing because of a minor infraction which could be taken care of at the next port.

Later on, when these men were phased out of the Coast Guard due to attrition, resignations, retirements, etc., a new breed of inspector appeared on the scene. When a young graduate from the Coast Guard academy or one of the maritime academies joined the Coast Guard, his first assignment was to an inspectors' school for approximately eight weeks training, and then he was assigned to a district Coast Guard inspection office. After a few inspections aboard merchant ships with another "experienced" inspector, he was on his own.

This young inspector was now in a position to tell captains, chief engineers, chief mates, and first assistant engineers, whose time working on their license probably totaled more years than the inspector's age, what they were doing wrong!

I have always believed that because the marine inspector is dealing with senior officers of a ship during a biennial inspection, midperiod inspection or a dry-docking survey, the Coast Guard should provide an inspector of "equal rank" and not junior officers or enlisted men. In any business ashore, a company vice president talks to another vice president, the general manager talks to another general manager, not to underlings in a company.

In the following pages I have highlighted several instances to illustrate reasons for the frustrations Merchant Marine officers feel toward our United States Coast Guard Marine Inspection Offices.

In one extreme case, I ran across an inspector during a dry-docking and biennial inspection in a Korean shipyard who threatened to delay the sailing of the ship because the required fish hooks in the lifeboat fishing kits were rusty! We had no spares aboard, so I told him I would purchase some ashore.

He told me that wouldn't do because they had to be Coast Guard approved and have the Coast Guard stamp on the package. In desperation I tried to explain that Korea was a country bounded on three sides by oceans and that fishing was their principal occupation. I told him that the fish hooks I purchased would more than likely be equal to or exceed the requirements of the Coast Guard.

He would have no part of it, but we soon solved our problem when a port engineer from another American ship found some spare approved fish hooks aboard his ship and gave them to us.

As I said this was an extreme case. I believe the inspector was peeved at us because we required his attendance aboard our ship for various inspections during a holiday weekend when he had been invited to a picnic with some young ladies he had met in a local bar the day before we arrived!

I was handling the SS *American Apollo*, one of our newer container ships of the Lancer Class, in my role as port engineer while the ship was undergoing its USCG Biennial Inspection. After completing the examination of the firesides and watersides of each boiler, I asked the inspector to return the following morning, at which time we would have steam up in both boilers, ready to set and seal the safety valves.

Instead of the same inspector returning, however, a new, much younger inspector appeared on board, telling me our assigned inspector had been dispatched to another job. The young man said he was experienced in safety valve testing so his boss told him to report to us.

I asked him if he had brought an inspector's gauge with him, and if so, did he wish to use it or rely on our ship's gauges. He replied, somewhat indignantly, "Oh no, none of that, I have a U.S. Coast Guard inspection gauge which you must use."

He removed a bright, shiny, chrome plated gauge from a velvet lined case and handed it to me, instructing me to handle it carefully because it was brand new. I examined it and told him we couldn't use it for this test because its range was only 0-800 pounds and the highest setting of our safety valves was 1050 pounds.

Without giving it a second thought, he said, "I don't care, you must use my gauge!" I advised him that the hand of the gauge would run off the scale at such a high pressure, therefore he would not have a true reading of the actual relieving pressure or the blowdown, both of which are required to be recorded in the Coast Guard records. I also advised him that it could permanently damage the gauge by distorting the Bourdon tube, as well as possibly run the internal gear beyond its limits and it might not restore itself to zero when the pressure is removed.

He still insisted on using it, so I mounted it to a special built-in fitting installed for that purpose and steam was brought up on the boiler. His next remark was, "I didn't realize these boilers carried so much pressure; wait until I tell my wife tonight that the Coast Guard had me test a thousand-pound boiler. Up to now, all I've been permitted to do was up to 600 pounds!"

Once again I thought, "This is another situation typical of what I've been through so many times before; an immature inspector without experience." We ran the pressure up to 1050 pounds and the safety valves relieved properly and reseated normally after the required blowdown. His gauge had gone beyond its limits and the hand had started around the dial again until it rested against the rear side of the zero pin!

I closed the valve to his gauge, removed it from the mounting, and examined it. Instead of its hand returning around the dial to come to rest at zero, it lingered at the 200 pound mark. I remarked that it could be permanently damaged.

He said, "I have to return this to my boss, I don't know how I m going to explain it!" In the meantime, we used our ship's gauges to determine the settings of the valves and he accepted them.

When he mentioned about having to tell his boss, I felt sorry for him so I took his gauge to the ship's machine shop, removed the mechanism from the case, reset the internal gear train so the hand rested at zero, and reassembled it. I instructed him to be sure it was recalibrated at his office before using it on another inspection. At least when he returned it to his boss, the boss would not suspect anything was wrong.

The young inspector thanked me. I said, "Don't forget this; if we ever meet again on another inspection, you owe me one!"

Mr. Alan Fife, an independent marine surveyor and ex-chief engineer, highly respected in the marine industry, was acting in behalf of an owner in the Hampton Roads area several years ago putting a ship through its Coast Guard biennial inspection.

When it was time to set the safety valves, one of the valves chattered loudly upon reaching its blowoff pressure instead of blowing cleanly. The inspector remarked, "I don't like the sound of that valve."

Alan replied, "Well, don't forget, Inspector, we are here to set them, not tune them!"

One of our frustrations with the Coast Guard marine inspection was the inequity between USCG vessel operation and commercial shipping operation.

A U.S. Lines Lancer Class container vessel was dry-docked in Newport News Shipyard undergoing a routine dry-dock survey and the Coast Guard hull inspector observed an "indent" in one of the steel plates of the hull. The indent was minor in nature in my opinion, and only set in about three inches for an area six feet square in the steel plate which was three quarters of an inch thick. The damaged area was several feet above the deep load line, and posed no problem as far as seaworthiness was concerned. I told him it probably happened from the ship striking a pier heavily while tying up, or perhaps a barge had struck us while tied up alongside while receiving cargo. In any case, the ship had no record of its occurrence.

He told me we would have to remove the damaged steel and install a new steel plate in the area. I questioned him on this, telling him we would probably have it faired or renewed at the next dry-docking in two years when the vessel would be undergoing its special survey dry-docking as required by the rules of the American Bureau of Shipping.

He insisted that we do the repair at this time, so I argued with him that the only reason it stood out was because the ship was comparatively new and this was the only indent in an otherwise smooth hull, but it really did not make for an unseaworthy ship. On older ships, hulls would be full of indents far worse than this from years of pier strikings, barges banging against them, etc. and something this size would be overlooked in favor of more serious dents.

A few hours after our discussion, a USCG Cutter tied up at the lay berth next to the dry dock. The starboard side of the Cutter had been stove in for a distance of about 20 percent of the length of the hull and to a depth of approximately five inches. One could see the outline of the frames behind the damage, and clearly they were affected by the damage. They were distorted and set in. In the area of the damage were also two portholes through which I could see the living quarters of the crew.

I assumed it had entered the yard to affect repairs but was told by one of their officers that they had come in for stores and were due to leave the next morning for patrol duty again!

The white hull paint and the block letters USCG had obviously been rubbed off in the way of the damage, however, this area was newly painted over with fresh paint and lettering.

When I questioned "my" hull inspector about the potential danger to the Cutter from that damage, he replied, "We in marine inspection have nothing to do with our own boats, they do their own inspecting!" I told him that hull was in a definitely weakened condition and with men billeted behind the damage it made it even more serious. Any encounter with heavy weather or the ship pounding could easily cause a crack in its thin shell plating and possibly rupture the hull!

He again said, "We have nothing to do with them. The Cutter is considered a 'Public Vessel' like Navy ships and our office has no control over them."

I must have made my point with him though because he backed off from making me renew our steel!

For many years the Coast Guard would never give the merchant crew credit for intelligence, another frustration. We were never permitted to carry acetylene and oxygen or have an electric arc welding machine on board our ships to make repairs. Their excuse, "We're afraid someone inexperienced might attempt to weld or burn on a pressure vessel or a fuel tank and start a fire or be injured!"

We countered with, "Coast Guard vessels use them! Are their crews more intelligent than ours?" Years later, they agreed to allow this equipment on board, after many engineers had taken welding courses, but prior to this many ships had certified welders aboard, but still were not allowed to use them.

An inspector once told me the reason he was so strict as a marine inspector was "at least I can sleep at night!" I could not, nor would I, fault him for that reasoning, but later the opportunity arose where I was able to point out to him the fault with living by the regulations.

It was a month later aboard a Lancer Class ship undergoing a USCG Biennial Inspection in February on one of the coldest days of the year. The same inspector asked me to have someone from our crew start the diesel engine in the starboard lifeboat to demonstrate its operation.

Somewhat smirking, I said, "OK, Inspector, we'll start it and call you when we get it going."

"Oh no, I have to be present when you start it," he said.

"This is February, Inspector, our lifeboat engine is a diesel and very difficult to start in cold weather, so give us a little time," I replied.

"If you had to use the boat for a rescue or to abandon ship in an emergency, you wouldn't have time to nurse it along to get it going!" he said.

"Exactly, Inspector, but we can start it on first try if you're not present!"

This bewildered him, "What the hell are you driving at?"

I explained that the engine is cranked with air pressure and upon cranking it is supposed to start. The air pressure is built up hydraulically through a unit called an accumulator, which takes the place of a battery starter.

The accumulator holds 3000 pounds of air pressure which would normally be enough to turn over the engine in warm weather and start it, but in this freezing weather, it most likely won't. With the 3000 pounds we could get three attempts at cranking, but after that we have to hand pump the pressure up to 3000 again to attempt it once more.

After explaining this to him, he insisted on our starting it cold. We opened the fuel valve, opened the air valve and it cranked, but didn't fire as predicted. We had two more attempts, but still it wouldn't fire off. He then asked how we would have started it if he weren't present.

"We would have squirted a couple of shots of ether into the air intake and it would start up at once," I said.

"What! Ether is prohibited onboard ship, you know that, it's too volatile, Coast Guard regulations!" he said excitedly. "We know that, too, that's why I said we would call you when we had it running. That way you wouldn't know how we started it."

During this discussion two crew members continued pumping up the accumulator and finally, after several minutes, the pressure reached 3000 pounds. With the pressure now built up, I asked the inspector if we could start the engine using the ether and he said, "OK, try it so I can see for myself."

The chief engineer squirted two shots of ether into the air intake, opened the air valve and off it went with a roar! I explained the air pressure would now build up again, ready for the next start through a recharging mechanism, much like a battery recharges in an automobile after starting the engine.

"I see your point, but regulations still prohibit carrying ether on board," he said.

"Coast Guard vessels carry it on board," I said, guessing, why can't we?

"Regulations," again.

"Let me ask you something, Inspector. If you were a crew member on here and your 'abandon ship station' was 'operate lifeboat engine,' wouldn't you be happy to know you could start it using ether and not waste time, especially if you were one of those in the boat?"

"I'm sorry, but I have to go by regulations."

I asked him to step over to the deck locker next to the lifeboat and showed him a full case of ether. "This ether remains on board unless I get it from you in writing in the form of an 835 in which you direct me to remove it," I said, "but remember what you said to me last month about being able to sleep at night!"

He finally backed off, telling me indirectly that it wasn't permitted aboard, however if we removed it voluntarily he would be satisfied, and he would not have to put anything in writing. If after he left the ship, it was put aboard again and stowed in the deck locker, he really wouldn't know about it, and he'd still be "able to sleep at night!"

Every three years on June 15, the Collective Bargaining Agreement between the National Maritime Union and United States Lines would terminate unless previous negotiating sessions had managed to produce a new pact. This was usually the case, so with few exceptions, labor peace between the two was maintained and the continuity of operations assured.

The NMU and other labor unions on board the ship were quite understanding when U.S. Coast Guard Regulations had to be followed to assure the safety of the crew, ship, and its cargo. Requirements such as conducting weekly fire and abandon ship drills were an accepted rule.

These drills were usually held at 10:20 A.M. or 3:20 P.M., immediately after coffee time, thus the day workers could attend during their eight-hour work day. But those men who were "off watch" were required to attend at no extra compensation in spite of it being in excess of their eight-hour day. They never complained because it was an understanding with their union that these safety drills were for everyone's benefit.

Recently a junior grade, lieutenant Coast Guard inspector aboard a U.S. flag ship wasn't satisfied with the way a fire drill had progressed in his presence so he wrote a requirement on Form CG-835 to "Conduct no less than fifteen fire drills in the next nineteen days and log each one in the deck logbook."

This unusual and incongruous requirement could generate all sorts of labor problems on the ship, requiring off-duty men to attend in excess of their eight hours nearly every day. These men could claim overtime for attending them because the NMU could reasonably claim this exceeded the understanding and "spirit" of the labor contract.

A requirement or penalty such as this absurd number of drills is not spelled out in the rules and regulations. It was done at the whim of a junior officer of the Coast Guard with no consideration given to the possible costly ramifications to the company.

Form CG-835 is a printed form which is used by inspectors to write requirements to correct deficiencies onboard ship. Over the years they have become known simply as an "835." One young inspector, feeling jovial, once told me he was giving me a "sixteen seventy." I asked what that was and he jokingly replied, "It's two 835s!" I said, "Your sense of humor belongs in a kindergarten with the other children."

On another occasion I was supervising the emergency dry-docking of one of our container ships in Rotterdam. The vessel had run aground leaving England and was in its third day in the Dutch shipyard. That morning I was in the chief engineer's office, holding a meeting with underwriters representatives and the American Bureau of Shipping Surveyor, when we heard the two young Coast

Guard inspectors assigned to the dry-docking from the Rotterdam office of the USCG outside the chief's office.

One said to the other, in a loud voice, "When we see Mr. Murphy, we'll tell him we just put two holes in the hull of number one lifeboat with our test hammers to see his reaction."

When they entered the office, they were surprised to see an assemblage of dignified surveyors and inspectors talking seriously about our vessel's bottom damage and its costs. These men, all Dutchmen, looked strangely at them, not thinking their remarks a bit funny. Glaring at the inspectors, I said, "Will you kids grow up, do you think we are running a candy store operation here?"

They quickly apologized realizing this was no joking matter and left the office. From that point on, they proved to be quite humble in their dealings with us, and maybe even matured somewhat that day!

I once had an assignment to put the SS *American Charger* through its USCG Biennial Inspection. The machinery inspector assigned to the ship was a young USCG ensign, a recent graduate of Kings Point. As we made our way to the engine room on the first day of the inspection, he told me how enthused he was to be able to inspect this particular ship because he had served in it as an engineering cadet three years earlier.

"Just think, Mr. Murphy, I was a cadet on here and now I'm the Coast Guard inspector for it."

My immediate thought was "Are there any skeletons down below in the engine room he might have knowledge of?" The previous chief engineer, Alan Corbett, was a very competent man, and a conscientious engineer. I wondered if he had perhaps installed any questionable piping to save fuel or fresh water and maybe had the cadet assist him in its installation.

As we walked around the engine room, observing the machinery in operation, he said, "I'd like to look at the rear of the starboard boiler for a moment." We walked over in that direction and he pointed to a sheet metal patch riveted to a panel of the air heater.

Pointing to it he said, "See that patch? When Mr. Corbett was on here, he taught me how to use epoxy. We had a leak in the air heater coil and we traced it to this corner. He had me hacksaw a square opening in the casing right there. When we removed the piece of metal, we could see the leak squirting out of the coil, but we couldn't reach it to braze it because of its location. He mixed up some epoxy paste and we could just reach inside the opening enough to apply the epoxy to the leak."

"Well, you must have done a good job because it hasn't leaked since," I said.

"Yeah, I learned a lot from Mr. Corbett," he said.

"I know, we miss him after his retirement last year." I said.

"Mr. Murphy, I hate to tell you this, but I can't permit an epoxy repair to remain as a permanent repair. You will have to remove it and braze the leak! The Coast Guard doesn't allow epoxy repairs on any ship as permanent repairs, especially on a boiler!"

I stood there dumbfounded. Had I heard right? "Inspector, we are permitted to use it in a number of places, for your information. For example we can use it on the underwater section of the bow plating to prevent erosion of the steel from the speed of the ship through the water, also on the forward section of the rudder and rudder horn for protection against the wash of the propeller. In the engine room we use it on the top of our atmospheric drain tank to prevent that steel from corroding due to the hot humid atmosphere in that location."

"Well, I can't allow it on a boiler."

"It's not on the boiler, it's in the air heater and that's not part of the boiler. They are two separate units. The air heater is only mounted on the top section of the boiler for convenience and proximity to the forced draft fan," I explained. I then walked him to the other side where I pointed out the manufacturer's nameplate for the air heater and then to another location where he could see the nameplate for the boiler.

"See, Inspector, two separate manufacturers, two separate pieces of machinery. Also, the pressure in the air heater is only ten pounds, so an epoxy patch is OK," I said.

"Well, I guess I can let it go, then."

Disgusted, I said, "Inspector, if I were you, I wouldn't repeat any of this conversation to anyone. To be proud of a repair you made as a cadet three years ago, and now as a Coast Guard inspector you want it removed is ludicrous."

From that point on, I wondered what other skeletons he might remember from three years ago, but apparently the air heater leak was the only one.

I was attending one of our chartered ships while it was in a Japanese shipyard. It was undergoing an extensive overhaul to ready it for deployment to Diego Garcia where it was to remain for four years without returning to the United States. In addition to a routine dry-docking, it was completing many other regulatory requirements, such as testing and examination of all cargo handling gear, completion of special survey, and a USCG Biennial Inspection.

I had informed the Coast Guard inspector of the importance of completing all requirements found during the inspection. After leaving Japan, there would be no other opportunity to complete them, since the ship would be at an ammunition berth where no repairs were permitted. And once the ship arrived at Diego, there were no repair facilities nor USCG Inspection Office to clear any requirements. The inspector on the scene in Japan had been flown there by U.S. Lines for the sole purpose of conducting the inspection.

Elaborate plans were made to coat the underwater sections of the hull with an exotic anti-fouling paint which would prevent marine growth from forming for that period of time. Also, large steel blanks were fabricated to be bolted over the inlets and overboards on the hull to enable the engine room sea valves to be opened after two years as required by law. All these arrangements being made to allow the ship to comply with inspections normally due in two years.

Near the end of our stay in the yard, at coffee time one morning, a third assistant engineer asked the inspector if he had issued any 835s yet, and he replied, "No, but I will. I always leave a few, otherwise my boss will never know I was on the job. It's my policy to always leave at least one or two on every inspection I perform!"

I took him aside and explained to him that we couldn't tolerate even one 835; the ship was leaving for four years and there would be no way to correct any deficiencies found after leaving the yard. I said, "Don't hold anything back, if you have found anything you're saving, let's have it. Never mind trying to impress your boss."

He then handed me a sheet of paper with several minor requirements written on it. They were nuisance items which I put in hand immediately, and upon completion of our yard stay, the ship had no outstanding requirements!

On another occasion, I flew to Port Canaveral, Florida, to meet one of our MSC chartered ships which had just arrived from Bremerhaven, Germany. During their passage I had talked to the chief engineer by phone and he informed me of a number of difficulties he had with the automation systems in the engine room. I told him I would meet the ship there, and bring along a technician from Nortech Marine, an electronics service group, who could trouble shoot the systems.

Trouble shooting electronics aboard ship is difficult because so much depends on machinery being in operation while testing the systems. Because much of his problem lay with the throttle assembly, we thought it would be best if both of us rode the ship from Canaveral to Charleston, South Carolina, during which time its operation could be observed and any problems corrected.

Working throughout the night, Luis Tur, the technician, managed to correct all the problems, and upon docking in Charleston, we were ready to leave for home. While he and I were in the engine room gathering up our tools, the engine room phone rang. It was the chief engineer calling to tell me a U.S. Coast Guard inspector was in his office and wished to speak to me.

I went to the office and asked if I could help him. It was a Sunday, we had no inspections due, and I was puzzled by his presence.

"I'm the weekend duty officer from the marine inspection office and have come aboard to investigate a claim that your ship has fuel oil in its fire line system!"

"That's weird," I said, "How in the world could anything as absurd as that happen. The two systems are completely isolated."

"All I know is that we had a report from a crew member about it," the inspector said.

Upon questioning the master, chief mate, and others, we concluded it was a disgruntled crew member who reported the erroneous story. We operated the fire pumps in the inspector's presence, shot water from every fire hydrant on board and convinced him everything was normal. The mate did say that there was some fuel on the surface of the water in the harbor in Bremerhaven while they were there. He also said they conducted a fire drill while at the pier so the pumps probably picked some of the fuel at the time because they observed some traces of fuel on the main deck after the drill was completed.

The inspector accepted this, and after examining our systems below, agreed it could have been a prank call.

While leaning on the chief engineer's file cabinet in his office, however, he picked up some papers lying there and began reading them during our discussions about the fuel system. These papers were "request for repairs forms," a form to be submitted by the chief engineer requesting repairs to be done by a shore gang. He had typed these requests for me so I could take them back to the company office to support the work done by the technician. On it was listed all the repairs completed by the technician the night before.

The inspector left the chief's office to go to the bridge and returned in a few minutes, "I have written an 835 for your ship, Mr.

Murphy, will you sign it please?"

"What's the 835 for, I thought we were clear of the fuel problem?" I asked.

"Oh, the fuel is not the problem, now. This 835 is to require you to complete every item on the chief's repair list for the automation."

"OK, Inspector, I'll sign it." And I did, acknowledging its receipt.

He went on to say, "Well, I'll leave you gentlemen. I have the weekend duty and have to stick around the house, so I'm having a group of neighbors over for a cookout this afternoon. You can have an inspector in New York clear these requirements when they are completed to his satisfaction. Have a nice day."

I spoke up, "Just a minute, Inspector, I'd like to have them cleared right now, by you!"

"How could I clear them, they haven't even been started."

"I beg your pardon, but they were not only started, they are complete. We've had a technician on it all through last night while the ship was underway and everything is complete, so I'm asking you to clear them at this time!"

"That'll take a couple of hours, I have to get to my cookout!" he said.

"I could care less, Inspector. After all, the only reason you knew we had any electronic repairs was because you eavesdropped on the chief's paperwork."

I then asked if he had filled in the bridge card, a document in a frame located in the wheelhouse which records the coming and going of any Coast Guard inspectors who may board. They are required to fill in the date and reason for boarding each time and to record any 835s issued during the visit.

"Yes, I did fill it in, and now I'll have to fill it in again if I clear these items." This concerned him because he knew no inspectors ever filled it in for requirements and then cleared them the same day during the same visit! I knew I had him, and he did too!

"Can I talk to the technician about this?" he asked.

"Sure, I'll call him on the phone and he'll be right up here."

Lou appeared and after a short discussion between them, in which he told the inspector what he accomplished with the automation during the night, what he had found wrong and corrected, the inspector cleared all the items right there in the chief's room without ever entering the engine room!

As he left, I thanked him, and said, "Enjoy your cookout and have a nice day, Inspector!"

Lou said he thought he detected a twinge of sarcasm in my voice.

For many years Boston, Massachusetts, was a routine port of call for our ships on the North Atlantic and Far East routes. Much of the cargo from European ports was destined for areas inland from there, as well as the New England area, so it made for a convenient stop for the ships en route to New York. Our Far East ships usually called there after their initial call at New York.

It served another advantage for us because U.S. Lines eventually became the only American flag company with off-shore ships to call there. The Coast Guard Marine Inspection Office in Boston had little to do in the way of inspections because no other American Flag ships used the port. When a U.S. Lines ship entered the port for cargo operations (which normally would require a stay of twelve to fifteen hours), a group of inspectors would descend on the ship to use the vessel as a classroom.

Whether the mates were busy working cargo or the engineers busy doing routine work, the Coast Guard would insist on a fire and boat drill being held. This would disrupt the routine. Many times key crew members and officers were ashore, but they insisted on a drill anyway with those remaining on board.

It was also not unusual to require the ship to conduct what amounted to a midperiod inspection, requiring everyone to leave their work and perform tests in the inspector's presence. If something malfunctioned, they would not permit the ship to leave until the problem was corrected, even though the company storeroom in New York held the spare parts needed to correct the situation. I recall one time aboard the SS *American Argosy*, the inspector asked me to trip the two main generators off the main switchboard to prove the emergency diesel generator would start. I refused, so he then asked me to manually start the emergency generator seven times in a row to prove the batteries were OK.

He and I went to the generator room where I operated the starting mechanism for him and it started instantly. I was then told to secure it, and restart it again, and again it kicked off. I repeated the starts two more times, but after the fourth start, it would not crank fast enough to fire and failed to start. I told him such an enormous engine required a considerable amount of power to start, and he should at least let me keep it running long enough to recharge the batteries between starts.

He insisted on seven consecutive starts, but I told him it would not get any better until the batteries recharged. He then insisted the batteries must be weak, and we would have to install new batteries or the ship could not leave Boston.

I called our office in New York, and was told not to waste time arguing, but to buy new batteries locally and have them installed in order to get the ship out on schedule. It was now near 5:00 P.M. and stores were closing, so I called Bethlehem Steel Shipyard who purchased new heavy duty truck batteries locally and installed them. After an initial charge, the engine fired off the required seven times for him. The irony of this is that we had an extra supply of batteries in our storeroom in New York if he would have only allowed the ship to leave. This little matter of batteries cost the company a considerable amount of money, not only for their price, but for the shipyard labor involved. The physical size of the new batteries was different from those which were replaced and the steel shelving holding them had to be altered. And most important, the company experienced the loss of the vessel's time while lying idle in port.

Our U.S. Lines office in Boston was only staffed with cargo operations people. However, it was routine for the company to dispatch a port engineer from New York to the port each time a ship called there just to get it through the Coast Guard inspectors who we could be assured would pay it a visit.

After many similar incidents when the ship's sailing was delayed because of the U.S. Coast Guard, the company made the ultimate decision and elected to eliminate Boston from its schedules. Management found it was quicker, and thus more economical to discharge and load the Boston cargo at New York using barges plus trucks and rail to transport it to Boston. Also as a result, the company found it necessary to lay off some of our Boston office employees, not to mention the longshoremen who lost work.

When the Boston Marine Inspection Office learned we no longer included their port on our schedules, they immediately informed their New York Office of the fact, and suggested to them we were trying to conceal serious operational problems. During the first few arrivals in New York from Europe we were then visited by them until they realized we had nothing to hide! The irony of the matter was that every ship had just crossed the Atlantic Ocean and suddenly was found unsuitable to proceed for another sixteen hours to New York!

All major American shipyards had a resident USCG inspection team assigned to it to expedite examinations and inspections required on American flag ships. Having them stationed there saved time for the yards and the company and assured both that an inspector would be on hand most anytime he might be needed. Otherwise without him available, it would be necessary to call the local marine inspection office to have an inspector dispatched to the job, and they weren't always available, or might require a day's lead time to arrange his visit.

This arrangement worked to the yard's advantage, but not necessarily to the owners'. Occasionally a particular inspector stationed in a yard was not one who got along with our company or people, or was one who had previously given our ships a difficult time during an earlier stay in that yard. I recall a few times when management wished to dry-dock a ship in a particular yard to suit scheduling, but would first call the yard to see if a certain inspector was still in residence there. If so, we would inform the yard of our desire to use their facility but we were reluctant to do so if a certain individual was still stationed there as a resident inspector. When this word reached the office of the general manager of the yard, a fast phone call was made to the local marine inspection office and that inspector transferred temporarily to another station.

While the Coast Guard's rules and regulations may appear to be hard and fast to enable an owner to be guided by their requirements in preparing a ship for the many inspections due by certain dates, they are by no means cast in stone. The rules are often changed arbitrarily by the local inspection office as they deem necessary. For instance, it is a requirement to examine boiler valves and their mounting studs every eight years. This is a big and costly undertaking requiring the removal of as many as twelve studs per valve for a total number of thirty to forty valves per boiler. The internal examination of each valve is usually a visual one where seat and disc are examined for any corrosion or erosion to the internals.

The examination of the studs is a different story, however. Some inspection offices require their inspectors to dangle each stud from a string, tap the stud with their test hammer, and listen for a ring or a thud. If it rings clearly, the stud is apparently not cracked. If a thud is heard, it is discarded.

I've tried this a number of times using studs with a known crack and they sounded like a church bell! Still some inspectors insisted this was the way they were told to test them.

Other inspectors have insisted on dye checking each one whereby each stud is wire brushed clean, a dye penetrant painted on it, and then a developing solution applied which would show up a crack as a thin line in the dye. This I have found to be the most dependable, nondestructive test.

Still others claim their office requires one stud from each valve be subjected to a bending test. The stud is placed in a clamp and a hydraulic press bends the stud to a right angle. The root (base) of the thread is examined for porosity or cracking, and if found, the entire eight, ten, or twelve studs from that flange rejected. This is not only a destructive test, but also an expensive one because all the remaining studs may be perfect. Also, if the test stud is found to be good, it doesn't mean the others are, and besides the tested stud is now destroyed anyway.

Thus when conducting a U.S. Coast Guard eight-year valve survey in any port, the port engineer must call the local inspection office to determine which procedure is the norm for that Coast Guard district.

Another discrepancy found among Coast Guard districts is the procedure for performing a hydrostatic test on a boiler after completing repairs. The rules require that a hydrostatic test be applied after repairs to the steam side of any boiler, and the test must be equal to 1 1/4 or 1 1/2 times the working pressure depending on the type of repair.

Of course, this excess pressure cannot be built up without gagging the safety valves or blanking them off. This is where a discrepancy enters the scene. Some ports will allow the owner to remove a couple of studs between the boiler flanges and the safety valve flanges and insert a steel blank to avoid subjecting the valves to the excess pressure. This is a quick and dependable method of preparing for the test, since a total of four safety valves could be involved on each boiler. Other ports will not permit this, however, requiring that the USCG seals be removed, the hand releasing gear of all safety valves removed, and each valve gagged for the test. Upon completion of the hydrostatic test, the safety valves must be retested individually, the hand releasing gear reattached, and the valves again sealed by an inspector. This is time consuming and could cause the vessel to remain in port at least an extra day after the completion of repairs.

Here again the port engineer must determine beforehand what the local policy is for that district, and of course, once a policy is in effect, no one is about to change it whether it benefits the ship owner or not!

As I mentioned earlier, it was often frustrating working with inexperienced U.S. Coast Guard marine inspectors. Usually, inspectors who had served in the Merchant Marine and afterward joined the USCG under Public Law 219 were experienced and aware of the difficulties confronting the company, such as maintaining schedules in order to avoid extra cost for waiting longshoremen, tugs, and pilots. It was not necessarily the young inspectors who were inexperienced however. I have dealt with many of high rank who were sometimes assigned to marine inspection roles.

Once a commander headed the marine inspection of a large East Coast shipyard several years ago when I was supervising the dry-docking of one of the U.S. Lines Mariner Class ships. The yard had unshipped the vessel's damaged propeller from the ship and was to reinstall our fleet spare. I asked the commander if the Coast Guard was interested in witnessing the fit of the spare propeller to the shaft.

"We certainly are, Mr. Murphy, I intend to witness it myself. What time do you anticipate the fit?"

"The yard estimates between 2:00 and 3:00 tomorrow morning," I said.

"Is that 2:00 or 3:00 A.M.? Why it takes me almost an hour to get to the yard from home." After giving it some thought he asked if the American Bureau of Shipping (ABS) surveyor and I would be present. When I replied, "yes," he said, "Well, in that case, if you two witness it, that will be OK for the Coast Guard."

I then informed the night superintendent to call only the ABS surveyor and me when ready. The yard was well experienced in fitting propellers and knew not to call us unless they were satisfied the fit was proper.

Fitting a propeller to a shaft is a cumbersome and sometimes lengthy procedure. The propeller, weighing some twenty tons and twenty feet in diameter, is unwieldy when suspended on chain falls. The inside tapered hub of the propeller and the external taper of the shaft are first cleaned with a solvent, then a light coating of bluing applied to the shaft taper.

A group of riggers, known as the wheel gang, then maneuver the propeller onto the shaft using the falls. They then install the nut on the shaft, and steel wedges are driven against each other between the nut and the rear side of the hub using heavy sledgehammers. This is done while standing on planking about twelve feet above the dry-dock floor.

Being a member of the wheel gang is one of the most respected jobs in the yard. These men are called upon to work around the clock, in all weather, from blistering summer heat to below freezing temperatures while a cold, wintry wind blows in on them from the river.

The propeller is then eased back off the shaft enough to examine the percentage of the coverage by the bluing in the propeller taper, indicating the contact between the two. If unsatisfactory, the high spots are ground off in the propeller hub, and the procedure repeated. When the fit is satisfactory, the nut is driven up permanently and "keepers" installed to keep the nut tight.

The wheel gang was not satisfied with the fits taken during the night so we were not disturbed. When I arrived in the yard in the morning, I was told that we could expect a final fit about 10:00 A.M. that morning, so I informed the commander of this. He replied, "Very well, I'll be present."

At 10:00 A.M. the inspector, ABS surveyor and I climbed the staging to the plank platform, about fifteen feet from the dry dock. As we were climbing around the area to position ourselves to witness the riggers slugging the wedges, the commander, out of earshot of the ABS surveyor, said to me, "You know, I've only seen one of these fits before this, and that was years ago. Just what are we looking for anyway?"

After explaining it to him I thought, "Here's a guy who was adamant about the Coast Guard witnessing this procedure, then decided it wasn't that important when he found it would be in the early hours of the morning, and then when he finally observed it, didn't know what he was looking at anyway!"

His entire career in the Coast Guard included little inspection experience. Had our inspector served in the Merchant Marine he undoubtedly would have had an opportunity to witness many of these fits.

Another inspector in that yard informed me the following day I would have to renew a section of pipe on the main deck of that same ship. He had nearly punched a hole through it with his test hammer because it was badly wasted he told me. I asked what pipe it was and he said he didn't know, but would show it to me. It was a short vertical section of pipe about two inches in diameter rising from the deck and was capped with a valve and painted light blue. When I heard the words "light blue," I immediately became suspicious.

Upon examination, I found the area of the pipe just above the deck penetration badly beaten and distorted from his hammer. Disgusted at seeing this, I scraped the blue paint from it to show him it was not steel pipe, but soft copper tubing. It was the fresh water filling line for the vessel! I told him my ten-year-old son could dent and mangle it with a toy plastic hammer.

I further informed him that the U.S. Public Health Service required it to be painted light blue so as to identify it as fresh water, that he should have known that, and that it could be made of copper.

Embarrassed, he examined the mangled area and determined that he had not holed it, therefore we would not have to renew it. I told him I had no intention of renewing it, but if I had to, the USCG would get the bill for it!

He apologized but I was still angry. I told him to inform all the inspectors in his yard office of what he had done so one of them wouldn't come to the ship, see the mangled pipe, and beat on it some more.

Later that afternoon, I visited their office and in his presence asked if he had told them about the tubing. They said that he had and they would be aware of it. I felt a somewhat selfish satisfaction in doing that and left their office, not quite so angry!

The *American Argosy* was laid up for one voyage at a lay berth in Newport News Shipyard in August for lack of cargo. This was common practice for company ships which were not subsidized and therefore not required to make a minimum number of voyages per year. The company took advantage of these lay-up periods to perform repairs and hold inspections and surveys which had been postponed or would be due in the near future.

During this particular period which lasted for five weeks, the crew and officers were laid off with only the master, chief engineer, and me on board. All machinery was shut down and the plant dead with shore power tied in for lights and emergency bilge pumping if needed.

One Sunday afternoon, the three of us were standing on the boat deck enjoying a cup of coffee and watching the traffic in the James River. Looking out over the river, we noticed a sheen on the water near its middle.

This indicates oil floating on the water's surface. After discussing it among ourselves, we decided we should call the USCG 800 Oil Spill number to report it, as the law required, lest we be blamed for causing it if it should drift toward the *American Argosy*.

Soon the Coast Guard oil spill team arrived on the scene. After interviewing us, they filed their report in which they stated the circumstances as to why it was reported, that it did not originate from our vessel, that our plant was secured, and that no transferring of fuel was taking place. They also reported that the cooperation of U.S. Lines personnel was excellent and that the spill obviously was not the fault of the reporting ship. Further they reported that it was so slight that no sample could be obtained and that no clean up was warranted.

The following June, the *American Argosy* was again laid up at the same berth for the same reason. Conditions were the same as the previous August, no crew, plant dead, etc. One Sunday afternoon, I was on the pier and discovered a dribble of fuel oil slowly oozing out the side of the ship from a fuel oil overflow line and forming a puddle on an electrical splice box on the stringpiece. The ship had laid up with a one-degree port list, and residual fuel which had lain in the pipe had softened due to the ninety-degree summer heat.

I informed the captain and chief. Together we used winches and managed to breast the ship slightly from the pier to find the oil streak on the hull ended abruptly at the point where the hull was lying against the pier. The oil had run onto the pier and onto the splice box.

We immediately called the 800 number again, as well as the yard superintendent, who immediately dispatched a cleanup crew to the scene. When the Coast Guard arrived much of the mess had been cleaned up, but they began their investigation. We breasted the ship from the pier as before to prove no fuel entered the water, and they were convinced the spill was minimal. One even remarked, "Why did you call us, nothing got into the water." We told them we thought it was our duty to report all spills. Their estimate and ours was that perhaps a bucketful had leaked out.

A Coast Guard petty officer quizzed the cleaning boss and was told they were receiving double time for Sunday, plus "dirty money," plus a minimum of four hours each for cleaning the exterior of the splice box. Doing some quick arithmetic, he wrote an estimate of the cleaning job for his report.

The cleanup crew also cleaned the side of the hull while the ship was clear of the pier, as well as the interior of the overflow pipe. The chief engineer then pumped some salt water ballast from one of the ship's tanks to bring the ship to an even keel. The Coast Guard was satisfied: no harm done, cooperation excellent, clean up completed, no fuel in the river, etc.

Several months later, long after the ship left the yard to resume its normal schedule, we received a letter in our New York office from the Hampton Roads Coast Guard Office which stated, "In view of the fact that your vessel, SS *American Argosy*, was involved in two fuel spill incidents within the span of one year in this district, we feel a fine of $500 is appropriate."

My boss, Dick Bower, was furious, as was I, and asked me what went on there during those two periods. When I told him, he told me to call our attorneys for advice. An hour later I told him they said to forget about it; it would cost more to send an attorney to fight it, pay his round trip air fare, meals, and hotel for one night than the $500 fine. Their advice, pay the fine. I asked Bower about me going to their office to fight it, but he said he couldn't because I was scheduled to dry-dock a ship in Taiwan. End result? We paid the fine!

Looking back on this writing I find I haven't treated the United States Coast Guard too kindly, but I should point out that my aggravation and frustrations were only with the marine inspection offices. Like most Merchant Marine personnel I have the greatest respect for their search and rescue missions, aids to navigation, environmental supervision, as well as their many other responsibilities such as ice breaking, waterways management, recreational boating supervision, the interception of aliens attempting to crowd our shores, and most importantly, the policing of coastal waters to prevent narcotics smuggling.

Their responsibilities in these many varied operations would seem to overwhelm this smallest of the services, but they perform their tasks admirably. It seems whenever a new action poses a threat to our country's security or safety, the problem is dumped onto the Coast Guard for handling and more than likely without any increase in their operating budget or personnel, and they take it in stride.

CHAPTER FORTY-FIVE

FINISHED WITH ENGINES

After working for forty-three years in U.S. Lines, I have come to realize I enjoyed the best of many worlds: the fine people with whom I worked in the ships, the office, shipyards, and vendors, as well as a chance to see the world as few have had the opportunity to see it, by ship and plane. The fun times and the sadness, it was a full life.

I'm sure it would have been different if it were not for my lovely wife, Priscilla, who raised our boys, made all the teacher conferences, acted as family chauffeur, and was both a father and mother to them in my absence. Perhaps it would have been different, too, if I had been assigned to a ship on a shorter trade route and had the opportunity to be home more often. Those four-and five-month trips to the Far East and Australia were trying times for us with a growing family.

As I look back now, I would like to have been home more with them. But I also had an opportunity to see some of the strife and poverty on this planet and come to appreciate life as we know it here, the finest country in the world bar none.

I saw young kids in Korea, the Philippines, and Vietnam on board our ship race each other to the stern where the garbage barrels were stowed to get first dibs on the still hot garbage just dumped into them. They put it into a pail or tin can and took it home to feed their brothers and sisters.

I saw the skinny, scraggly dressed longshoreman in sandals made from discarded rubber tires leaving the ship after his ten-hour shift with a half-dozen sticks of wood broken from our dunnage during discharge of cargo. He tied them together with a string and carried them home to feed a fire to cook the family's meager supper.

I saw the longshoreman with his high rubber boots standing hip deep in grain in the cargo hold guiding the wheat or corn or barley to waiting grain suckers. When he left the ship to go home, his boots were full to the brim with the grain cargo to be emptied after he passed through the pier gates into a paper bag carried in his pocket. Later it would be ground into a powder by his wife to bake bread.

While in other ports, I had many opportunities to appreciate our good fortunes at home. Once a visit from church authorities representing an orphanage in Pusan, Korea, who asked our crew for any old clothing was so inspiring that most crew members wrote letters to relatives and friends back home to save their old clothing and to collect some from neighbors for pickup by the individual when he returned home for a few days leave.

Upon our next call at Pusan, the orphanage had to send a truck to the pier to pick up the many bags of clothing collected. Our ship continued the practice for many trips, and the response from families of crew members was overwhelming, even to the point where it was expanded to include canned goods and other nonperishable food items!

In some ports youngsters as well as adults would approach the cooks in the galley offering to wash the deck or scrub pots and pans or do other menial chores in exchange for a meal of leftovers!

During the Christmas season, the company would conduct Christmas parties aboard its ships in various world ports for underprivileged kids, with the local U.S. Lines office people making the arrangements.

The company was also a participant in the "Adopt A Ship Program," sponsored by the Women's Propeller Club of the United States. This program was begun many years ago to familiarize some of the nation's grammar schools with the American Merchant Marine, as well as to encourage them to learn about the customs and peoples of the world.

Classrooms were invited to submit their names to the program and then randomly selected to participate. My ship, the *Pioneer*

Ming, was selected to be "adopted" by the sixth grade class of a school in Clinton, Iowa.

The students were just as enthusiastic about their selection as we were to be a part of it. They knew they were only one of a few lucky classes selected from hundreds who had submitted their names because of the comparatively few American ships on the oceans. A few classes were disappointed because the crews on their ships showed little or no interest in participating, but happily, all U.S. Lines crews were enthusiastic about the program with encouragement from the company.

Letters and photos were exchanged between the students and the ship's officers and crew members. We sent a large map of the world to them which the teacher hung on the wall in their classroom, accompanied by an itinerary of our voyage which stated miles between ports, speed of the ship, and the course to be followed. A different student was assigned the task of replacing a pin at our daily position at noon each day, just as the noon position is used on board as the basis for the day's run.

Many crew members purchased souvenirs abroad and sent them off to the students on a regular basis. The program proved to be a valuable aid to education, judging by the letters received from the teacher. She told us in one letter that the program in her class had been expanded so that the entire grammar school was participating by sharing our letters.

We were pleased to hear this because it meant promoting our Merchant Marine to a midwestern state which had no waterfront activity except small river traffic, and it was teaching the kids about importing and exporting goods which they use every day.

Unfortunately, today the program is almost nonexistent because there are so few American ships on the oceans.

Going to sea gave me the opportunity to travel to places on this globe not usually seen by most people such as Pitcairn Island, Diego Garcia, and Tahiti, and even my trip around the world by plane!

I had the privilege of serving in one ship whose master was Robert A. Smith, a nephew of Captain Smith of the ill-fated Titanic. We were aboard the SS *Pioneer Star*, tied up to our pier in Manhattan, and nearly ready to leave for Australia. Captain Smith was making his last three trips before retirement, and had a fascination for Pitcairn Island of *Mutiny on the Bounty* fame.

He requested a letter from our office to be presented to the postmaster in the General Post Office in Manhattan which stated he was the master of the SS *Pioneer Star* which would be leaving for Australia in a few days. The letter authorized the post office to hand over any mail for Pitcairn to him for delivery to the island. This was no problem because U.S. Lines had a mail contract with the postal department, anyway.

The post office was glad to get rid of the small amount of mail it was holding because there was no regular mail service to Pitcairn. The island is a remote mountain top rising out of the Pacific Ocean more than three thousand miles east of New Zealand which was settled by the mutineers in 1789. It has no harbor, pier, anchorage, or landing strip, nor is it on any regular trade route, except when ships alter their course slightly en route to Australia from Panama.

Weeks later approaching the island, we contacted their radio operator, a New Zealander on active Navy duty, about their mail. He came back to us by voice radio which we could pick up but had to reply by Morse code because we were not yet fitted out with voice radio. As we neared the island, he began a narration which described the voyage of the *Bounty*, the mutiny, the nearby islands where the mutineers found the women who would occupy the island with them, Bounty Bay where the famed ship was burned and sunk, the cliff where John Adams was to jump to his death, and many other interesting facts of the story.

After our arrival, two longboats left the shore manned by a total of about eighty men rowing them. They secured their boats alongside and boarded the *Pioneer Star*. They had brought with them carved statues of flying fish, walking sticks, and numerous other souvenirs made on the island. They wanted no money for these (they had no store on the island), but would accept flashlights, batteries, diesel fuel, matches, soap, soap powder, and any old dunnage we might be able to spare.

We were turning slow circles about a half mile off the island while they were aboard. I left my room to go to our engine department storeroom, to fill a bag with soap, while Fletcher Christian, the sixth or seventh, I don't remember which, and others stayed in my room. Upon my return, I thought how foolish of me to leave them there where they could have ransacked my quarters, but nothing was touched. On my bookshelf was a copy of *Mutiny on the Bounty*, which I had purposely bought in New York when I learned we were stopping at Pitcairn. I intended to have it autographed by the descendants. I completely forgot it was there until an hour after they left the ship and we were on our way!

We stayed there about an hour and a half, delivered their mail to them, watched them load their long boats with the dunnage and then said our good-byes with everyone posing for pictures. They were a very religious group of men and had been first approached by missionaries soon after they landed on the island and set up housekeeping.

As a precaution, however, we had counted the number of men who had boarded the ship, and assured ourselves the same number left. Also, a stowaway search was completed before we were too far from the island. To be "marooned" as they were on such a tiny piece of land in the middle of nowhere for your entire life might not have been for all of them! Also, they asked for copies of *Life* magazine to take ashore, thus they knew there was another way of life out there beyond their tiny island.

As they pulled away in their longboats on the smooth, quiet Pacific, they sang in blended voices, "God be with you 'til we meet again." I don't think there was a dry eye on board the *Pioneer Star* as they slowly rowed away from us.

I enjoyed going to sea, working aboard ship, seeing the many countries of the world, so in 1961 when Joe Cragin, superintendent engineer asked me to consider working ashore in the engineering office, I had to give it some serious consideration. I realized it would mean an end to spending countless days on those many monotonous oceans and a big cut in pay from chief engineer to port engineer, but at least I would still be working aboard a ship. I really didn't have to think about it for long before I decided to go for it.

It had a distinct advantage, I might even have a chance to be home every night, or at least more often than I previously had. It would mean flying to a job in a foreign port for a dry-docking or collision repairs, but at least I wouldn't be spending days at sea on a ship standing on it beam's end during heavy weather with my life jacket propped under my mattress to form a wedge with the adjoining bulkhead so I wouldn't be tossed out. And I wouldn't be tuned in to the broadcast band on my radio listening to East Coast stations announce that the big storm that hit the area has passed "harmlessly" out to sea.

When I came ashore in 1961, the company required that I withdraw from the Marine Engineers' Beneficial Association because office people were nonunion. I guess Cragin must have detected a slight change in my expression when I heard that, because he said, "Don't worry George, U.S. Lines will be around a lot longer than that union you belong to!" How wrong he was.

In 1968, U.S. Lines was taken over by Walter Kidde Co., a conglomerate with many varied holdings, but this was their first venture into steamship operations. John McMullen was selected to be our new president. Good benefits had been available at U.S. Lines, including a generous severance pay policy for many years which allowed office personnel to receive a month's pay for each year worked up to a total of one year's salary.

After the Kidde takeover this policy ceased, creating a feeling of uncertainty among the employees. Soon after, a review of engineering office personnel showed several to be at the top of their earning scale for that particular job, including the assistant superintendent engineer, Bob Lurye, so the layoffs began. In addition to Lurye, Arthur Garypie and Tom Cameron soon followed. Those of us who were still employed at this point knew our days were numbered so a call went out to the MEBA to rush over to the office with pledge cards! The MEBA had already signed up the port engineers from several other companies, and had knocked on our doors a few times, but we always rejected them because our pay was on a par with that of the union members.

Not long after, an election was held under the National Labor Relations Board rules and we won union representation. We did find it necessary to picket the office for one day. I, like the others, felt weird saying "Good morning" to our vice presidents and managers as they crossed our picket line. But most shook hands with us and encouraged us to hang in there, so we knew we had their support. Of course, none of them had any idea how long they would survive the new management.

Before joining the MEBA, we had started taking delivery of our new Challenger II Class vessels, the company's first venture into automation and bridge control. Nick Bachko, vice president of engineering, and I rode the first ship out of the builder's yard in Chester, Pennsylvania, to New York, and tied up at Pier 74 in the North River.

For several months prior to this delivery, the MEBA had been requesting the company to start an "automation school" to train engineers in the operation of the new class of ship. But the company balked at this, maintaining the union should bear the expense of operating the school. Thus when the ship docked that night about 5:00 P.M., Jesse Calhoon, MEBA president, boarded the ship to speak to the engineers. Dick Bower, superintendent engineer, also boarded.

A meeting was held in the chief engineer's office with Calhoon, Bower, the chief engineer, Nick Bachko, and me. Calhoon again asked Bower if he had any intention of starting a school. When Bower replied the answer was no, Calhoon said, "Sorry, Dick, but all the ship's engineers are exhausted tonight from the strenuous trip to New York so they are all going home to get a good night's rest! I expect you'll have to shut down the engineering plant for the night because we have no night engineer to stand the night watch, simply because no one has been trained in automation!"

Bower was just as clever as Calhoon so I sat back to see how he would field this remark. Bower thought for a moment, and then said, "We have a night engineer for the ship, he's sitting right next to you!"

Calhoon looked at me, "Him?"

"Yeah, George Murphy is our night engineer for tonight!"

With a faint smile, I said, "OK, boss."

Bower was determined not to let Calhoon get the better of him, even at my expense. As Calhoon left the office, he laughed at us, knowing I had no experience except that which I had picked up during the eighteen-hour trip from Chester. He said, "Mr. Murphy, I'll be staying at the New Yorker Hotel tonight, five blocks up on Thirty-fourth Street. I have a room facing the river so just before you lose the plant tonight, blink the ship's lights to me!"

"Mr. Calhoon, I plan to have lots of lanterns hanging all over the ship tonight so if I lose the plant, you'll never know it!"

I stood the fifteen-hour watch, relying on the engine department crew members who had been aboard for a month in the yard to carry me through, and at 0800 the lights were still burning!

Bower and Calhoon soon reached an agreement and an automation school was started up, each sharing a portion of the cost.

Rejoining the MEBA was at least a guarantee that I would receive my severance pay, because that was one of the conditions on which we would rejoin. As a result, many of our temporary help who had been employed to assist in the new construction program received severance pay at the termination of the program. For the rest of us, the company turned over the money that had been paid into the company pension plan on our behalf to the union pension fund. In my case, it added seven more years, so my time in the union pension plan became continuous from 1943.

In my opinion, many factors contributed to the demise of U.S. Lines in 1986: Poor (and stubborn) management, labor unions, the Coast Guard, and a proliferation of container ships.

Often when ownership of a large corporation changes, many high-level positions are eliminated or the individuals holding those positions are replaced. This was the case in U.S. Lines not only after the Walter Kidde takeover, but also after McLean Industries took over from Kidde.

When McLean came on the scene, many in the company felt somewhat relieved because after all, he was the "father of containerization." This caused a major upheaval in the shipping industry throughout the world and after his development of containerization at Sealand, he was now our owner and Sealand's biggest competitor!

Soon after he took over, he brought many "bean counting types" into the company, and it didn't seem too long before they were having a big influence in the running of many departments. My interest was strictly in the operations department which included the engineering group.

A new vice president of operations, a former naval officer, soon came on the scene and began cleaning house. One of the first to go was his predecessor, a lifelong employee of U.S. Lines, Ken Gundling, a very capable businessman and one who always ran an extremely efficient department.

Next on his list was my boss, Dick Bower, superintendent engineer, who had been in the company since he graduated from Pennsylvania Nautical School in 1939. Dick was seated in his glass-enclosed office one Thursday evening about 6:00 P.M., with a spreadsheet laid out on his desk, and was about to list the names of all the company ships in the left column to begin what was always his biggest annual task, making out a budget for the coming year for forty-five ships.

The new vice president walked by his window and saw him at his desk, so he stuck his head in the door and told Dick that he didn't fit into the company's future plans; that he had intended to tell him the following day but as long as he was still there that evening he would give him the news then.

Dick laid his pencil down on his desk, put on his coat, and walked out. He called all his port engineers that night at home to tell us the news. He still maintained a touch of humor though. He told us it was too bad they hadn't waited for two more weeks when he would have completed the budget, but now they could stumble through it! It was bittersweet humor and we all felt badly for him.

Others were soon to follow and many of us could see the direction the company was taking; it was just a question of time. Many poor judgments were made after these layoffs, for example: Our container ship, SS *American Apollo*, struck a rock while transiting the cut in the Panama Canal and suffered considerable bow damage.

After a preliminary survey at the canal, a top-level manager suggested it proceed to Trinidad for repairs. That individual was soon overruled, reasoning if the ship could proceed to Trinidad, it could go on to the Savannah, its first scheduled port of discharge. This individual was instructed to order the ship to Savannah thus helping our customers. A survey was conducted at each subsequent port on its discharge schedule and a permit to proceed procured until the cargo was discharged as scheduled, finally ending up in New York, her last port of discharge.

Middle management suggested the vessel proceed to Newport News, Virginia, for repairs, but higher management elected to dry-dock it in the Graving Dock at the Bayonne Military Ocean Terminal for survey. Underwriters' representatives, U.S. Coast Guard inspectors, American Bureau surveyors, U.S. Lines personnel, and shipyard estimators representing several yards scrambled over the damage, writing damage surveys, making notes, taking dimensions, and then the yards were invited to submit bids for the repairs.

The vessel lay there for several days while bids were considered, causing the ship to lose valuable time and at considerable cost. One of our newer executives, one of the accounting types, suggested removing the bow section from one of our smaller general cargo ships which was laid up and attaching it to the forebody of the

American Apollo. This made as much sense as asking a mechanic to replace the front end of a Mack truck with that of a small Ford!

Our previous management would have sent a couple of shipyard representatives to Panama to conduct a preliminary survey, take measurements, fly back to their yard to start fabricating a new bow section, and have it well underway by the time the cargo was discharged. And more than likely it would have been done in Newport News where weather was usually mild enough to perform the considerable amount of welding involved since it was the winter season. This would have saved a considerable amount of money, and had the blessing of underwriters as well.

Top management selected a shipyard in Maine to be awarded the contract, however, this yard did not have a dry dock large enough to handle a container ship of this size. They reactivated a shut down shipyard in Boston for the work. Steel work in the North in the dead of winter! Since the Boston yard had no local employees, i.e., welders, burners, pipe fitters, electricians, etc., these craftsmen and other dry-dock workers and the numerous other trades needed to make a shipyard functional were bussed to Boston from Maine on a weekly basis and put up in local motels near the yard.

Materials had to be trucked to the yard from Maine, and the new bow sections barged from there. The costs were increasing astronomically each day! When the ship eventually left the yard at completion of repairs, the invoice was worked up and submitted for consideration.

Because striking the rock was a peril for which we were insured, underwriters were to be a party to the negotiations in settling the invoice. The shipyard had broken down the bill into labor costs and materials, as well as the costs of trucking, barging, bussing, and the motels of the workers. Underwriters immediately denied the trucking, barging, bussing and motels, and only allowed a fair price for the actual cost of the repairs based on what would be a fair price in an active yard with resident workers available.

There was a lot of expertise available in the old U.S. Lines. Being a steamship company over seventy-five years old, there wasn't too much that could happen to a ship that hadn't happened previously. Such was the situation with the *American Apollo*. The ship missed its next scheduled sailing due to the accident and, ninety-one days later, missed its next assigned slot due to the delays in the yard in Boston!

Another example of corporate thinking came to light when one of our new accountants suggested in September that we purchase no more spare parts for any ship until after the start of the new year. He suggested this because so many of the ships had gone over their budget for the year! This was an asinine suggestion which, if taken seriously, would have tied up a third of our fleet!

After Bower's discharge, the port engineers were handed the task to make up the budget for those three or four ships assigned to each of us. Two weeks later, in the company auditorium, we had to lay out our proposals for the coming year before company officials. Management was overwhelmed at the figures we presented, asking us to justify them. We pointed out which ships were scheduled for dry-docking, Coast Guard inspections, Special Surveys, known repairs which had been put off, plus a myriad of other factors involved in keeping a ship at sea for a year, and in class with the regulatory people. Using current billing rates, we also showed the costs of doing the repairs domestically, as well as in a foreign yard.

Management began chopping at our numbers, crossing out items, and questioning us on most others. We informed them they were at liberty to cut anywhere they wished, but these were bare-bones budgets. About nine months later their revised budgets were out of money!

Later after I had returned to our home office from a dry docking in the Hyundai yard in Ulsan, Korea, I was called on the carpet to explain why many of the repairs I had supervised had gone over my budget. Attending the conference held in the boardroom at Cranford were ten or twelve men and me.

Present were Captain Bill McManus, the director of marine operations; Jim McQuaid, vice president of purchasing; Ray McPhail, superintendent engineer and my boss; plus the vice president of operations, and others who were from the accounting department. The first item they questioned was why I paid $7,000 to weight test a lifeboat when my estimate showed only $700. I was glad they chose that item first because I was ready for it.

Lifeboats are tested in a weighted condition by either filling them with sufficient fresh water to equal the required weight for the test, or by loading sand bags in the boat to reach that weight. The boat is then lowered from the davits by gradually releasing the handle of the mechanical hand brake attached to the lifeboat winch and allowing the boat to slowly fall by its own weight. This tests the davits, cables, brake, lifeboat hooks, sheaves, and other fittings. As the boat nears the water, the brake is applied to slow its movement and the boat is eased into the water where the hand releasing gear is tested to free the boat from the davits.

I found it necessary to explain this test to the vice president and the accountants because only McManus, McPhail, and McQuaid knew what I was talking about. Each of them witnessed many tests in their lifetime, even McQuaid who had spent many years in the shipyard as an estimator. I told those assembled that based on this basic test, I allowed $700 in my budget for it.

I then explained what went wrong with the $700 test. The USCG inspector was on the scene. The ship's master, chief mate, and most of the deck department were also standing around witnessing it. The sand bags had been loaded, the required weight was determined to be in the boat, and the boatswain was standing by the brake.

After assuring ourselves it was safe to lower, I gave the order to release the brake slightly. The boatswain slacked it off and the boat began to lower itself, but suddenly it gained speed in its downward travel. He leaned more on the handle but it kept accelerating in speed. In a flash, the boat was falling rapidly, and began spitting out red-hot brake rivets in all directions. Smoke began pouring out from beneath the brake band which was wildly throwing red-hot fragments of brake lining while emitting a loud, ear splitting, screeching noise!

Everyone in the vicinity scattered, nearly falling over each other to get out of the way of the shrapnel. Everyone except two people, the boatswain and me. I jumped over the guardrail and put all my weight on the brake handle with the boatswain, shouting to him over the noise to stay with it, the weight of the two of us should slow it down.

"I've seen this happen before, Bosun, we can stop it if we stay with it," I screamed! By now any brake lining was long gone and it was metal to metal, brake band to drum, and the brake band was glowing cherry red!

The travel of the boat began to slow and we managed to stop it about one foot from the water, after traveling more than thirty feet straight down! We then eased it into the water where it was towed to the pier.

After the noise stopped and the smoke cleared, the inspector and others appeared back on the scene, now somewhat embarrassed, seeing the boatswain and me still there. The brake band assembly was removed from the winch and taken to the shipyard machine shop where a complete new brake assembly had to be fabricated. The brake drum was found to be badly scored and had to be machined to a new smooth surface.

After this, we examined the brake assembly on the other lifeboat and found it to be in very poor condition, so we renewed it also.

"$7,000 is cheap for the work entailed," I said, "and if it hadn't been for the boatswain and me, we'd be looking at a bill for $70,000 to purchase a new Coast Guard approved lifeboat!"

"Furthermore, there are only three men in this entire group who understand what the hell I'm talking about and what we were up against, Captain McManus, Jim McQuaid, and Ray McPhail; the rest of you don't have a clue," I said defiantly.

McManus spoke up and said, "You're right, George, I've seen lifeboats run away during a test, and we'd be lucky if we just had to buy a new boat; someone could have gotten injured or killed!" McPhail and McQuaid quickly agreed!

The vice president then thanked me for the information and adjourned the meeting.

With the new management of Malcom McLean, many U.S. Lines employees didn't know where they stood with new executives taking over. The new owners assured everyone that all hands would be secure in their positions, at least until they had a chance to observe the operations of the company.

One of the first things that came about was a letter to all hands about a dress code for the office people. This proved to be a useless document because although it spelled out that all men must wear suits and ties and the women be suitably attired for a business office, nothing had to change because everyone dressed that way as a matter of routine, and had done so for years!

Another obnoxious notion they came up with was to hire a company whose personnel would spend time with each office and department to attempt to streamline it and point out deficiencies in its operations.

One of our executives came into the port engineers' office one Monday morning accompanied by a young man in a gray flannel suit.

"Which one of you has the next ship coming in?"

"I have," replied Don Kadlac, "tomorrow morning."

"OK, this is Mr. Jones. He is an efficiency expert and he will accompany you on board, stay with you for the day to see just what a port engineer's duties are, and then forward a report to us with his recommendations."

Don said, "OK, I'll meet you on board at 0700 hours in the morning, at our Howland Hook container pier."

"At 0700, that's 7:00 A.M. isn't it?"

"Yup, 7:00 A.M."

The following morning, Don boarded the ship and Mr. Efficiency boarded shortly after. Don introduced him to the chief engineer, and then excused himself while he went into the chief's bedroom. When he came out, he was dressed in old coveralls, carried a flashlight, and a notebook.

"OK, let's go, we're going up into the stack, Chief, to check on the whistle." Don and Mr. Efficiency left the chief's office, went up one deck, and opened a small dogged access plate at the base of the outer smokestack. It was an oval-shaped opening about twenty inches high and fourteen inches wide. Don climbed through and then stood aside while the efficiency man followed.

Inside, Don pointed his flashlight up toward a grating at the top of a long vertical ladder and said, "We have to climb up there to examine the whistle, so follow me!"

"Damn, I can't climb up there, I'll get my suit dirty. This place is full of soot; I'll wait here for you!"

Don climbed the ladder and could be seen shining his flashlight around the area of the whistle and, in a few moments, descended to the level where Mr. Efficiency stood.

They then returned to the boat deck where Don opened a door to the engine room fiddley, the uppermost section of the engine room, as well as the hottest! Don grasped the handrails of the topmost ladder and deftly slid down the rails, never touching a step until he landed at the foot of the ladder. Mr. Efficiency saw this and couldn't believe what he had just witnessed. Don beckoned for him to come down, so he started down the steep ladder, but after two steps, turned around and descended the ladder backwards, holding tightly to the rails. At the next landing, Don again "rode the rails," while Mr. Efficiency climbed down backwards again.

This went on for four more levels until they were in the lower engine room next to the main engine. By now the efficiency expert was dirty with soot and perspiration. Don led him to the shaft alley, a narrow confining enclosure housing the propeller shaft, and cranked open the shaft alley watertight door. Don had earlier asked the chief to close the door to make a deeper impression on Mr. Efficiency. Of course, Don could have taken him to the engine room using outside ladders instead of the hottest section of the engine room, but chose not to. After pumping open the hydraulic door and stepping over the sill, Don closed the door behind him to make the guy feel claustrophobic, and they walked aft on the grating until they reached the stern gland area where the propeller shaft goes out through the stern. The stern tube was a wood-bearing type, and thus dripping a trickle of water. Don explained to him that the shaft was lubricated with seawater and that small leakage was normal. He also pointed out to him the escape trunk, about two-feet square and twenty-feet straight upward directly over them. Don explained that they would climb the escape should anything occur while down there which would require abandoning ship, and he explained that they were about fifteen feet below the outside water level.

Under the leaking gland was a sheet metal collecting tray which caught the water and funneled it to a bilge well under the shaft. Don descended the short ladder leading to this area and invited the man down with him to show him what he had to check on in the area, but the guy backed off, again citing getting his clothes any dirtier.

When Don climbed out of the area after a phony examination, he explained that he now had to enter the fire side of one of the boilers for an examination. At this the guy backed off.

"Mr. Kadlac, I've seen enough. I'm hot and dirty, I think I'll go back to the office in Cranford and make out my report," Mr. Efficiency said.

Don replied, "OK, maybe I'll see you back there later this week when I finish my work on this ship."

Thanks to Don, we never laid eyes on him again!

The labor unions must take their share of blame for the downfall of the company also. Many factors were involved in labor agreements between the five unions represented aboard ship and U.S. Lines, as well as involvements with the longshoremen unions. A major problem in the contracts for all the unions was the staggered contract termination dates.

Some unions terminated their contracts in the middle of summer, just when the Christmas trade was at its peak and at a time when a strike would be costly to the company. Others terminated during the dead of winter when a strike would mean vessels laying up in freezing weather, causing untold damage to the piping systems, cargo winch grounds, and shorts in electrical systems. Still others terminated during the peak period of travel for passenger ships.

The unions were at fault for featherbedding on crewing the ships, especially passenger ships, insisting on more crew than necessary to safely operate the ship. And the longshoremen were at fault for reluctantly refusing to reduce work crews while the company was attempting to enter the container ship era without incurring severe penalties such as the guaranteed annual wage. I am well aware that the unions were looking out for their members to keep them employed as long as possible, but nevertheless these demanding work rules added to the woes of the company. I recall one U.S. Lines vice president making the remark after signing a contract, "We should now be assured of labor peace for at least four months, until the next contract expires!"

I would be remiss if I stopped the blame at this point because it is my sincere belief that our own United States Coast Guard must also bear some responsibility for the company's failure. The quality of vessel inspections left a lot to be desired. As pointed out earlier, the young officers detailed to inspect the merchant vessels were for the most part inexperienced, immature, and regarded vessel inspections as a necessary evil in their Coast Guard careers. Their inexperience proved costly to many companies.

Many of the Coast Guard's new construction requirements were drawn up by the naval architects of the American Bureau of Shipping, but the Coast Guard would not permit an ABS surveyor to clear many requirements concerning them. They had to be cleared by an inspector from the marine inspection office who more than likely wasn't familiar with the requirement.

The U.S. Coast Guard and the American Bureau of Shipping have the same rules for a tailshaft examination, but still it requires a surveyor from each regulatory body to pass on it. The load line certificate, required aboard every American flag vessel, is a Coast Guard issued document, however a surveyor from the ABS is permitted to endorse it annually as required by law. Similarly, tests and examinations of cargo handling gear are required by the Coast Guard but surveyors representing the American Bureau of Shipping are allowed to conduct these examinations and endorse the certificates. If these, why not others? Redundancy costs dollars. Now many years too late, the United States Coast Guard is entertaining thoughts for allowing the American Bureau of Shipping surveyors to conduct some of the Coast Guard inspections.

While the rules and regulations are hard and fast for the safety of American flag vessels, their interpretation and intent are often abused by inspectors. For example, in the *Coast Guard Safety Manual*, as part of 46 CFR Ch.1, 91.25-50, it is written: "(a) Nothing in this subpart shall be construed as limiting the inspector from making such tests or inspections as he deems necessary to be assured of the safety and seaworthiness of the vessel."

I have seen this paragraph abused so often by inspectors that it in itself has cost U.S. Lines a small fortune in unnecessary inspections, purchases, sailing delays, etc. Often it has been necessary to call the officer in charge of marine inspection in a particular port to curb the inspector in order to permit the ship to sail to the next port where longshoremen have been ordered and would have to be paid if the vessel didn't appear for its regular schedule.

The answer to the problem, however late, is for the Coast Guard to furnish experienced inspectors who have been to sea as licensed officers and could appreciate the problems faced by the company in attempting to stay in business. Or the Coast Guard could grant the surveyors from the American Bureau of Shipping a broader range of testing on behalf of the Coast Guard.

Such a program was instituted when, under Public Law 219, Merchant Marine officers were granted commissions in the Coast Guard to bolster the marine inspection service. The program was quite successful but short lived. Most of the officers selected for this program were masters and chief engineers, who had a good working knowledge of these problems from personal experience and reflected the intent of the inspection policy as outlined at the start of Chapter Forty-four.

Yes, good years, good times, probably the best of times in a diminishing industry. I was fortunate to be a part of it when there were many major shipping companies competing, all under the American flag. Companies such as Grace Line, Moore-McCormack, Delta, Prudential, American Export, American President, Dollar Line, Isbrandtsen, Lykes, and Waterman were plying the waters all over the world.

Ships were general cargo types, resulting in a port stay of several days. This enabled ship's crews to perform the necessary maintenance work and gave them an ample opportunity to see the interiors of many foreign lands instead of just waterfronts.

General cargo piers were usually located in the center of most cities, instead of miles outside, such as the container terminals of today. And the port stay of container ships is usually only a matter of hours.

Shipyards were abundant in most ports, Bethlehem Steel with a yard in Hoboken, two in Brooklyn, another in Staten Island, as well as two in Baltimore, and others in Texas, California, Seattle. Todd Shipyards Corporation, with its headquarters in our own building at One Broadway, and a yard in Brooklyn, Hoboken, New Orleans, Texas, California, and Washington.

These giants of the shipbuilding and repair industry suffered directly because of the failure of so many steamship companies, such as U.S. Lines, who found it more economical to do their sur-

and repairs in foreign yards, in spite of paying a fifty-percent customs duty on the repairs.

The final blow to U.S. Lines came about when McLean contracted to build twelve new container ships in a Korean shipyard. These were to be the largest container ship in the world capable of transiting the Panama Canal. Our company had a group of engineers in house who were well experienced in new ship construction, having supervised a total of more than thirty general cargo and container ships as well as two passenger ships in three different shipyards. But management told them "Hands Off," it would be completely supervised by outsiders, another costly venture.

The ships, capable of carrying a total of 2400 forty-foot containers, faced an enormous logistics problem. The problems included calling at each port once and discharging and reloading containers in each; carrying short-term loads between some ports as well as long-term loads from New York to the Far East; and trying to avoid overstowage which would result in moving a container from the bottom of a stack only after the removal of those five above it, then putting it on the pier, and restowing the five back in the hold. All these moves cost dollars.

Another problem was overcarriage of containers where a container was missed at a port, only to be found later, and then it had to be transported to its destination by another carrier. More dollars.

All of these problems had to dealt with while keeping foremost in one's mind the stability of the ship with a deck load nearly forty-five-feet high!

All of the foregoing contributed to the company's failure, in my opinion, but probably the final blow came when company executives refused to consider suggestions, thoughts, and recommendations from middle management personnel who survived the earlier purge of company officials.

The executive branch had plans for a round-the-world service, in an eastbound direction, using twelve Econ vessels, the term given to the newly constructed ships built in Korea. The intention was to schedule one sailing each week which, with ten ships, would have shown a profit.

After ten of the ships had been delivered, the service was commenced with a weekly sailing from New York, each voyage lasting seventy days. This arrangement proved to be a profitable one, and would have allowed management to reassign other company container ships to other routes, sell them to other companies, or scrap them.

When the final two ships were delivered, management elected to add them to the round-the-world schedule instead of laying them up or assigning them to other routes, plus adding two more ports to the schedule. At this time they also had to reduce the speed of the ships to keep them on a weekly schedule, so the seventy-days schedule was now increased to eighty-four days.

With the addition of the two ships there was no increase in cargo or revenue, and the transit time for cargo was slowed by the reduced speed, much to the disapproval of our shippers. The two extra ships and longer schedules translated into fourteen additional days of added vessel operating expenses plus the added extra cost of equipping these two ships, crewing them, and maintaining them.

The rates for cargo (and consequently the profits) were diluted because of the additional ships and soon the company had to file for Chapter 11. Attempts were made to restructure the company and many rumors abounded about various companies and banks promising to bail the company out of its dilemma. But these attempts failed and the ships were eventually seized for nonpayment of bills and the company forced to close its doors after more than seventy-five years in existence.

Also, many in the office questioned the wisdom of sending ships to Europe when we already had a European service to several cities using smaller container ships, as well as a Far East service from the East Coast of the United States, also served by smaller ships. Except for the trade between northern Europe and Singapore, these new behemoths would be competing with our own ships!

Additionally, the new ships were competing for cargo in a world market that was to see countless numbers of container ships added to the world's fleets almost monthly! There just was not enough cargo to go around.

Ironically, after the company's failure, these new ships were taken over by the banks who ultimately sold them to Sealand, our original competitor only a few years ago, and formerly operated by McLean!

There were many disgruntled employees when the word came down that the company was filing bankruptcy. Many employees had to settle for reductions in vacation pay, compensatory time, and reduced pensions.

I had applied for my pension earlier in 1984, giving the union two-years lead time as I was required to do. Thus in 1986, when the ax fell, I was not directly affected by it and my retirement coincided with the company failure. Many others, however, felt let down, disappointed, bewildered. They questioned how a prestigious steam-ship company, over seventy-five years old, which at one time operated a total of more than sixty cargo ships and four passenger ships, could have failed. In retrospect, many longtime employees said they could see it coming soon after the last management took over.

The words of Joe Cragin keep coming to my mind when he said back in 1961, "Don't worry, George, United States Lines will be around a long time after that MEBA you belong to..."

GLOSSARY

AB, Able bodied seaman.

BR, Room steward who cleans rooms and makes beds.

Bicycle Shop, Any small repair facility specializing in marine repairs.

Bilge keel, A longitudinal fin fitted to exterior of the hull at the turn of the bilge to reduce rolling.

Black Gang, Engine room workers.

Camel, A fender or type of cushion between ship and pier.

Captain, Nickname for ship's master.

Captain Kangaroo, Children's TV entertainer.

Captain's table, Name commonly used in many cities for a seafood restaurant.

Charley Noble, Galley smoke stack.

Chips, Ship's carpenter.

Christmas Tree, Cluster of lights mounted on flying bridge.

Christmas Tree, Group of valves mounted together in engine room.

Collision Mats, Pancakes.

Cookie, Ship's cook.

Costume, Uniform.

Deep Six, To throw overboard.

Donkey Boiler, Boiler in use in port at low steaming rate.

Dunnage, Wood used for shoring cargo.

Eight thirty-five, (835) USCG requirement.

Eighty-six (86), Cadet signal for officer approaching.

ETA, Estimated time of arrival.

ETD, Estimated time of departure.

Expert, In a shipyard anyone from out of town.

FWE, Finished with engines.

Flags, Navy signalman.

Forty Thieves, .Customs searchers.

Fox Tail, Small dust brush.

Gadget, Cadet.

Golden Rivet, Imaginary last rivet driven in ship construction, sometimes used as ploy to get young female passengers to shaft alley to sight same.

Guns, Gunner, Gunners mate in Navy.

High Pressure, Officers' hat.

Hockle, Bight or kink in rope, sometimes referred to as an asshole.

Homesteader, Crew member who is a steady employee.

Hooligan Navy, U.S. Coast Guard.

Horse Cock, Bologna, "baloney."

MAC, Military Airlift Command.

Marad, U.S. Maritime Administration.

Master, Individual in charge of vessel.

MMP, Masters, Mates and Pilots, a labor union.

MEBA, Marine Engineers' Beneficial Association, a labor union.

MSC, Military Sealift Command.

Morgan Line Strawberries, Prunes, so called because Morgan Line served them at every breakfast, and the pits were thrown overboard. On the homebound voyage the mate on watch would attach a piece of chewing gum to the end of a heaving lead, and drop the lead into the water until it hit bottom. Upon retrieving the lead, if a prune pit was found imbedded into the gum he knew he was on course.

Night Engineer, Engineer from ashore who assumes the watch at night and on weekends in port to allow the ship's engineers to go ashore.

Night Mate, Similar to night engineer, but on deck.

Old Joe, Syphilis

Old Man, Nickname for the master.

OSHA, Occupational Safety and Health Administration.

OS, Ordinary seaman.

Pork Chop, Lifeboat davit.

Rat Man, U.S. Public Health Inspector who inspects ship for rodents.

RMO, Recruitment and Manning Organization, World War II Merchant Marine personnel office.

Red Hand, Commercial name for brand of epoxy.

Red Lead, Cadet name for ketchup.

Rose Box, Cargo hold or engine room bilge well.

Saloon, Officers' dining room.

Scuttlebutt, Drinking fountain, rumors on ship.

Sea Lawyer, Any sailor who is an expert on everything.

Sea Story, Tales told by sailors, some of which appear in this book.

Shave and a haircut, A fast dry-docking where only the underwater portion of the hull is cleaned and painted.

Short Stop, Cadet name for someone who intercepts a condiment at mealtime for his own use before passing it along when requested by another.

Skipper, Nickname for master.

Slop Chest, Ship's store.

Sparks, Ship's Radio Operator, sometimes ship's electrician.

Squeeze the Boiler, Hydrostatic pressure test on boiler.

Toe the mark, Toe the line, to stand in line.

USCG, United States Coast Guard.

WSA, War Shipping Administration.